Tolstoy

PLAYS

T0289346

Tolstoy

PLAYS: VOLUME THREE, 1894–1910

Leo Tolstoy

Translated from the Russian by Marvin Kantor

with Tanya Tulchinsky

Introduction by Andrew Baruch Wachtel

Northwestern University Press

Evanston, Illinois

Northwestern University Press

Evanston, Illinois 60208–4210

Copyright © 1998 by

Northwestern University Press.

All rights reserved.

Printed in the United States of America

ISBN cloth 0-8101-1598-0

  paper 0-8101-1599-9

Library of Congress

Cataloging-in-Publication Data

Tolstoy, Leo, graf, 1828–1910.

  [Plays. English]

  Tolstoy : plays / Leo Tolstoy ; translated by

  Marvin Kantor with Tanya Tulchinsky; introduction by

  Andrew Baruch Wachtel.

    p. cm. — (European drama classics)

    Contents: v. 1. 1856–1886. — v. 2. 1886–1889. — v. 3. 1894–1910.

    v. 1 ISBN 0-8101-1109-8. — ISBN 0-8101-1110-1

  (pbk). — v. 2. ISBN 0-8101-1394-5 (cloth). — ISBN 0-

  8101-1395-3. (paper) . — v. 3. ISBN 0-8101-1598-0. (cloth).

  — ISBN 0-8101-1599-9 (paper).

    1. Tolstoy, Leo, graf, 1828–1910—Translations into

  English. I. Kantor, Marvin. II. Tulchinsky, Tanya. III.

  Wachtel, Andrew Baruch. IV. Title. V. Series.

  PG3366.A19   1994

  891.72'3—dc20   94-22919

                                               CIP

Contents

Introduction

In his 1897 treatise *What Is Art?* Tolstoy claims that to be considered worthy of the name, a work of art must first and foremost be the expression of a genuine and sincere feeling. For only such works can infect the reader or spectator and thereby produce the communication of emotion that it is art's task to provide. But although genuineness of feeling is necessary, its mere presence is not sufficient to guarantee the creation of a good work of art. For that, further conditions need to be met; the good work must promote progress—defined as the most advanced religious, or perhaps better, ethical ideals of a given epoch—and it must be accessible without the need for advanced training on the part of the reader or spectator.

The dramatic works published in this volume were written during the period that began around 1890 and ended with Tolstoy's death in 1910.[1] For the most part, Tolstoy's creative energies at this time were devoted to the production of religious and philosophical texts, although his prodigious energy and unconquerable internal need to create artistic works led to the novel *Resurrection,* the novella *Hadji Murat,* and a number of important short stories, as well as these dramas. All of these works can be seen as attempts on Tolstoy's part to produce texts that would meet the strict criteria for good art he laid out in *What Is Art?* In principle, they would have formed a kind of countercorpus to his work published before 1881, almost all of which he summarily rejected.

As a guarantee that these dramatic works would express a genuine feeling, Tolstoy adopted a fairly sure method: the majority are to a significant extent autobiographical, which ensures that the feelings expressed had indeed been experienced by the author. Of course, in this respect the late dramas do not differ from many earlier Tolstoyan texts. *Childhood,* the author's debut work, was for example heavily based on Tolstoy's own experiences (although the experiences of others and purely fictional sections were freely interpolated).[2] And the character of Konstantin Levin, hero of *Anna Karenina,* is heavily indebted to his creator. The connection of *Anna Karenina* to the late plays is particularly interesting, because in all of these works Tolstoy uses his fictional text in a very unusual way. Rather than providing a literary description of something he had already experienced, the text appears to have allowed Tolstoy either to reexperience and refigure situations whose outcome in life had been unsatisfactory or—and this is even more interesting—to preexperience actions that he himself would later undertake. In this respect, one can see the Levin plot of Tolstoy's novel and most of his later plays as attempts by the author to provide a literary sideshadow on his own life.[3]

In the plays *Peter the Breadman, And the Light Shineth in Darkness,* and *The Living Corpse* Tolstoy is particularly concerned with exploring artistically the problem of renunciation of and escape from the world. As anyone who has studied Tolstoy's biography, religious teaching, and later fiction is aware, the question of how much contact the enlightened individual should have with the world (including not just the public world but the private universe of his own family) was central during the last three decades of his life. In the story "Father Sergius," for example, Tolstoy depicts his hero as a man of great ability and stupendous willpower, but afflicted with an overweening sense of pride. Despite all his achievements as a monk-healer, Sergius does not find personal salvation until he renounces everything and disappears to an anonymous life among the people. Tolstoy himself frequently expressed a desire to escape from his own family, and his actual flight in 1910 (which led to his death at the Astapovo station) can be seen as a real-life attempt to incarnate this model of behavior.

In the three major plays in this volume, Tolstoy handles the theme of renunciation and escape with various degrees of realism, autobiographicalism, and thoroughness. *Peter the Breadman,* which is set in third-century Syria, appears at first to be nothing more than a resetting of an ancient Byzantine tale. Nevertheless, it is clear that what attracted Tolstoy to the subject was precisely Peter's decision to break entirely with his old way of life and his family, to conquer his pride by selling himself into what could be seen as demeaning slavery but is here interpreted as freely given service to others. I will have a great deal more to say a bit later about the heterogeneous sources of *The Living Corpse,* but in the present context suffice it to say that Fedya Protasov's decision to renounce his wife and family—indeed, his entire former way of life—is clearly related to this same thematic cluster. Of course, because the play is set in contemporary Russia, Fedya's indictment of the order of things becomes a great deal more concrete than is the case in *Peter the Breadman.* But while *The Living Corpse* is in this respect more realistic than *Peter the Breadman,* it is far less thoroughgoing. While Peter does humble himself and completely transform his life, Fedya's success is at best equivocal, for in the real world of late-nineteenth-century Russia he finds it impossible to remake himself completely.

Although the central characters of *Peter the Breadman* and *The Living Corpse* share some of Tolstoy's central concerns, they can at most be considered autopsychological rather than explicitly autobiographical figures; that is to say, they think and behave the way Tolstoy would or would have liked to in the given situations, but these situations differ significantly from Tolstoy's own.[4] *And the Light Shineth in Darkness,* by contrast, is perhaps the most directly autobiographical work Tolstoy ever produced. Although it is unfinished, the play is nevertheless a powerful evocation of its author's position, at least as Tolstoy himself understood it. And while Nikolai Ivanovich Saryntsev's preaching can get tedious, the pain he feels as a result of the insoluble collision between the life he created for himself before his recognition of the "true path" and the new life he desires provides as illuminating a portrait of the later Tolstoy as we have. For unlike Fedya Protasov and Peter the Breadman, Saryntsev and Tolstoy find it impossible to break completely with their former lives. And it is important to note that this is due not to weakness of the will or fear of the loss of creature comforts; rather, it is a recognition of how much suffering their renunciation of the world would cause to those whom they have loved and continue to love.

As we noted above, according to Tolstoy's own aesthetic rules the communication of genuine feeling was a necessary but not sufficient condition for the true work of art. In addition, the work had to express the leading religious/ethical notions of the time. For Tolstoy in this period the leading religious idea was his own version of Christianity, a faith he proselytized with great energy. Although most of its basic tenets, including nonresistance to evil, a rejection of all governmental and religious authority, the injunction to avoid alcohol, tobacco, and sex, and a conviction that communal peasant life is the ideal, appear in various guises in the plays mentioned above, they are foregrounded in what can be called the nonnarrative dramatic dialogues that make up the remainder of the volume. The playlets entitled *The Wisdom of Children* were clearly imagined as dramatic only in form. Tolstoy uses the voices of children to express what he sees as truths that adults, because of their contamination by the habits and prejudices of daily life, cannot see. In *The Traveler and the Peasant*, Tolstoy sets up a conversation between someone very like himself (thereby continuing the autobiographical theme of the later plays) and a peasant. Here, the Tolstoyan wisdom that was provided by naive children in *The Wisdom of Children* is proffered by the sage traveler. Finally, in *The Cause of It All*, Tolstoy is more specifically concerned with the scourge of drunkenness (a subject he had explored in his earlier play *The First Moonshiner*—see Tolstoy, *Plays*, vol. 1—as well as in the essay "Why Do Men Stupefy Themselves?"). Of these three didactic works, this is the only one that even gestures toward a dramatic plot. And although it is unfinished, the final scene in which Mikhaila, at the urging of his wife, allows the tramp to go on his pathetic way rather than exacting retribution has a certain dramatic power. These dramatic scenes are also linked because they are all designed to meet the second criterion for good art as well: more or less universal accessibility. Nevertheless, perhaps because they are unfinished, or perhaps because the dramatic form is not as suitable as prose for works of this type, these sketches are ultimately unsuccessful curiosities rather than convincing artistic works.

Unquestionably, the most important drama in this volume, and along with *The Realm of Darkness* Tolstoy's most compelling play, is *The Living Corpse*. The initial impulse for the work was neither didactic nor autobiographical but purely literary. Tolstoy saw a production of Chekhov's *Uncle Vanya* and hated it.[5] In particular, he disliked Chekhov's plays for their lack of "a knot, a center, from which everything and to which everything would flow." The same complaint cannot be made about *The Living Corpse*, for it is clearly constructed around a central knot—the fake suicide of the main character, Fedya Protasov, and his "resurrection" as a "living corpse." As it turns out, the thematic knot formed by the act of fake suicide and subsequent "resurrection" has been of cardinal importance for Russian thought and has appeared frequently (and with complicated variations) in Russian culture and society. Indeed, it would not be an exaggeration to say that it has been one of a handful of paradigms central for the development not just of Russian literature, but of Russian cultural history in general. For Tolstoy, and for his readers, Fedya's fake suicide would have recalled a panoply of heterogeneous subtexts. Fedya's act is, therefore, not simply the intratextual central point in the play, it is also the point to which intertextual meaning flows and from which Tolstoy engages his varied intertexts.

The theme of fake suicide and subsequent resurrection draws extratextual meaning in *The Living Corpse* from at least four different kinds of intertexts: a real-life situation, literary texts by other authors, religious/philosophical concepts, and Tolstoy's own earlier work. As readers of the play will recall, Fedya Protasov is a good-natured but weak-willed aristocrat married to Liza. At the beginning of the play we discover that, for the umpteenth time, Fedya has run off to the gypsies and squandered all the family money. Although she loves her husband, eventually, at the urging of her mother, Liza resolves to cut her ties with the irresponsible Fedya and to marry her longtime admirer, Viktor Karenin. For this, of course, she must obtain a divorce. But Fedya does not wish to subject himself to the demeaning lies that would be required to free his wife.[6] Instead, at the instigation of the gypsy woman, Masha, he decides to escape the impasse by faking suicide. He pretends to drown himself, and Viktor and Liza (who evidently really believe he has killed himself) are married. Everything goes awry, however, when Fedya's identity is discovered. All three characters are brought to trial, and when Fedya finally decides that there is no other way out of the situation he takes his own life.

The most obvious source for Protasov's fake suicide and the complications that flow from it was a real-life story, well known both to Tolstoy and to a relatively large circle of Moscow society. In 1881, E. P. Simon, the daughter of an acquaintance of Tolstoy's, married N. S. Gimer, a middle-ranking clerk in the Ministry of Justice. Gimer turned out to be a drunkard, and, after two years of marriage, having given birth to a son, E. P. Simon-Gimer left her husband. Her mother then introduced her to P. P. Akimov, a white-collar employee of the railroad. Simon-Gimer never divorced her first husband, but lived as Akimov's common-law wife for approximately seven years. Unfortunately, it turned out that Akimov was no better than Gimer, and Simon-Gimer finally left him in 1890.[7] Sometime in the early 1890s she met and fell in love with S. I. Chistov. Having resolved to marry Chistov, she attempted to get a divorce from her first husband, but for reasons which remain unclear the divorce was not granted. At this point Simon-Gimer became desperate. She paid her first husband to fake his own suicide. He pretended to drown himself, and the "widow" was soon remarried. However, the scheme was uncovered as soon as Gimer attempted to obtain a new passport. Simon-Gimer's second marriage was annulled, and she and her first husband were put on trial in 1897. The two were sentenced to Siberian exile, but, as a result of the intervention of high-placed friends, the sentence was commuted to a year in prison and then suspended.

Clearly, the *The Living Corpse* parallels the Simon-Gimer story in a number of respects. Nevertheless, many crucial elements of the Simon-Gimer case do not correspond to the plot of Tolstoy's play. The most prominent changes include Liza's ignorance of the fact that Fedya's suicide is a sham, and a shift from the middle-class circles of Simon-Gimer to the upper-class society of the Protasovs and the Karenins. Nevertheless, for Tolstoy's contemporaries, the resemblances would have been sufficient to call the notorious Simon-Gimer case to mind. The silent presence of this prototype undoubtedly helped lend Tolstoy's play the ring of truth he so valued in a work of art. In addition, Tolstoy could have expected his potential audience to know just where and how his version of the story differed from the original. As a result, the real-life situation could serve as a kind of neutral ground (a control group, as it were) against which other intertexts would stand out in high relief. Finally, to turn to Tolstoy's own creative process for a moment, while the real-life prototype did not in the end provide either the plot or the characters of *The Living Corpse,* the Simon-Gimer story did call up a host of associations without which he might never have written the play. In particular, Gimer's fake suicide and its consequences echoed a number of literary texts in which a fake suicide was used as an important plot motif. Thus, the Simon-Gimer story served as a first step, the initial block of the intertextual foundation on which *The Living Corpse* was constructed.

The best-known literary text that the Simon-Gimer story called to mind was one to which Tolstoy had taken a violent dislike many years before: Chernyshevsky's novel, *What Is to Be Done?* It should be noted that far from being an obscure text (as it might now seem to non-Russian readers), in Russia this novel was certainly the most notorious and probably the most widely known work of the nineteenth century.[8] For Tolstoy, *What Is to Be Done?* was to be abused whenever possible, but it was to be used frequently as well.[9] There is one overt reference to the novel in *The Living Corpse*. In Act IV, Vignette 1, Scene 5, Fedya is thinking about shooting himself when Masha the gypsy enters the room.

MASHA (*grabbing the letter*). You wrote that you killed yourself, right? You didn't write about the gun—just that you killed yourself?

FEDYA. Yes, that I'll be no more.

MASHA. All right, all right, all right. Did you ever read *What Is to Be Done?*

FEDYA. I think so.

MASHA. It's a boring novel, but there's one very, very good thing there. He, that, what's his name, Rakhmanov, goes and pretends that he drowned himself . . .[10]

However, the parallels between *What Is to Be Done?* and *The Living Corpse* extend far beyond this scene. The plot outlines of the two works are remarkably similar. Both center on a love triangle involving a woman and two men. In the novel and in the play the first and second husbands of the main female character are not strangers and rivals but friends. Indeed, in both cases the two men were friends even before the initial marriages. In both works, when it becomes apparent that the first marriage is unviable, the supplanted husband cedes his wife directly, and more or less willingly, to the second. Finally, in both cases, the first husband liberates his wife by faking suicide and disappearing.[11]

At the same time, there are extremely important areas in which the novel and the play diverge. These are not so much on the level of the plot as on that of the plot's meaning; this becomes particularly obvious when we examine the outcome of the fake suicide in the two works. In *What Is to Be Done?* Kirsanov (the second husband) and Vera Pavlovna live happily ever after. Lopukhov (the first husband) eventually returns to Russia where, without any trouble, he passes for Charles Beaumont, the American employee of a British firm, marries the girl of his dreams, and gets back in contact with his old friends. The potential problems raised by Lopukhov/Beaumont's strangely split existence—that is, the question of how two individuals with overlapping but not identical personalities, psychologies, and life experiences manage to coexist in the same body—are not addressed. This character is able to retain some Lopukhov memories and personality traits, while conveniently sloughing off all aspects of his past that would be troubling for his Beaumont existence. For example, although it is true that he loved Vera Pavlovna and was a close friend of Kirsanov's, he was led to his fake suicide by feelings of bitterness toward both of them. After his return, however, he recalls only their former friendship and has evidently completely forgotten the acrimonious days before his disappearance. Nor, on a more quotidian plane, does the fact that he is still legally married to Vera Pavlovna prevent him from marrying Katya Polozova. In effect, Chernyshevsky allows Lopukhov/Beaumont to have the best of two lives without any of the problems that might conceivably plague this strange hydralike being.

The questionable logic of Lopukhov's personal reincarnation is echoed on the novel's sociological level. Chernyshevsky believes that social transformation is right around the corner; the "new people" (of whom Lopukhov is one) will usher in a utopia similar to the one that Vera Pavlovna envisions in her fourth dream. Once again, however, the problem of the connection between the old order and the new is never seriously addressed. Nor is the mechanism for passing from one to the other revealed overtly. The reader is evidently meant to believe that change will occur swiftly, but without the use of force, as a result of the dictates of logic. A closer examination of the text indicates that Chernyshevsky conceived this mechanism in religious terms. In this regard, it is crucial that Lopukhov's reappearance is described in terms that link him directly with Christ.[12] Christ, of course, as man/God handles a double identity (before and after his crucifixion) without any difficulty. Evidently, Lopukhov/Beaumont, in his imitation of Christ, is meant to function as a kind of metonym for Chernyshevsky's model for the revolutionary transformation of Russian society in general. The motif of fake suicide is therefore linked on the one hand to questions of revolution and, on the other, to the problem of resurrection.[13]

For Tolstoy, Chernyshevsky's resolution of the fake suicide plot must have seemed glib to the point of puerility. Long before he wrote *The Living Corpse,* Tolstoy had come to the conclusion that the problem of resurrection was not primarily physical, but rather philosophical. In the play, once he becomes reincarnated as a "living corpse," Protasov is unable to figure out who he is, how to reconcile the radical break between his past and present selves; that is, he is neither able to forget his past completely and start afresh nor able, like Lopukhov, to integrate selected parts of his past with his present condition. While Tolstoy accepts Chernyshevsky's linkage of personal and social transformation, he turns the argument on its head. Just as Protasov is unable to take on a new identity after his resurrection, so society is unwilling or unable to modify its rigid attitudes toward marriage and divorce in the face of his actions. In prosecuting Protasov, Liza, and Karenin, the judicial system reveals a fatal inability to reconcile law and justice. At the same time, Tolstoy eliminates the parallels between the resurrected hero and Christ that underlie Chernyshevsky's novel. Ultimately then, *The Living Corpse* can be seen as a parody of *What Is to Be Done?* in the sense that it uses the same literary material in order to radically reevaluate it.[14]

If Chernyshevsky's novel served primarily as a model to be rebutted, a different Russian literary text used the fake suicide theme in a way that was probably more to Tolstoy's liking: Sukhovo-Kobylin's "comedy-joke," *Tarelkin's Death*.[15] As in *What Is to Be Done?* and *The Living Corpse*, a fake suicide forms the central plot element in *Tarelkin's Death*. Here, a thieving petty bureaucrat (Tarelkin) fakes suicide in order to avoid his creditors and to extort money from his corrupt superior, Varravin. However, Varravin uncovers Tarelkin's scheme and, after a series of grotesquely funny machinations, forces the now identity-less Tarelkin to make his miserable way in the world, literally from nothing.

Two themes in *Tarelkin's Death* are important for *The Living Corpse* but were absent or only latently present in the Simon-Gimer case and in *What Is to Be Done?* The first is a sharp parody of the criminal justice system, and the second is an overt concern with questions of death, resurrection, and personal identity.[16] Sukhovo-Kobylin's bitter satire was considered so inflammatory that, although the play was published in 1869, it was not allowed to be staged until 1900. The playwright portrays a judicial system (and particularly a police system) that is rotten to the core. Officials are either too stupid to understand what is happening around them or so venal that they can easily be bought off. The scenes in *Tarelkin's Death* in which the police interrogate the "resurrected" Tarelkin play out a grotesque version of the senseless and tragic situation that Tolstoy describes in Act VI of *The Living Corpse*.

More central, however, is the contrast between the consequences of the fake suicide in the two plays. After his supposed death, Tarelkin takes on the identity of his former neighbor, Sila Silych Kopylov. Unfortunately for him, it turns out that Kopylov has also died, and when this fact is discovered, the "resurrected" Tarelkin is without any identity:

> RASPLYUEV. There's no doubt about it. Kopylov died. Died of apoplexy! Died in the village of Do-Nothing, was cut open, and buried in the ground!! (*Whacks a piece of paper.*)
>
> VARRAVIN. How horrible!
>
> RASPLYUEV. And now this again. Tarelkin died! He died—and he was buried in the ground by me!! (*strikes his chest*)—by me!!! And now this 'un: Who is he?!!
>
> VARRAVIN. Hold on! I know who he is! It's . . . it's life's greatest peril . . . Listen to me. . . . Do you know what a werewolf is? (Act II, Scene 7)

Tarelkin, raised from the dead, becomes at one and the same time two people and no one. His situation is, in effect, exactly the opposite of that of Lopukhov/Beaumont.[17] Tarelkin retains only the unnecessary traits of his former existence and is unable to take on those of his "new" incarnation.

> TARELKIN. What can I say?—I told you—I'm Kopylov.
>
> RASPLYUEV. You're lying, you devilish soul! He died. Here are the papers. (*To Kachala*) Twist his arm! . . .
>
> TARELKIN. Oy-oy-oy,—well O.K., I'm Tarelkin—oy, Tarelkin!
>
> RASPLYUEV. (*Forcefully*) You're lying—Tarelkin—Why General Varravin himself—what are you wasting my time for, anathema. (*To Kachala*) Twist!
>
> TARELKIN. O gods, ay . . . I'm . . . I'm . . . both of them.
>
> VARRAVIN. (*To Rasplyuev*) And both of them are dead. (Act II, Scene 7)

In many respects, Fedya Protasov's position after his fake suicide is similar.

> FEDYA. I don't exist.
>
> PETUSHKOV. Just what do you mean?
>
> FEDYA. No. I'm a corpse. That's right.

Like Tarelkin, like Lopukhov, Fedya simultaneously does and does not exist in the real world. But whereas Lopukhov is able to forge ahead, to become resurrected as a living being, Tarelkin and Fedya Protasov fail to reconcile their "before" and "after" identities. Still, there is a crucial difference between the situations of Fedya and Tarelkin/Kopylov. Tarelkin is a cheat, and an extortionist, and while there is a certain abstract tragedy in his final situation, the spectator essentially does not care what happens to this grotesquely comic character. But Fedya and his situation are perceived as genuinely tragic. Despite his resurrection, Fedya remains the same weak-willed, good-hearted, ineffectual drunkard he was before.[18] Now, however, these traits cannot save him, and the logic of his position leads inexorably to his real death. Thus, as was the case with *What Is to Be Done?* it seems that Tolstoy evoked a literary subtext as a source of parody. The same sorts of situations reappear, but they are evaluated differently.

Tolstoy broke with his literary predecessors not in his use of the fake suicide theme, but in regard to the subsequent fate of the resurrected "suicide." His purpose in recalling early texts was polemical; by reusing and reevaluating the same theme, Tolstoy emphasizes what separates his ideas from those of his forebears. But while literary texts are clearly vitally important for understanding the meaning of the theme of fake suicide in *The Living Corpse,* they were by no means the only ones that would have come to the minds of Tolstoy and his readers when the subject of resurrection was broached. In 1881, during one of his extended visits to Moscow, Tolstoy became acquainted with the librarian of the Rumyantsev Museum, Nikolai Fedorovich Fedorov. The two men became quite friendly and saw each other frequently whenever Tolstoy was in Moscow. As it turned out, in addition to being a librarian, Fedorov was a strikingly original philosopher. One of the core beliefs of his philosophical system was the necessity for mankind to harness the powers of nature and science in order to accomplish the actual physical resurrection of all those who had ever lived on earth. The accomplishment of this task was, in Fedorov's view, the prerequisite for creating the kingdom of heaven on earth: "Christianity believes in the triumph over death; but that belief is dead and that is why death exists; that belief will remain dead as long as it remains separated from all of mankind's other forces, that is, until all the forces of all people join together for the general goal of resurrection."[19]

Fedorov's ideas, particularly those concerning resurrection, struck a chord with many Russian thinkers of the second half of the nineteenth century. Dostoevsky, for example, speaking for himself and for the philosopher Vladimir Solov'ev, wrote a letter to Fedorov's chief disciple, N. P. Peterson, in which he expressed the hope that Fedorov understood the resurrection of mankind literally and not allegorically.[20] It is perhaps not surprising that Dostoevsky was attracted to Fedorov's ideas, particularly since there is some evidence that he saw his own life in terms of a pattern of death and resurrection. It will be recalled that Dostoevsky was officially sentenced to death for his part in the so-called Petrashevsky affair, and that he was actually led out to be executed before it was announced that his sentence and those of his comrades had been commuted.[21] After this symbolic death Dostoevsky spent the next four years in prison. The last line of his autobiographical novel describing these years, *Notes from the House of the Dead,* may be taken to indicate Dostoevsky's own view of the experience: "Freedom, new life, resurrection from the dead. . . . What a glorious moment!"[22]

Tolstoy was also well aware of Fedorov's philosophy, as is demonstrated by a letter he wrote to V. I. Alekseev in November, 1881. "He [Fedorov] has formulated a plan for the general affairs of all humankind, which has as its goal the resurrection of all people in the flesh. First of all, it's not as crazy as it seems. (Don't be afraid, I never did and do not now share his views, but I understand them so well that I feel myself able to defend them against the claims of all other beliefs having an external goal.)"[23] What was it about Fedorov's theory that bothered Tolstoy, despite his evident sympathy both for the philosopher and his views? I believe that the problem lay in Fedorov's belief that resurrection would automatically lead to transformation. Like Chernyshevsky, Fedorov never seems to wonder about why and how the moral transformation of mankind will be effected. Evidently, as far as he is concerned the physical fact of general resurrection ensures a remaking of the world for the better. As we will see, however, for Tolstoy the act of resurrection is not social but personal, and a positive outcome for the process is by no means guaranteed. Thus, the Fedorov subtext is also invoked in *The Living Corpse.* But Tolstoy does not parody it as he does other literary texts. Instead, by concentrating on the failure of resurrection in the case of an individual, Tolstoy calls Fedorov's excessively optimistic system into question.

Although a recognition of Tolstoy's use of the intertexts cited above is vital to an understanding of *The Living Corpse,* there is another group of texts that play an even more important role in the play: Tolstoy's own earlier works. Tolstoy used the theme of death and resurrection frequently throughout his career. One might recall, for example, Prince Andrei's near death and subsequent resurrection at the battle of Austerlitz and then again at Borodino in *War and Peace,* as well as Pierre Bezukhov's moral death and resurrection in the same novel. Tolstoy's late novel, *Resurrection,* is obviously built around this theme, which had an autobiographical dimension as well: Tolstoy's *Confession* is structured around it (as, of course, are many confessions since Augustine). However, the work in which death and resurrection is featured most prominently, and the work which is most important for *The Living Corpse,* is *Anna Karenina.* Connections between these two works can hardly be missed, considering that Liza's second husband is Viktor Karenin (not Anna's Aleksei, but close enough) and his mother's name is Anna Karenina. Of course, Tolstoy did occasionally recycle character names innocently,[24] but the choice of the name Karenin here was certainly not accidental.

In an article entitled "A Real-Life Story and a Literary Plot," A. Maryamov demonstrates a number of ways in which *The Living Corpse* can be seen as a commentary on *Anna Karenina.* In Maryamov's view, the resurrection of Anna in the person of Viktor's mother, a society woman *comme il faut* in all the wrong ways, indicates yet another attempt by Tolstoy to reject his early work. "To revive his former heroine merely in order to afflict her with senile amnesia and to force her to forget the most searing moments of her own life—that is indeed a horrible vengeance. The only thing that could have brought Tolstoy to this kind of vengeance was a stubborn conviction which forced him, in a cruel battle with himself, to reject his earlier book."[25] While certain aspects of this interpretation are appealing, I believe that it is impossible to characterize the relationship between these two works in particular, and between the artistic work of the "early" and "late" Tolstoy in general, as one of simple rejection.

As I try to show in a different essay, the plot of *Anna Karenina* revolves around the figurative deaths and resurrections of all four main characters.[26] There are, however, two possible outcomes to this process. The deaths and resurrections of Kitty and Levin occur in a context of Christianity. They lead to moral regeneration, and ultimately, new life and happiness. Those of Vronsky and Anna are in a pagan context and lack a moral/religious component. After their resurrections, neither Anna nor Vronsky chooses the path of redemption, and eventually they are condemned to despair and new death.[27]

While it is possible to find Fedya to be a sympathetic character, he is undoubtedly a morally ambiguous figure. For although he abhors the false values of his class and has a number of admirable qualities, he is also untrustworthy, a drunkard, and a spendthrift. Most damning of all, when given the chance to be reborn, a chance that opens up the possibility of moral regeneration even to Tolstoy's greatest sinners, he fails, as illustrated by his actions after his resurrection. Fedya evidently rejects the pure and disinterested love of Masha the gypsy (an act which mirrors his rejection of his loving wife before the fake suicide), even though by his actions he has already made life among the gypsies untenable for her. In addition, he is arrested only because he cannot resist narrating his melodramatic history while drunk in a public place.

Thus, like Tarelkin and Gimer, Fedya loses his identity after his fake suicide and is unable to gain a new one after his "resurrection." Death and resurrection does not result in Fedya's spiritual renewal as it manifestly does for Kitty and Levin, Nekhlyudov and Pierre, all of whom find their "true" identity as a result of this process. On the contrary, Fedya chooses the way of Vronsky and Anna. In Tolstoy's moral and literary universe, this must inevitably lead to his real death, which comes by suicide in the final scene of the play. Thus, if any character in *The Living Corpse* can be said to represent a resurrected Anna Karenina, that character is surely Fedya Protasov. At the same time, Protasov lives not just by and in himself and in the reflected light of Anna, but in varying relations to Gimer, Tarelkin, Lopukhov, and all of Tolstoy's other resurrected personages. Fedya is composed of bits and pieces of all, the confused sum of his heterogeneous parts.

Thus, *The Living Corpse* draws its meaning through an ingenious juxtaposition of a varied group of subtexts. Tolstoy uses the plot element of the fake suicide to comment on the way that theme had previously been used in Russian culture. At the same time, he greatly broadens the philosophical implications of this this plot element by emphasizing its potentially tragic aspects and by integrating it with one of his favorite topics: death and resurrection. Thus, fake suicide and death and resurrection become part of a single theme cluster, which is further complicated by questions surrounding the resurrected character's tragic loss of identity. As a result, Fedya's fake suicide really becomes the "central knot from which and to which everything flows," making *The Living Corpse* a true drama in Tolstoyan terms.

Andrew Baruch Wachtel
Northwestern University

Translators' Preface

Virtually everything we wrote in the preface to volume 2 concerning Tolstoy's use of substandard language, dialect, and corruptions applies to several of the plays and the fragment contained in this volume, specifically, *The Wisdom of Children, The Traveler and the Peasant*, the untitled fragment, and *The Cause of It All.* This has made translation into English a daunting task. We decided not to follow the path of previous translators, who have, without exception, rendered these plays into more or less standard, colorless, literary English. Such use of English ensures that the flavor and tone of the original will be utterly lost. Therefore, we have, as in the previous volume, attempted an explicit "colloquial" rendition, one that is unmarked as to regional, ethnic, or racial origin. The dialect "transcription" we utilize emphasizes the way the plays should *sound.* This choice has resulted in a potential problem: the transcription takes some getting used to, since as a piece of English writing it *looks* affected and "kinda" awful on the page. To some extent this is also true of the original scripts for Russian readers, who have to make their way through a maze of corruptions, dialectisms, and distortions. Once again we hope our transcription will not prove to be too much of a burden on the reader.

We would like to take this opportunity to thank Andrew Wachtel and Géza von Molnár for their help in the preparation of this volume.

Peter the Breadman

A Drama in Five Acts 1884–1894

Wanderer
Beggars (3)
Beggarwomen (2)
Peter the Breadman (Methodius)
His wife
Woman fool in Christ (Dunyushka)
Physician
Woman
Elizar
   a slave
Buyers (2)
Slavemerchants (2)
Egyptian
Merchant
Mute

Tolstoy did not provide a list of the dramatis personae for this play. It has been prepared by the translators for the convenience of the reader.

ACT I

The action takes place in Syria during the third century.

SCENE 1

A square before a house. There sit two female and three male BEGGARS; *residents walk by; the* BEGGARS *ask for and receive alms.*

SCENE 2

Enter indigent WANDERER.

WANDERER. Greetings, friend.

FIRST BEGGAR. Where are you from?

WANDERER. From Cairo. Are things going well?

FIRST BEGGAR. Bad, too few rich people.

WANDERER. What do you mean too few? These here are such rich houses (*points*). The man who owns this one must have thousands.

[FIRST] BEGGARWOMAN. Yes, he's got much wealth, but he'd sooner choke than give something to a beggar.

SECOND BEGGAR. Everyone knows Peter the Breadman. Ever since I've lived here, thirty years now, he's never given anyone so much as a crust of bread.

THIRD BEGGAR. And his wife and daughter are the same.

SECOND BEGGARWOMAN. No, his daughter's a little kinder. Their maid-servant said so.

FIRST BEGGARWOMAN. There isn't a stingier man in the world than this Peter; he'll never give anything to anyone.

WANDERER. What do you mean he won't? He'll give to the one who knows how to ask.

FIRST BEGGAR. Is that so! Just try.

WANDERER. I will too. There isn't a man who wouldn't give if I press him.

[FIRST] BEGGARWOMAN AND [FIRST] BEGGAR. You can't ask him enough, he just won't give.

WANDERER. Want to bet?

FIRST BEGGAR. How much?

They all crowd around the WANDERER.

WANDERER. Do you want to bet these three coins?

FIRST BEGGAR. It's a bet (*they strike hands and laugh*). Hand over the coins.

(*The* WANDERER *and* FIRST BEGGAR *give the coins to the* FIRST BEGGARWOMAN.)

SECOND BEGGAR. Here he comes now. He's taking loaves of bread to the prince.

SCENE 3

Enter PETER *followed by a slave carrying a basket of bread.*

WANDERER (*approaching* PETER). For the love of Christ, help a homeless wanderer. You are our patron, have mercy. Benefactor, for the love of Christ, I'm dying of hunger...

PETER (*continues on his way without turning his head; the* WANDERER *presses him, falls to his knees, clutches the flaps of his robe*). Leave me alone.

WANDERER. Kind sir, please...

PETER. Get away.

WANDERER (*runs to his other side; falls to his knees*). Kind sir...

PETER. Go away or I'll kill you (*bends down and picks up a stone*).

WANDERER. Be merciful, have pity. (*Clutches his hand.*)

PETER. I said I'll kill you. Go away. (*Grabs a loaf from the basket, throws it at him, and exits.*)

SCENE 4

THE SAME *without* PETER.

WANDERER (*catches the loaf and runs to the* BEGGARS). What did I say? I won. Here it is, Peter's alms. (*Shows the loaf.*) Give me my coins.
SECOND BEGGAR. You're lucky, my friend. You won, so why not treat us.

Curtain.

ACT II

The interior of PETER*'s home.* PETER*'s wife and daughter are sitting in the foreground. In the background there is a bed on which* PETER *is lying, tossing about and delirious.*

SCENE 1

PETER. You bandits, you've ruined me. Why'd you put so much flour in? Pay the money. Slice it. The king. Flowers have burst out. Good-bye. (*Calms down.*)

WIFE. It'll be the third day this evening, and he's still not better. I hope he won't die.

Enter FOOL IN CHRIST.

FOOL IN CHRIST. Hi there, woman. Still crying. You think you're going to bury your husband. Have no fear, he won't die. He's not ready yet. He's been gathering money for thirty years, now it's going to take just as many years to throw it around. Then he'll be ready, only then.

WIFE. Enough of your foolishness, Dunyushka. You want something to eat?

FOOL IN CHRIST. I don't need to eat. Hey, old man, you asleep? (*The daughter exits;* PETER *listens carefully.*) A rich man can't enter the kingdom of heaven. You can't wriggle in, you'll get snared. And if you can't wriggle in, you'll land in hell with the devils.

SCENE 2

Enter PHYSICIAN. THE SAME *and the* PHYSICIAN, *without the daughter.*

PETER (*jumps up and shouts*). What do you want? Do you want to choke me also?

PHYSICIAN. Calm down, your sickness will pass. (*Takes him by the hand and seats him on the bed.*)

FOOL IN CHRIST. You're a fool, a fool, you're doing dumb things, you're spoiling my doings. I don't want to look. (*Exits running.*)

PHYSICIAN. Hold him. (*Feels and taps his body, and talks to himself.*) Nothing here. Here, it begins. I can hear it, right here. I'll drive this one out. All the sickness is here. You'll recover, just relax. Lie still. (*Takes out a bottle, gives him to drink, and hands another bottle to his wife to rub him down.*) Rub him down in the evening. Like this. (*The PHYSICIAN exits; the WIFE follows him.*)

SCENE 3

PETER (*alone, lies silently for a long time; suddenly jumps up and sits down*). What's this? It's death. I feel that I'm dying. Here, an angel has come for my soul. He said I'll recover. How can you recover from death? My God, what'll happen to me there? Is it really true that a rich man can't enter the kingdom of heaven? Is it really true that I'll be accountable for all my cruelty, for not giving to one who asks, for not having pity on the widow, the orphan, the sick, the needy? Is it really true? Why didn't I understand this? It'd be better for me to give not half but everything away than to go to those devils now. Here they are, here, already pulling my soul away. (*Looks up.*) And here they are, the scales which will weigh my good and evil deeds. Now on one side they placed the money I've taken away from widows and orphans, the wages I've not given to workers, the insults, curses, and blows. Now they piled up the platform on the scales, and already the scales have gone down, and they, the devils, rejoiced. Oh, oh, I'm lost. What will they now place on the other side?... What's this? A loaf of bread. Just one loaf, that loaf which I then threw at that irksome beggar. Good gracious, the scales have risen, the loaf outweighed all my evil deeds... So that's what charity is about! If only I don't die now. I'd know what I should do. Following the words of Christ, I'd give all that I have to the poor,[1] and would leave nothing for myself. (*Drops on the bed and falls asleep.*)

Curtain.

ACT III

In front of the veranda of PETER'S *home.* PETER *is on the veranda, around which there is a huge crowd of beggars and other people.* PETER *is distributing money from a sack.*

SCENE 1

FIRST BEGGAR (*to the* SECOND BEGGAR). You're now taking for the second time. (*They push each other.*)

SECOND BEGGAR. That's not true, it's you who's taken three times.

WOMAN. Oh, goodness gracious, I'm being crushed.

VOICE FROM THE CROWD. Don't rush ahead then.

THIRD BEGGAR. To me, to me, I've got five children, one younger than the other...

Various cries are heard.

PETER. Take, take, there's enough, just don't wrong one another. I wronged you all enough, forgive me, for the love of Christ.

SCENE 2

WIFE (*enters running*). What are you doing, you bandit? Do you want us to become beggars? You used to be much too stingy, but now you're much too generous. You bandit. (*Takes the sack away from him and pushes him into the house; shouts at the people and drives them away.*)

SCENE 3

Enter PETER THE BREADMAN *with his slave* ELIZAR.

PETER. So promise you'll do what I ask of you.

ELIZAR. I'll do everything, because now I love you more than I love my father and mother. I love you because I see the spirit of God in you.

PETER. You promise, you swear?

ELIZAR. I promise, I swear.

PETER. You see, my family won't allow me to distribute the last of what I have. I cannot use force against them, but I also cannot remain the way I was. I now understand my sin and want to atone for it, and to serve God alone. It is said: "Sell whatsoever thou hast, and give to the poor."[2] They won't let me distribute the remainder of what I have. I'm not free to dispose of it, but I'm free to dispose of myself, and I want to give myself to the people. So come with me to the bazaar where they sell slaves, bind my hands, and take me forth, and sell me as your slave. And the money you'll earn, give to the poor.

ELIZAR. Master, I cannot do this.

PETER. But didn't you promise and swear to me?

ELIZAR. Don't do this, I feel sorry for you.

PETER. Why didn't you feel sorry for me when I was doing evil and ruining myself? And now you feel sorry when I want to save myself.

ELIZAR. Let it be as you wish.

WIFE (*enters*). What are you doing here? Enough of your babbling about nothing. Come into the house. (*They exit.*)

Curtain.

ACT IV

The bazaar. Female and male slaves bound and shackled, and their SLAVEMERCHANTS. *The* FIRST SLAVEMERCHANT *with two [fe]male slaves;³ the* SECOND SLAVEMERCHANT *with an old male slave and his son, a boy slave;* ELIZAR *with* PETER. BUYERS.

SCENE 1

FIRST BUYER. How much are you asking for this one? (*Points to a female slave.*)

FIRST SLAVEMERCHANT. Twenty pieces of ten.

FIRST BUYER. What can she do?

FIRST SLAVEMERCHANT. She can dance, sing.

FIRST BUYER. Can she cook?

FIRST SLAVEMERCHANT. For cooking take the old one.

FIRST BUYER. I don't want her.

SECOND BUYER (*comes up to the old man and the boy*). How much for these two?

SECOND SLAVEMERCHANT. Thirteen pieces of ten.

SECOND BUYER. Who would give you that? (*Touches the old man's arm.*) He has no strength, and that one's too young.

SECOND SLAVEMERCHANT. I won't take less.

SECOND BUYER. No, I don't want them. (*Comes up to* PETER.) What kind of work is he good for?

ELIZAR (*quietly*). I can't, free me.

PETER. Remember, you swore, don't ruin me. (*To the* BUYER.) I'm good for all manner of work. I can do manual work, and I can also write and reckon.

SECOND BUYER. How much?

PETER (*whispers to* ELIZAR). Say: ten pieces of ten.

ELIZAR. Ten pieces of ten.

SCENE 2

Enter two EGYPTIANS.

FIRST EGYPTIAN (*to the* BUYER). Why are you buying him?

SECOND BUYER. I need someone for manual labor. But this one knows how to write and reckon, and such people are not suitable for hard labor.

FIRST EGYPTIAN. I need just such a person. In our precious stones business hard labor isn't necessary, but honesty, prudence, and loyalty are.

PETER. Take me, Master, you'll be satisfied. I'll serve you as a son does his own father.

FIRST EGYPTIAN. I like you. (*To* ELIZAR.) What's his price?

ELIZAR. Ten pieces of ten.

FIRST EGYPTIAN. Here's the money.

ELIZAR (*weeping*). I can't.

PETER (*embraces* ELIZAR). Good-bye. Give away the money as I told you.

ELIZAR. I'll do everything so that your soul can be at peace. Good-bye, dear Master.

PETER. Quiet. (*Exits with the* EGYPTIAN; ELIZAR *alone, weeps.*)

Curtain.

ACT V

*The action takes place in Egypt. A gatekeeper-*MUTE *admits a* PHYSICIAN *and a* MERCHANT, *and explains by signs that his master is coming shortly.* [MUTE] *exits.*

SCENE 1

PHYSICIAN. He must mean that his master is at home, and he's inviting us in. Let's go.

MERCHANT. Yes, I know that they are hospitable people.

SCENE 2

Enter FIRST EGYPTIAN.

FIRST EGYPTIAN (*addressing the* MERCHANT). I'm happy to see you in my home. You're welcome here. You must be tired from your journey, and will not refuse my hospitality.

MERCHANT. Thank you. My friend the physician and I have come from distant Syria to do business in your city, and we're happy to visit with you.

[FIRST] EGYPTIAN (*claps his hands and calls*). Methodius! (*To the guests.*) Please, be seated.

SCENE 3

Enter PETER *dressed as a servant-slave. Upon seeing the* PHYSICIAN, *he becomes frightened and turns away.*

PETER. What does my master command?

[FIRST] EGYPTIAN. Bring some bread, wine, and grapes for my dear guests. They're from your country. Do you happen to know them?

PETER. No, I don't. (*Exits.*)

PHYSICIAN (*to the host*). Have you ever been in our city?

[FIRST] EGYPTIAN. I was there eight years ago. At that time I bought the slave you've just seen.

PHYSICIAN. Now that was the time when something very unusual happened in our city, something that nobody can understand to this day.

[FIRST] EGYPTIAN. What was that?

PHYSICIAN. Well, one of the richest men in our city, Peter the Breadman, who owned huge gardens and much land, and who was the stingiest man in the country, suddenly turned to the Christian faith, and distributed everything he could. But since he couldn't distribute everything, he, they say, sold himself into slavery, and the price he received for that he gave away to the poor, and disappeared without a trace.

MERCHANT. His wife to this day keeps on sending people everywhere in search of him, but no one knows where he is or what he's doing.

[FIRST] EGYPTIAN. What a strange story. How old was he and what did he look like?

(*Enter* PETER *carrying a pitcher with wine and some fruit.*)

PHYSICIAN. He was around fifty, of medium height, and more on the thin side than the heavy one, like this slave. (PETER *covers his face and hurriedly exits.*) What a nice face this slave has.

[FIRST] EGYPTIAN. He is not a slave, he's pure gold. Since I've had him, all of my affairs have prospered. Many times have I offered him his freedom, but he doesn't want it. He's a slave, but he's one of the finest people I've ever known. Methodius, come here.

Enter PETER.

PHYSICIAN (*to the* MERCHANT). Look, he really resembles Peter the Breadman.

(PETER *runs toward the door.*)

PETER. Mute, open the door. (*The door opens;* PETER *runs out. Enter* MUTE.)

MUTE. That was a saint, for I saw a halo surround him as he went out the gate; then he disappeared.

[FIRST] EGYPTIAN. It's a miracle, the mute is talking.

MERCHANT AND PHYSICIAN. It is he, it is he, he vanished to prevent men from praising him.

Curtain.

The End.

And the Light Shineth in Darkness[1]

A Drama in Five Acts 1896–1897, 1900

Nikolai [Nicolas] Ivanovich Saryntsev
Marya [Marie, Masha] Ivanovna
  Saryntseva
  his wife
Styopa
Vanya
[Nikolenka]
[Misha]
  their sons
Lyuba [Lyubov Nikolayevna]
Missy
Katya
[Natasha]
  their daughters
Mitrofan Yermilovich [Yermilych]
  Vanya's tutor
Governess of the Saryntsevs
Nannie of the Saryntsevs
Aleksandra [Alina, Sasha] Ivanovna
  Kokhovtseva
  Marya Ivanovna's sister
Pyotr [Petya] Semyonovich
  [Semyonych] Kokhovtsev
  her husband
Lizanka [Liza]
  their daughter
Princess Cheremshanova [Catiche]
Boris [Aleksandrovich Cheremshanov,
  Borya]
  her son
Tonya
  her daughter
Little Girl
  her daughter
Vasily Nikanorovich
  a young priest
Aleksandr Mikhailovich Starkovsky
  Lyuba's intended
Father Gerasim [Fyodorov]
  a priest

Lawyer
Ivan Zyabrev
  a peasant
Malashka
  his daughter with her baby brother
Woman
  wife of Ivan Zyabrev
Yermil
  a peasant
Other peasant
Sevastyan
  a peasant
Pyotr
  a peasant
Woman
  wife of Pyotr
Policeman
Peasant men with scythes, peasant
  women with rakes
Carpenter [Yakov Nikanorovich]
General
Adjutant of the general
Colonel
Regimental clerk
Sentry
Two soldiers
Political officer[2]
Clerk of the political officer
Regimental chaplain
Head doctor, in a ward for the
  mentally ill in a military hospital
Staff doctor, in the same ward
Guards, in the same ward
Officer-patient
Pianist
Countess
Aleksandr Petrovich
Footmen of the Saryntsevs [Afanasy]
Students, ladies
Dancing couples

ACT I

The set depicts the enclosed terrace of a wealthy country home. In front of the terrace are flower beds, a lawn tennis court, and croquet lawn. The children are playing croquet with their GOVERNESS. *Sitting on the terrace are* MARYA IVANOVNA SARYNTSEVA, *an attractive, elegant woman of forty; her sister,* ALEKSANDRA IVANOVNA KOKHOVTSEVA, *a fat, determined, and stupid woman of forty-five; and her husband,* PYOTR SEMYONOVICH KOKHOVTSEV, *a fat, flabby man dressed in a summer suit, and wearing a pince-nez. They are sitting at a table set with a samovar and coffee pot, and drinking coffee;* PYOTR SEMYONOVICH *is smoking.*

SCENE 1

MARYA IVANOVNA, ALEKSANDRA IVANOVNA, *and* PYOTR SEMYONOVICH.

ALEKSANDRA IVANOVNA. If you weren't my sister but a stranger, and Nikolai Ivanovich weren't your husband but an acquaintance, I would find this original, and very cute, and, perhaps, I myself would go along with it. *J'aurais trouvé tout ça très gentil.* But when I see your husband acting like a fool—really, a fool—then I can't stop myself from telling you what I think. And I'll tell him, your husband, too. *Je lui dirai son fait, au cher* Nikolai Ivanovich. I'm not afraid of anyone.

MARYA IVANOVNA. I'm not offended, not at all. Can't I see it myself? Only I don't think it's that important.

ALEKSANDRA IVANOVNA. You don't think so, but let me tell you that if you just leave things as they are, you can wind up being paupers, *du train que cela va.*

PYOTR SEMYONOVICH. Come now, paupers, with their means!

ALEKSANDRA IVANOVNA. Yes, paupers. Please don't interrupt me, my dear. Whatever you men do is always fine with you...

PYOTR SEMYONOVICH. Oh, I don't know, I'm only saying...

ALEKSANDRA IVANOVNA. But you never know what you're saying, because when your fellow men start acting like fools, *il n'y a pas de raison*

que ça finisse. I'm only saying that if I were in your place, I wouldn't allow it. *J'aurais mis bon ordre à toutes ces lubies.* What's this business? A
husband, the head of a family, has no occupation, dropped everything,
and just gives everything away *et fait le généreux à droit et à gauche.* I
know how it'll end. *Nous en savons quelque chose.*

PYOTR SEMYONOVICH (*to* MARYA IVANOVNA). But *Marie,* explain to
me, what's this new trend? Now liberals want regional councils, a con-
stitution, schools, reading rooms and *tout ce qui s'en suit*—I understand
this. And Socialists back *les grèves,* an eight-hour day—I understand this
too. But what is this? Explain it to me.

MARYA IVANOVNA. But he told you yesterday.

PYOTR SEMYONOVICH. I must admit I didn't understand. The Gospel,
the Sermon on the Mount, the Church isn't necessary... But then how
can you pray, and all that?...

MARYA IVANOVNA. The main thing is that he'd destroy everything and
put nothing in its place.

PYOTR SEMYONOVICH. How did it start?

MARYA IVANOVNA. It started last year, when his sister died. He loved her
very much, and her death had a great affect on him. He became very
gloomy, talked about death all the time, and got sick himself, as you
know. And then, after his bout with typhus, he changed completely.

ALEKSANDRA IVANOVNA. Still, in the spring he came to see us in
Moscow, and was very nice, and played whist. *Il était très gentil et comme
tout le monde.*

MARYA IVANOVNA. Yes, but he was already entirely different.

PYOTR SEMYONOVICH. How, specifically?

MARYA IVANOVNA. Well, completely indifferent to his family, and an *idée
fixe*—the Gospel. He would read it for days on end, didn't sleep nights,
would get up, read, make notes, excerpts, and then he began going to
bishops and monks—all to seek advice about religion.

ALEKSANDRA IVANOVNA. So did he fast and prepare for confession and
communion?

MARYA IVANOVNA. Until then he hadn't done this since we got married,
must be twenty-five years ago. But now he did once fast, confess, and
take communion in a monastery, and decided immediately after doing
so that this ritual isn't necessary, nor is going to church.

ALEKSANDRA IVANOVNA. That's what I'm saying, there's no consistency whatever.

MARYA IVANOVNA. Yes, a month ago he wouldn't miss a single service and kept every fast, and then suddenly none of this is necessary. So go on and talk to him.

ALEKSANDRA IVANOVNA. I already did and I will again.

PYOTR SEMYONOVICH. Yes. But that's not that terrible...

ALEKSANDRA IVANOVNA. For you nothing is that terrible, because you men have no religion.

PYOTR SEMYONOVICH. No, please let me speak. I'm saying that that is not the point. If he rejects the Church, why does he need the Gospel?

MARYA IVANOVNA. To live according to the Gospel, and the Sermon on the Mount, and give everything away.

ALEKSANDRA IVANOVNA. Always extremes.

PYOTR SEMYONOVICH. But how can you live if you give everything away?

ALEKSANDRA IVANOVNA. And where did he find in the Sermon on the Mount that you have to shake hands with footmen? It says: "Blessed are the meek," but there's nothing about shaking hands.

MARYA IVANOVNA. Yes, of course, he gets carried away as always, just as he once got carried away by music, hunting, and schools. But that doesn't make it easier for me.

PYOTR SEMYONOVICH. So why did he go to town?

MARYA IVANOVNA. He didn't tell me, but I know that it's about the trees that were stolen. The peasants have cut trees down in our forest.

PYOTR SEMYONOVICH. The stand of fir you planted?

MARYA IVANOVNA. Yes, they were fined and sentenced to jail, and today, he told me, their case is being reviewed,[3] and I'm certain he went for that.

ALEKSANDRA IVANOVNA. He'll forgive them, and tomorrow they'll come and cut the trees in the park.

MARYA IVANOVNA. It's already started. They've broken all the apple trees and trampled the unripe fields; he forgives it all.

PYOTR SEMYONOVICH. That's odd.

ALEKSANDRA IVANOVNA. That's exactly why I'm saying you cannot leave things as they are. If it goes on like this, *tout y passera.* I think you have to, as a mother, *prendre tes mésures.*

MARYA IVANOVNA. But what can I do?

ALEKSANDRA IVANOVNA. What can you do? Stop him, explain to him that this cannot go on. You have children. What kind of example is this for them?

MARYA IVANOVNA. Of course, it's hard, but I just bear it and hope it'll pass, like his previous infatuations.

ALEKSANDRA IVANOVNA. Yes, but *aide toi, et Dieu t'aidera*. You have to make him understand that he's not alone, and that he cannot live like this.

MARYA IVANOVNA. Worst of all is that he no longer cares about the children. I have to decide everything all by myself. And on the one hand I have a nursing infant, and on the other older children, girls and boys, who need supervision and guidance. And I'm all alone. He used to be such an affectionate, thoughtful father, but now he doesn't care. Yesterday I told him that Vanya isn't studying and will fail again, and he said it would be much better if he would leave school altogether.

PYOTR SEMYONOVICH. And go where?

MARYA IVANOVNA. Nowhere. That's what's so awful: everything is no good, but what's there to do, he doesn't say.

PYOTR SEMYONOVICH. That's strange.

ALEKSANDRA IVANOVNA. What's strange about it? It's simply your usual way: condemn everything and do nothing yourselves.

MARYA IVANOVNA. Styopa has now graduated and has to choose a career, but his father doesn't say anything to him. He wanted to get a position in a minister's office—Nikolai Ivanovich said he shouldn't; he wanted to go into the horse guards—Nikolai Ivanovich was completely against it. So he asked: "Then what am I to do, not work the land?" And Nikolai Ivanovich said: "Why not work the land, it's much better than office work." So what's he to do? He comes to me and asks, and I have to decide everything. But all the prerogatives are in his father's hands.

ALEKSANDRA IVANOVNA. Well you have to tell him all this straight-out.

MARYA IVANOVNA. Yes, I have to, I'll talk to him.

ALEKSANDRA IVANOVNA. And tell him straight-out that you cannot go on this way, that you're doing your duty, and he has to do his; if not— let him hand everything over to you.

MARYA IVANOVNA. Ah, that's so unpleasant.

ALEKSANDRA IVANOVNA. I'll tell him if you want. *Je lui dirai son fait.*

(*Enter a* YOUNG PRIEST, *nervous and uneasy, carrying a book; shakes hands with everyone.*)

SCENE 2

THE SAME *and* YOUNG PRIEST

PRIEST. I've come to see Nikolai Ivanovich, so to speak, I've brought his book.

MARYA IVANOVNA. He's gone to town; he'll be back soon.

ALEKSANDRA IVANOVNA. Now what would be the book that you borrowed?

PRIEST. Oh, it's a work by Mr. Renan, so to speak, *The Life of Jesus.*[4]

PYOTR SEMYONOVICH. Is that so! What books you read!

PRIEST (*nervously lights a cigarette*). It was Nikolai Ivanovich, he gave it to me to read.

ALEKSANDRA IVANOVNA (*contemptuously*). Nikolai Ivanovich gave it to you to read! So, do you agree with Nikolai Ivanovich and Mr. Renan?

PRIEST. Certainly not. If, so to speak, I agreed, I wouldn't be, as they say, a servant of the Church.

ALEKSANDRA IVANOVNA. And if, as they say, you're a faithful servant of the Church, why don't you convince Nikolai Ivanovich?

PRIEST. Everyone, it could be said, has their own ideas about these matters, and Nikolai Ivanovich, it could be said, is right about many things, but he's wrong, it could be said, about the main thing, the Church.

ALEKSANDRA IVANOVNA (*contemptuously*). So what are the many things Nikolai Ivanovich is right about? Is it right then that you must, according to the Sermon on the Mount, give your property away to strangers, and let your family go begging?

PRIEST. The Church sort of sanctifies, so to speak, the family, and the Fathers of the Church sort of blessed the family, but the highest perfection, so to speak, requires the renunciation of worldly goods.

ALEKSANDRA IVANOVNA. Yes, ascetics did this, but I think ordinary mortals should simply do what is fitting for every good Christian.

PRIEST. Nobody can know what summons awaits him.

ALEKSANDRA IVANOVNA. You are, of course, married, aren't you?

PRIEST. Certainly.

ALEKSANDRA IVANOVNA. And do you have children?

PRIEST. Two.

ALEKSANDRA IVANOVNA. Then why aren't you renouncing worldly goods, but smoking those lousy cigarettes instead?

PRIEST. On account of my weakness, it could be said, my unworthiness.

ALEKSANDRA IVANOVNA. Yes, I see, instead of talking sense into Nikolai Ivanovich, you support him. I'll tell you straight-out, that's wrong!

SCENE 3

THE SAME *and* NANNIE.

NANNIE (*enters*). Don't you hear Nikolushka crying? Please go and nurse him.

MARYA IVANOVNA. I'm coming, I'm coming. (*Gets up and exits.*)

SCENE 4

THE SAME *without* NANNIE *and* MARYA IVANOVNA.

ALEKSANDRA IVANOVNA. I feel so terribly sorry for my sister. I see how she's struggling. It's no joking matter to run a household—seven children,[5] one still nursing, and then these here fantasies to boot. I really think there's something wrong here. (*Points to her head.*) Now I ask you, what is this new religion you have found?

PRIEST. I don't understand, so to speak...

ALEKSANDRA IVANOVNA. Please stop playing games with me. You understand very well what I'm asking.

PRIEST. But please...

ALEKSANDRA IVANOVNA. I'm asking, is there such a faith that professes that you must shake hands with every peasant, and let them cut down trees, and give them money for vodka, and abandon your own family?

PRIEST. I don't know any...

ALEKSANDRA IVANOVNA. He says it's Christianity. You're an Orthodox priest, so you must know and must tell me whether Christianity commands us to encourage robbery?

PRIEST. But I...

ALEKSANDRA IVANOVNA. Then why are you a priest, and why wear long hair and a cassock?

PRIEST. But Aleksandra Ivanovna, we are not asked...

ALEKSANDRA IVANOVNA. What do you mean not asked? I'm asking. He told me yesterday that the Gospel says: "Give to him that asketh thee."[6] So in what sense is that to be understood?

PRIEST. In its obvious sense, I believe.

ALEKSANDRA IVANOVNA. And I think not in its obvious sense, but as we were taught; everyone's fate is determined by God.

PRIEST. Of course, however...

ALEKSANDRA IVANOVNA. Well now it's quite clear that you're on his side, just as I was told. And I'll tell you straight-out, that's bad. It's one thing for a schoolmarm or some kid to go along with him, but you, in your position, must bear in mind what your responsibility is.

PRIEST. I try to...

ALEKSANDRA IVANOVNA. What kind of religion is it if he doesn't go to church and doesn't recognize the sacraments? And you, instead of talking sense into him, read Renan with him, and interpret the Gospel as you like.

PRIEST (*nervously*). I cannot answer. I'm, so to speak, shocked, and will hold my tongue.

ALEKSANDRA IVANOVNA. Oh, if I were the bishop, I'd teach you to read Renan and smoke those lousy cigarettes!

PYOTR SEMYONOVICH. *Mais cessez au nom du ciel. De quel droit?*

ALEKSANDRA IVANOVNA. Please, don't lecture me. I'm certain the reverend father isn't angry with me. Well, I've had my say. It would be worse if I kept it in. Right?

PRIEST. Forgive me if I didn't express myself properly, forgive me.

(*An awkward silence. The* PRIEST *walks aside, opens the book, and reads. Enter* LYUBA *and* LIZANKA. LYUBA, *a beautiful, energetic girl of twenty, daughter of* MARYA IVANOVNA; LIZANKA, *a little older than* LYUBA, *daughter of* ALEKSANDRA IVANOVNA. *Both carry baskets, wear kerchiefs, are on their way to gather mushrooms. They exchange greetings,* LYUBA *with her aunt and uncle,* LIZANKA *with her father and mother, and the* PRIEST.)

SCENE 5

THE SAME, LYUBA *and* LIZANKA.

LYUBA. Where's Mamá?

ALEKSANDRA IVANOVNA. She just went to nurse the baby.

PYOTR SEMYONOVICH. See that you bring back a bunch. This morning our girl brought marvelous white mushrooms. I'd go with you but it's too hot.

LIZANKA. Come on, Papá.

ALEKSANDRA IVANOVNA. Go, go ahead, you're getting too fat.

PYOTR SEMYONOVICH. All right, I'll just take my cigarettes. (*Exits.*)

SCENE 6

THE SAME *without* PYOTR SEMYONOVICH.

ALEKSANDRA IVANOVNA. Now where are all our youngsters?

LYUBA. Styopa rode his bike to the station. Mitrofan Yermilych went to town with Papá, the little guys are playing croquet, and Vanya is here on the porch, fooling around with the dogs.

ALEKSANDRA IVANOVNA. So, has Styopa made a decision?

LYUBA. Yes, he brought in his application, he's volunteering. He was disgustingly rude with Papá yesterday.

ALEKSANDRA IVANOVNA. Well, it's hard on him, too. *Il n'y a pas de pa-*

tience qui tienne. The boy has to make a life for himself, and he's told go work the land.

LYUBA. Papá didn't tell him that. He said...

ALEKSANDRA IVANOVNA. It doesn't matter. Styopa has to make a life for himself, and whatever he thinks of, it's all wrong. Ah, here he comes.

(*Enter* STYOPA *riding on a bicycle.*)

SCENE 7

THE SAME *and* STYOPA.

ALEKSANDRA IVANOVNA. *Quand on parle du soleil, on en voit les rayons.* We were just talking about you. Lyuba says you weren't very nice to your father.

STYOPA. Not so. There was nothing in particular. He gave me his opinion, and I gave him mine. It's not my fault that our convictions differ. Lyuba, you know, understands nothing but has an opinion about everything.

ALEKSANDRA IVANOVNA. So what did you decide?

STYOPA. I don't know what Papá decided. I'm afraid he doesn't know very well himself, but as for me, I've decided to volunteer for the horse guards. Everything is turned into a problem here. But it's all very simple. I've graduated, and I have to serve my time. To serve it in the army with drunken and crude officers wouldn't be much fun, so I'm joining the guards where I have friends.

ALEKSANDRA IVANOVNA. Yes, but why didn't Papá agree?

STYOPA. Papá? What's there to say about him? He's now under the influence of his *idée fixe,* and sees nothing but what he wants to see. He says military service is the vilest form of service, and so one shouldn't serve at all; that's why he won't give me any money.

LIZANKA. No, Styopa, he didn't say that; I was here, you know. He said, if you can't avoid serving, let them draft you; but to volunteer is to choose this form of service yourself.

STYOPA. But it's I who'll serve, not he. He served his time already.

LIZANKA. Yes, but he says it's not that he's not giving any money, it's that he cannot take part in something which is contrary to his convictions.

STYOPA. It's not a matter of convictions, one has to serve, and that's it.

LIZANKA. I'm only saying what I heard.

STYOPA. I know you always agree with Papá. Aunt Alina, you know Liza's always on Papá's side.

LIZANKA. If something's right...

ALEKSANDRA IVANOVNA. Yes, I know Liza's always on the side of all kinds of nonsense. She can sniff out nonsense. *Elle flaire cela de loin.*

SCENE 8

THE SAME *and* VANYA. (VANYA, *in a red shirt, enters, running, carrying a telegram, followed by dogs.*)

VANYA (*to Lyuba*). Guess who's coming?

LYUBA. Why should I? Give me the telegram. (*Reaches for it;* VANYA *does not let go.*)

VANYA. I won't give it to you, and I won't tell. It's someone who'll make you blush.

LYUBA. Nonsense! Who's the telegram from?

VANYA. See, you blushed, you blushed. Aunt Alina, she blushed, didn't she?

LYUBA. What nonsense! Who's it from? Aunt Alina, who's it from?

ALEKSANDRA IVANOVNA. The Cheremshanovs.

LYUBA. Aha!

VANYA. That's it! Huh! So why're you blushing?

LYUBA. Aunt Alina, show me the telegram. (*Reads.*) "Three of us arriving on mail train. Cheremshanovs." That means the princess, Boris, and Tonya. Well, I'm very glad.

VANYA. That's it, very glad! Styopa, look how she's blushing.

STYOPA. Now stop bothering her, you keep going on and on.

VANYA. Yeah, because you're busy making eyes at Tonya. You'd better draw for it, since a sister and brother can't marry a brother and sister.[7]

STYOPA. Stop talking rubbish. Leave it alone. How many times have you been told already!

LIZANKA. If they're coming with the mail train, they'll be here soon.
LYUBA. That's right. So we won't leave.

SCENE 9

THE SAME *and* PYOTR SEMYONOVICH.

LYUBA. Uncle Petya, we're not going.
PYOTR SEMYONOVICH. Why not?
LYUBA. The Cheremshanovs are coming soon. Let's play one set of tennis
   in the meantime. Styopa, do you want to?
STYOPA. All right.
LYUBA. Vanya and me against you and Lizanka. Okay? Then I'll go get the
   balls and round up the kids. (*Exits.*)

SCENE 10

THE SAME *without* LYUBA.

PYOTR SEMYONOVICH. Well, so much for going.
PRIEST (*preparing to leave*). It was a pleasure.
ALEKSANDRA IVANOVNA. No, Father, wait, I'd like to talk to you. Be-
   sides, Nikolai Ivanovich will be back soon.
PRIEST (*sits down and lights another cigarette*). It'll probably be long, won't
   it?
ALEKSANDRA IVANOVNA. There, someone's coming. Must be him.
PYOTR SEMYONOVICH. Which Cheremshanova is this? Could her
   maiden name be Golitsyna?
ALEKSANDRA IVANOVNA. Of course. The same Cheremshanova who
   used to live in Rome with her aunt.
PYOTR SEMYONOVICH. I'll really be glad to see her. I haven't seen her
   since Rome when we sang duets together. She sang very well. She has
   two children, doesn't she?
ALEKSANDRA IVANOVNA. Yes, she's bringing them along.

PYOTR SEMYONOVICH. I didn't know they and the Saryntsevs were that close.

ALEKSANDRA IVANOVNA. Not close, they just lived together abroad last year. And it seems to me *la princesse a des vues sur Lyuba pour sons fils. C'est une fine mouche, elle flaire une jolie dot.*

PYOTR SEMYONOVICH. But the Cheremshanovs themselves were rich.

ALEKSANDRA IVANOVNA. They were. The prince is still alive, but he's a hopeless drunk, and has squandered everything. She appealed to His Highness, salvaged a few scraps, and left him. But in spite of that she did an excellent job with her children. *Il faut lui rendre cette justice.* Her daughter's an excellent musician, and her son finished the university, and is very nice. Only I don't think Masha's very happy. It's not a good time for guests now. Ah, here's Nicolas.

(*Enter* NIKOLAI IVANOVICH.)

SCENE 11

THE SAME *and* NIKOLAI IVANOVICH.

NIKOKAI IVANOVICH. Hi, Alina, Pyotr Semyonych. Ah (*to the* PRIEST) Vasily Nikanorovich. (*Shakes his hand.*)

ALEKSANDRA IVANOVNA. There's still some coffee left. Do you want some? It's a bit cold, but can be warmed up. (*Rings.*)

NIKOLAI IVANOVICH. No, thanks. I'm fine. Where's Masha?

ALEKSANDRA IVANOVNA. Nursing the baby.

NIKOLAI IVANOVICH. Is she all right?

ALEKSANDRA IVANOVNA. Pretty good. So, have you taken care of your business?

NIKOLAI IVANOVICH. Yes, I have. You know, if there's any tea or coffere, I'll have some. (*To the* PRIEST.) Ah, you've brought the book. Did you read it? I was thinking about you all the way back.

(*Enter* FOOTMAN, *bows.* NIKOLAI IVANOVICH *shakes his hand.* ALEXANDRA IVANOVNA *shrugs her shoulders and exchanges glances with her husband.*)

SCENE 12

THE SAME *and* FOOTMAN.

ALEKSANDRA IVANOVNA. Heat up the samovar, please.
NIKOLAI IVANOVICH. Never mind, Alina. I don't want any, but if I feel like, I'll drink it as it is.

SCENE 13

THE SAME *and* MISSY.

MISSY (*upon seeing her father, she comes running from the croquet lawn, and throws her arms around his neck.*) Papá, come with me.
NIKOLAI IVANOVICH (*caressing her*). Right away, right away, just let me have a bite to eat. Go and play, I'll come.

SCENE 14

THE SAME *without* MISSY.

ALEKSANDRA IVANOVNA. So, were the peasants found guilty at the session?

(NIKOLAI IVANOVICH *sits down at the table, and avidly drinks tea and eats*).

ALEKSANDRA IVANOVNA. So, were they?
NIKOLAI IVANOVICH. Yes, they were, but they themselves admitted their guilt. (*To the* PRIEST.) I thought you'd find Renan not very convincing...
ALEKSANDRA IVANOVNA. But you didn't agree with the verdict?
NIKOLAI IVANOVICH (*annoyed*). Of course I didn't. (*To the* PRIEST.) For you the question is not the divinity of Christ, or the history of Christianity, but the Church...

ALEKSANDRA IVANOVNA. How come? They admitted their guilt, *et vous leur avez donné un démenti.* They didn't steal, they just took it.

NIKOLAI IVANOVICH (*begins speaking to the* PRIEST, *but turns resolutely to* ALEKSANDRA IVANOVNA). Alina, my dear, don't needle me with insinuations.

ALEKSANDRA IVANOVNA. But I'm not...

NIKOLAI IVANOVICH. And if you really want to know why I cannot prosecute the peasants for the wood they needed and cut...

ALEKSANDRA IVANOVNA. I suppose they also need this samovar.

NIKOLAI IVANOVICH. So if you want me to tell you why I cannot allow these people to be put in jail and be ruined because they cut down ten trees in a forest that is considered to be mine...

ALEKSANDRA IVANOVNA. Everyone thinks it is.

PYOTR SEMYONOVICH. Ah, arguing again. I'd better take the dogs into the garden. (*Exits from the terrace.*)

NIKOLAI IVANOVICH. Even if I were to consider that forest mine, which I cannot possibly do, we have nine hundred acres[8] of forest, with about five hundred trees per acre, which makes four hundred fifty thousand trees—isn't that right? They cut down ten trees, that is, one forty-five-thousandth of the trees. Now, is it worth, can you really tear a man away from his family and put him in prison for that?

STYOPA. Yes, but if you don't seek damages for the one forty-five-thousandth, then very soon the remaining forty-four-thousand-nine-hundred-ninety-ninths will also be cut down.

NIKOLAI IVANOVICH. But I only said that for your aunt. Actually I have no right to this forest—the land belongs to everyone, that is, it cannot belong to anyone. And we didn't put any work into this land.

STYOPA. Yes we did, you saved money and looked after this forest.

NIKOLAI IVANOVICH. How did I get these savings? And I didn't look after the forest myself... Anyway, you can't prove this to someone who feels no shame at knocking another person down.

STYOPA. No one's hitting anyone.

NIKOLAI IVANOVICH. And if a man feels no shame at exploiting another's work without doing any work himself, then you can't prove this to him, and all the political economy you learned at the university serves only to justify the situation we find ourselves in.

STYOPA. On the contrary, knowledge puts an end to biases.

NIKOLAI IVANOVICH. Anyway, for me that doesn't matter. The only thing that does matter is that I know if I'd been in Yefim's place, I'd have done the same thing that he did, and would despair if I were imprisoned. Therefore, since I wish to do to others as I wish done to me, I can't charge him, and am doing my best to get him released.

PYOTR SEMYONOVICH. If that's the case, then you can't own anything.

ALEKSANDRA IVANOVNA. Then it's much more profitable to steal than to work.

STYOPA. You never answer an argument. I say that a man who saves has the right to enjoy his savings.

NIKOLAI IVANOVICH (smiling). Now I really don't know whom to answer. (To PYOTR SEMYONOVICH.) No, you can't own anything.

ALEKSANDRA IVANOVNA. But if you can't own anything, you can neither have clothing nor a piece of bread, and have to give everything away, you can't live.

NIKOLAI IVANOVICH. No, you can't live the way we do.

STYOPA. That means we have to die. That means that the teachings aren't suited for life.

NIKOLAI IVANOVICH. Not at all, it's been given so that you can live. Yes, you have to give everything away. Not just the forest which we don't use and have never seen, but you have to give even your clothes away, and your bread, yes.

ALEKSANDRA IVANOVNA. Even the children's bread?

NIKOLAI IVANOVICH. Yes, even your children's bread, and not only bread, but yourself as well. That is the essence of Christ's teachings. You have to make every effort to give yourself.

STYOPA. That means to die...

NIKOLAI IVANOVICH. Yes, if you give your life for your friends,[9] that would be a beautiful thing both for you and for others. But the point is that man is not mere spirit, but spirit in flesh. And his flesh moves him to live for his own sake, while the spirit of light moves him to live for God and for others. Our lives are not conducted in the manner of animals but rather along a middle course, and the closer to a life for God, the better. Therefore, the more we strive to live for God, the better; and the animal part of life will take care of itself.

STYOPA. Why a middle course, an accommodation? If it's right to live this way, then you should give everything away and die.

NIKOLAI IVANOVICH. That would be beautiful. Try to do this, and it'll be good for you and for others.

ALEKSANDRA IVANOVNA. No, that's not clear, not simple. *C'est tiré par les cheveux.*

NIKOLAI IVANOVICH. Well, what can you do? It can't be explained in words. Anyway, that's enough.

STYOPA. Right, that's enough, and I don't understand it. (*Exits.*)

SCENE 15

THE SAME *without* STYOPA.

NIKOLAI IVANOVICH (*turns to the* PRIEST). So what impression did the book make on you?

PRIEST (*nervously*). How shall I put it? Well, the historical part is worked out adequately, but it's not entirely convincing, or credible, let's say, because the materials, let's say, are entirely inadequate. Neither the divinity nor nondivinity, let's say, of Christ can be proved historically; there's only one incontestable proof...

(*During this conversation first the ladies and then* PYOTR SEMY-ONOVICH *exit, leaving the* PRIEST *and* NIKOLAI IVANOVICH *alone.*)

NIKOLAI IVANOVICH. You mean the Church?

PRIEST. Well, naturally, the Church, and the testimony, let's say, well, of credible people, the saints, let's say.

NIKOLAI IVANOVICH. Sure, it would be great if there were such an infallible group of people whom we could trust; it would indeed be desirable. But the fact that it's desirable does not prove that there is.

PRIEST. I think it does prove this in particular. The Lord couldn't, well, leave, in His law, let's say, the possibility of distortion or misinterpretation, but must have left a kind of, well, guardian, let's say, of His truth so that this truth could not be distorted.

NIKOLAI IVANOVICH. Very well. Whereas at first you had to prove the truth itself, now you have to prove the credibility of the keeper of the truth.

PRIEST. Well, here, let's say, you need faith.

NIKOLAI IVANOVICH. Faith—you need faith, you cannot go on without faith, however not faith in what others tell me, but faith in what you yourself arrive at by dint of your own thought, your own reason... Faith in God, in the true, eternal life.

PRIEST. Reason may deceive, everyone has his own mind.

NIKOLAI IVANOVICH (*ardently*). Now that's horrible blasphemy. God has given us one sacred tool for knowing the truth, the only thing that can unite us all. And we distrust it.

PRIEST. How can we trust it, when there are, well, disagreements, let's say?

NIKOLAI IVANOVICH. Where are the disagreements: that two times two is four, that you don't do to others what you don't want done to you, and that everything has a cause? We all acknowledge truths of this kind because they all conform to our reason. But that God revealed Himself to Moses on Mount Sinai, or that Buddha flew off on a sunbeam, or that Mohammed flew to heaven, or that Christ flew there too—on matters of this kind we are all at odds.

PRIEST. No, we who hold to the truth are not all at odds; we are all united in one faith in God, Christ.

NIKOLAI IVANOVICH. No, not even in this are you united, but you have all gone your separate ways. And then, why should I believe you more than a Buddhist lama? Only because I was born in your faith?

(*The tennis players argue again.*)[10]

[FIRST VOICE]. Out.
[SECOND VOICE]. Not out.
VANYA. I saw it.

(*During the conversation servants set the table again for tea and coffee.*)

NIKOLAI IVANOVICH. You say the Church unites. On the contrary, the Church has always caused the greatest divisions. "How often would I have gathered you together, even as a hen gathereth her chickens..."[11]

PRIEST. That was until Christ. And Christ did gather all together.

NIKOLAI IVANOVICH. Yes, Christ did, but we divided all, because we understood Him in the wrong way. He destroyed all churches.

PRIEST. But didn't He say: "Tell it unto the church"?[12]

NIKOLAI IVANOVICH. It's not words that matter—moreover, these words don't refer to the Church at all—what matters is the spirit of teaching. Christ's teaching is universal, it includes all religions, and doesn't admit anything that is exclusive: neither the Resurrection, nor the divinity of Christ, nor the sacraments, nor anything that divides.

PRIEST. Then this, well, is your, let's say, interpretation of Christ's teachings; but Christ's teachings are founded entirely on His divinity and resurrection.

NIKOLAI IVANOVICH. That's precisely what's so awful about churches. They divide by asserting that they possess the whole, unmistakable, infallible truth. "It seemed good to us and to the Holy Ghost."[13] This began at the first Council of the Apostles. From that time they began to assert that they possessed the whole, exclusive truth. You know, if I say there's a God, the origin of the world, everyone will agree with me, and this acknowledgement of God will unite us. However, if I say there's a God—Brahma, or the Jewish God, or the Trinity—such a deity will divide us. Men want to unite and, therefore, devise ways of accomplishing this, but they disregard the one certain way of uniting—striving for truth. It's as if in an enormous building with light shining down in the center men were striving to unite in small groups in the the corners instead of all going toward the light. Then, all would unite, without even thinking of uniting.

PRIEST. But how would you guide the people without, well, a certain, let's say, truth?

NIKOLAI IVANOVICH. That's what's so awful. Each of us has to save his own soul, has to do God's work himself, but we are preoccupied with saving and teaching others. And what do we teach them? It's awful even to think about. Now, at the end of the nineteenth century, we teach them that God created the world in six days, then brought a flood, put all the animals in an ark, and all that noxious nonsense from the Old Testament. And then we teach them that Christ commanded to baptize all with water, and to believe in the abominable absurdity of atonement without which you cannot be saved; and then that Christ flew off to heaven and sat down there, in heaven which does not exist, on the right hand of the Father. We've gotten used to this, but it's awful. An innocent child, open to goodness and truth, asks what the world is and what are its laws, and instead of revealing to him the simple teachings of love and truth that have been given to us, we carefully stuff his head with all kinds of absurdities and abominations, and ascribe them to God. Now that's awful. Now that's the worst crime ever. And we, you and your Church, are committing this. Forgive me.

PRIEST. Yes, if you look, well, rationally, let's say, at Christ's teachings, that's true.

NIKOLAI IVANOVICH. No matter how you look at it, it'll be the same.

(*Silence. Enter* ALEKSANDRA IVANOVNA.)

SCENE 16

THE SAME *and* ALEKSANDRA IVANOVNA. (*The* PRIEST *bows and takes his leave.*)

ALEKSANDRA IVANOVNA. Good-bye, Father. Don't listen to him, he'll lead you astray.

PRIEST. No, test the Scriptures. The matter is too important, well, to disregard, let's say. (*Exits.*)

SCENE 17

THE SAME *without the* PRIEST.

ALEKSANDRA IVANOVNA. Really, Nicolas, you show him no mercy. Although he's a priest, he's still only a boy, and can't have firm convictions, or be self-assured.

NIKOLAI IVANOVICH. Give him time to be self-assured and become an inveterate fraud! No, what for? Besides, he's a decent, sincere person...

ALEKSANDRA IVANOVNA. But what whould become of him if he were to believe you?

NIKOLAI IVANOVICH. There's no reason to believe me, but if he'd see the truth, it'd be good, good for him and for everyone else.

ALEKSANDRA IVANOVNA. If it were good, everyone would believe you, but now, on the contrary, no one believes you, least of all your wife. She just can't believe you.

NIKOLAI IVANOVICH. Who told you that?

ALEKSANDRA IVANOVNA. Well, go ahead and explain this to her. She'll never understand, and I won't either, nor will anyone in the world understand that you should care for strangers and abandon your own children. Go ahead and explain this to Masha.

NIKOLAI IVANOVICH. Masha will most certainly understand. And forgive me, Alina, but if it were not for outside influences, to which she's very susceptible, she would've understood me, and gone along with me.

ALEKSANDRA IVANOVNA. In depriving her children for the benefit of drunken Yefim *et compagnie?* Never. So you're angry with me, forgive me, but I cannot help speaking my mind.

NIKOLAI IVANOVICH. I'm not angry. On the contrary, I'm even very glad that you've had your say, and given me a chance, challenged me, to express all my views to her. I was thinking about this on the way home today, and I'll tell her now; and you'll see that she'll agree with me, because she's intelligent and kind.

ALEKSANDRA IVANOVNA. Well, allow me to have my doubts.

NIKOLAI IVANOVICH. No, I have none. You see, it isn't some fantasy of mine, it's simply what we've all known, and what Christ revealed to us.

AKEKSANDRA IVANOVNA. Yes, you think Christ revealed this, but I think it was something else.

NIKOLAI IVANOVICH. It can't be anything else.

(*Shouts from the tennis players.*)

LYUBA. Out.

VANYA. No it's not.

LIZANKA. I saw it hit right here.

LYUBA. Out, out, out.

VANYA. Liar.

LYUBA. First of all, it's not polite to say "liar."

VANYA. And I say it's not polite to lie.

NIKOLAI IVANOVICH. Now just stop, don't argue, listen to me.

ALEKSANDRA IVANOVNA. Well, I'm listening.

NIKOLAI IVANOVICH. Isn't it true that at any moment we may die and go off to the void or to God, who wants us to live according to His will?

ALEKSANDRA IVANOVNA. Well?

NIKOLAI IVANOVICH. Well what can I do in this life other than just what the Supreme Judge in my soul, my conscience, God, wants of me? And my conscience, God, wants me to consider all men equal, to love all men, to serve all men.

ALEKSANDRA IVANOVNA. Your own children as well.

NIKOLAI IVANOVICH. Of course my own as well; but that I do what my conscience tells me. The main thing is to understand that my life does not belong to me, nor yours to you, but to God, who sent us into the world, and wants us to do His will. And His will...

ALEKSANDRA IVANOVNA. And you think you'll convince Masha of this?

NIKOLAI IVANOVICH. Certainly.

ALEKSANDRA IVANOVNA. And she'll stop raising her children properly and abandon them... Never.

NIKOLAI IVANOVICH. Not only will she understand, but you will too, that there's nothing else to do.

ALEKSANDRA IVANOVNA. Never!

(*Enter* MARYA IVANOVNA.)

SCENE 18

THE SAME *and* MARYA IVANOVNA.

NIKOLAI IVANOVICH. Well, how are you, Masha? I didn't wake you up this morning, did I?

MARYA IVANOVNA. No, I wasn't sleeping. So, did you have a good trip?

NIKOLAI IVANOVICH. Yes, very good.

MARYA IVANOVNA. Why do you drink everything cold? By the way, we have to prepare for the guests. You know Cheremshanova is coming with her son and daughter.

NIKOLAI IVANOVICH. Well, if you like having them, I'm glad.

MARYA IVANOVNA. I like her and the youngsters. Only it's kind of a bad time.

ALEKSANDRA IVANOVNA (*rising*). Go ahead, talk with him, and I'll go watch their game. (*Exits.*)

SCENE 19

THE SAME *without* ALEKSANDRA IVANOVNA. (*Silence, then* NIKO-LAI IVANOVICH *and* MARYA IVANOVNA *begin speaking at the same time.*)

MARYA IVANOVNA. It's not a good time because we have to talk.

NIKOLAI IVANOVICH. I was just telling Alina...

MARYA IVANOVNA. What?

NIKOLAI IVANOVICH. No, you talk.

MARYA IVANOVNA. I just wanted to talk about Styopa. Well then, something has to be decided. He's worried, poor thing, doesn't know what'll become of him. He comes to me, but I can't make this decision.

NIKOLAI IVANOVICH. What's there to decide? He can decide by himself.

MARYA IVANOVNA. But you know he wants to volunteer for the guards, and for this he needs your permission; and he has to have money to support himself, and you don't give him any. (*Upset.*)

NIKOLAI IVANOVICH. Masha, for God's sake, don't get upset, just listen to me. I'm not giving anything, nor am I refusing to give. To enlist in the military, I consider either a stupid, crazy act natural for a savage, if he doesn't understand how repugnant this deed is, or a despicable one, if it's done out of self-interest...

MARYA IVANOVNA. But now everything seems savage and stupid to you. He has to live, you know. You did.

NIKOLAI IVANOVICH (*angrily*). Yes, when I didn't understand, when no one told me, but it's not about me. It's about him.

MARYA IVANOVNA. Of course it's about you, you're not giving him the money.

NIKOLAI IVANOVICH. I cannot give him what does not belong to me.

MARYA IVANOVNA. What do you mean it doesn't?

NIKOLAI IVANOVICH. The work of other people does not belong to me. The money I give him I must take from others. I have no right to do that, I can't. As long as I manage this estate, I can only do it the way my conscience tells me. I cannot give the work of toilworn peasants for binges for hussars of the Lifeguard. Take over the estate, then I won't be responsible.

MARYA IVANOVNA. But you know I don't want to and, what's more, I can't. I have to raise the children, nurse them, and bear them. That's cruel...

NIKOLAI IVANOVICH. Masha, my dear! That's just not the point. When you began speaking, I also began, and I wanted to talk to you very openly. You see, we cannot go on like this. We live together, and don't understand each other. Sometimes it's as if we don't understand each other on purpose.

MARYA IVANOVNA. I want to understand you, but I don't, I don't. I don't understand what's happened to you.

NIKOLAI IVANOVICH. Then try to understand. Though now's not a good time, God only knows when that will be. Don't try so much to understand me, but yourself, try to understand your own life. You see, we cannot go on living like this, not knowing why we live.

MARYA IVANOVNA. But we've lived like this, and lived very well. (*Noticing an irritated expression on his face.*) All right, all right, I'm listening.

NIKOLAI IVANOVICH. Yes I've lived like this, just like this, that is, not thinking why I'm living; but the day did come, and I became horrified. All right, we're living on the toil of others, making others work for us, bearing children, and raising them to do the same. Now old age approaches, and death, and I ask myself: "Why have I lived?" So as to breed more parasites like myself? And, on the whole, this life isn't much fun. After all, it's only tolerable while you're full of energy, like Vanya.

MARYA IVANOVNA. But everybody lives like this.

NIKOLAI IVANOVICH. And everybody's unhappy.

MARYA IVANOVNA. Not at all.

NIKOLAI IVANOVICH. I at least saw that I was terribly unhappy, and was making you and the children unhappy, and I asked myself: "Did God really create us for this?" And as soon as I thought about it, I immediately felt that He did not. And I asked myself: "What did God create us for?"

(*Enter* FOOTMAN.)

SCENE 20

THE SAME *and* FOOTMAN.

MARYA IVANOVNA (*does not listen to her husband and addresses the* FOOTMAN). Bring some hot cream.
NIKOLAI IVANOVICH. And I found the answer in the Gospel—by no means do we live for ourselves. This came to me clearly when I began one day to think about the parable of the vineyard.[14] Do you know it?
MARYA IVANOVNA. I do, yes, the laborers.
NIKOLAI IVANOVICH. For some reason this parable showed me my mistake more clearly than anything else. Just as those laborers thought that the vineyard was theirs, I thought that my life was mine, and everything was awful; but I've just understood that my life is not mine, that I was sent into the world to do God's work.
MARYA IVANOVNA. So what? We all know that.
NIKOLAI IVANOVICH. Well if we know that, we cannot go on living like we live, since our entire life is not a fulfillment of His will, but, on the contrary, a continual transgression of it.
MARYA IVANOVNA. How is it a transgression when we live without doing harm to anyone?
NIKOLAI IVANOVICH. What do you mean without doing harm to anyone? That is precisely the understanding of life that those laborers had. After all, we...
MARYA IVANOVNA. Yes, I know the parable—that he rewarded all equally.
NIKOLAI IVANOVICH (*after a silence*). No, it's not that. Just think of one thing, Masha, we have but one life, and we can either live it morally or waste it.

MARYA IVANOVNA. I can't think and debate. I don't sleep nights, I'm nursing, I'm running the whole house, and instead of helping me, you speak to me of things I don't understand.

NIKOLAI IVANOVICH. Masha!

MARYA IVANOVNA. And now these guests as well.

NIKOLAI IVANOVICH. No, let's agree. (*Kisses her.*) Okay?

MARYA IVANOVNA. Yes, just be like you used to be.

NIKOLAI IVANOVICH. I can't, but listen to me.

(*The sound of bells and an approaching carriage is heard.*)

MARYA IVANOVNA. There's no time now, they're here. I have to go to them. (*Exits around the corner of the house.* STYOPA *and* LYUBA *follow her.*)

VANYA (*jumping over a bench*). I'm not quiting. We'll finish up later. Lyuba, so what about it?

LYUBA (*seriously*). Please, stop your nonsense.

(ALEKSANDRA IVANOVNA, *her* HUSBAND, *and* LIZANKA *come out on the terrace.* NIKOLAI IVANOVICH *paces thoughtfully.*)

SCENE 21

NIKOLAI IVANOVICH, ALEKSANDRA IVANOVNA, PYOTR SEMYONOVICH, *and* LIZANKA.

ALEKSANDRA IVANOVNA. So, did you convince her?

NIKOLAI IVANOVICH. Alina, what's going on between us is serious business. Jokes are out of place. It's not I who convinces, but life, truth, God, that's who, and, therefore, she cannot but be convinced, if not today, then tomorrow, if not tomorrow, then... It's really awful that no one ever has time. Who has come now?

PYOTR SEMYONOVICH. The Cheremshanovs. Catiche Cheremshanova, whom I haven't seen for eighteen years. The last time I saw her we sang together: *La ci darem la mano.* (*Sings.*)

ALEKSANDRA IVANOVNA (*to her husband*). Please, don't interrupt, and don't think I'll argue with Nicolas. I'm telling the truth. (*To* NIKOLAI IVANOVICH.) I'm not joking at all, it just seemed strange to me that you wanted to convince Masha just when she decided to have a talk with you.

NIKOLAI IVANOVICH. All right, all right. Here they come. Please tell Masha I'll be in my room.

Curtain.

ACT II

The same country home a week later. The set depicts a large hall. The table is set with a samovar, tea service and coffee pot. A grand piano and music rack with scores are by the wall. At the table sit MARYA IVANOVNA, *the* PRINCESS, *and* PYOTR SEMYONOVICH.

SCENE 1

MARYA IVANOVNA, *the* PRINCESS, *and* PYOTR SEMYONOVICH.

PYOTR SEMYONOVICH. Yes, Princess. It doesn't seem so long ago that you were singing the part of Rosina, and I... Now, I'm not even fit for Don Basilio...[15]

PRINCESS. Now our children could do the singing. But times are different.

PYOTR SEMYONOVICH. Yes, materialistic times... But your daughter plays very well, is quite serious about it. The youngsters can't still be asleep, can they?

MARYA IVANOVNA. Yes, they took the horses for a moonlight ride last night, and got back very late. I was nursing and heard them.

PYOTR SEMYONOVICH. And when will my wife be back? Have you sent someone to get her?

MARYA IVANOVNA. They left already, but it's too early. She should be here soon.

PRINCESS. Did Aleksandra Ivanovna really go just to get Father Gerasim?

MARYA IVANOVNA. Yes, she thought of it yesterday, and rushed off right there and then.

PRINCESS. *Quelle énergie! Je l'admire.*

PYOTR SEMYONOVICH. *Oh, pour ceci ce n'est pas ce qui nous manque.* (*Takes out a cigar.*) Anyway, I'll go have a smoke and take a walk around the park with the dogs till the youngsters get up. (*Exits.*)

SCENE 2

MARYA IVANOVNA *and the* PRINCESS.

PRINCESS. I don't know, my dear Marya Ivanovna, but it seems to me you're taking all of this too much to heart. I understand him. It's so high-minded. So what if he gives to the poor. As it is we think too much of ourselves.

MARYA IVANOVNA. If only he'd stop at that, but you don't know him, you don't know the whole story. It's not just helping the poor, it's a complete change, the destruction of everything.

PRINCESS. I don't want to interfere in your family life, but if you'll allow me...

MARYA IVANOVNA. Yes, I think of you as one of the family, especially now.

PRINCESS. I would advise you to state your demands directly and frankly, and to come to an agreement with him as to the limits...

MARYA IVANOVNA (*agitated*). There are no limits, he wants to give everything away. He wants me, at my age, to become a cook, a laundress.

PRINCESS. That can't be. That's astonishing.

MARYA IVANOVNA (*takes out a letter*). We're alone now, and I'm happy I can tell you all about it. He wrote me this letter yesterday. I'll read it to you.

PRINCESS. What, he and you live in the same house and he writes you letters? How strange!

MARYA IVANOVNA. No, I can understand that. He gets very upset when he talks. I've been worried about his health lately.

PRINCESS. So what did he write?

MARYA IVANOVNA. Here's what. (*Reads.*) "You reproach me for destroying our former life, and not offering anything else, nor saying what arrangements I would like to make for the family. Whenever we begin to talk about it, we get upset, and that is why I am writing this letter. I have already told you many times why I cannot go on living as I have; and in a letter I cannot convince you that one must not live this way, but in a Christian way. You may do one of two things: either believe in the truth and follow me of your own free will, or believe me, commit yourself to me, and follow me trustingly." (*Stops reading.*) I can't do either one. I don't think one has to live the way he wants to, I feel sorry for the children, and I can't trust him. (*Continues reading.*) "This is my plan: we will give our land to the peasants, keeping for ourselves fifty acres, the entire orchard, the vegetable garden, and the flooded meadow. We will try to work ourselves, but we will not force each other, or the children. What we keep should still bring us about five hundred roubles."

PRINCESS. Live on five hundred roubles with seven children. It's impossible.

MARYA IVANOVNA. Well, the whole plan is to turn the house into a school, and we ourselves are to live in the gardener's two-room cottage.

PRINCESS. Yes, I'm also beginning to think that there's something unhealthy about it. So what was your answer?

MARYA IVANOVNA. I said I couldn't do it; if I were alone, I'd follow him anywhere, but with the children... Just think, I'm still nursing Nikolenka. I said he can't ruin everything like that. I didn't agree to this when I married. I'm not young and strong anymore. It's not easy to bear and nurse nine children, you know...

PRINCESS. Yes, I never imagined this had gone so far.

MARYA IVANOVNA. That's how it is, and I don't know what'll happen. Yesterday he exempted the Dmitrovka peasants from paying the rent, and he wants to give them the land altogether.

PRINCESS. I don't think you should allow this. You have to protect your children. If he cannot manage the estate, let him hand it over to you.

MARYA IVANOVNA. But I don't want that.

PRINCESS. You must do it for the children. Let him transfer the estate to you.

MARYA IVANOVNA. Sasha, my sister, told him so. He said he has no right to do it, that the land belongs to those who work it, and that he has to give it to the peasants.

PRINCESS. Yes, I can see now that it's much more serious than I thought.

MARYA IVANOVNA. And the priest, the priest is on his side.

PRINCESS. Yes, I noticed yesterday.

MARYA IVANOVNA. That's why my sister went to Moscow. She wanted to consult with a lawyer, but mainly she went to bring Father Gerasim back, so that he could convince him.

PRINCESS. No, I don't think Christianity is about ruining your family.

MARYA IVANOVNA. But he won't believe Father Gerasim either. He's so headstrong, and when he talks, you know, I can't refute him. And what's so terrible is that it seems to me he's right.

PRINCESS. That's only because you love him.

MARYA IVANOVNA. I don't know, maybe, but it's terrible, terrible. Everything just remains unsettled. That's Christianity for you.

(*Enter* NANNIE.)

SCENE 3

THE SAME *and* NANNIE.

NANNIE. Will you please come, Nikolenka's up, he wants you.

MARYA IVANOVNA. I'm on my way. When I'm worried, he gets a bellyache. Coming, coming.

(NIKOLAI IVANOVICH *enters by another door with a paper in his hand.*)

SCENE 4

MARYA IVANOVNA, *the* PRINCESS, *and* NIKOLAI IVANOVICH.

NIKOLAI IVANOVICH. No, that's incredible.

MARYA IVANOVNA. What is it?

NIKOLAI IVANOVICH. Because of some fir tree of ours, Pyotr's being put in jail.

MARYA IVANOVNA. What?

NIKOLAI IVANOVICH. Just that. He cut it down, got turned in, and was sentenced to three months in prison. His wife has come.

MARYA IVANOVNA. So, can't you do something?

NIKOLAI IVANOVICH. Not now. The only thing to do is not to own the forest. And I won't. Now what's there to do? I'll go to him, see whether what we've done can be set right. (*Goes out on the terrace and meets* BORIS *and* LYUBA.)

SCENE 5

THE SAME, BORIS, *and* LYUBA.

LYUBA. Hi, Papá! (*Kisses him.*) Where're you going?

NIKOLAI IVANOVICH. I just got back from the village and I'm off to there again. They're now hauling a starving man off to jail because he...

LYUBA. Must be Pyotr.

NIKOLAI IVANOVICH. Yes, Pyotr. (*Exits.*)

SCENE 6

THE SAME *without* NIKOLAI IVANOVICH.

LYUBA (*sits down by the samovar*). Will you have coffee or tea?

BORIS. Either one.

LYUBA. It's always the same. I see no end to it.

BORIS. I don't understand him. I know the peasants are poor and uneducated, and must be helped, but not by encouraging thieves.

LYUBA. By what then?

BORIS. By all our activity. Serve them with all our skills, but you cannot give up your life.

LYUBA. But Papá says that's just what you have to do.

BORIS. I don't understand that. You can serve the people without ruining your own life. That's how I want to live my life. If only you...

LYUBA. I want what you want, and I'm not afraid of anything.

BORIS. And how about these earrings, this dress?

LYUBA. I'll sell the earrings, and the dress—doesn't have to be like this one—but still may be pretty.

BORIS. I'd like to talk with him some more. Do you think I'll be in his way if I follow him to the village?

LYUBA. Not at all. I can see he likes you, he spoke to you most of the time yesterday.

BORIS (*finishes his coffee*). Then I'll go.

LYUBA. Yes, go ahead, and I'll go and wake up Lizanka and Tonya. (*She and* BORIS *exit in different directions.*)

Curtain.

Change of scene. A street. IVAN ZYABREV, *covered with a sheepskin coat, is lying near his cottage.*

SCENE 1

IVAN ZYABREV, *alone.*

IVAN. Malashka!

(*From behind the cottage comes a little girl with her baby brother in her arms. The baby is crying.*)

SCENE 2

IVAN ZYABREV, MALASHKA *with the baby.*

IVAN. Water. I'm thirsty.

(MALASHKA *goes into the cottage, where the screams of the baby can be heard. She brings out water in a ladle.*)

IVAN. Why're you always beatin' the kid an' makin' 'im howl? Wait till I tell yer mother.

MALASHKA. Go 'head, tell 'er. He's howlin' cuz he's hungry.

IVAN (*drinks*). Why don't you ask the Demkins for some milk?

MALASHKA. I went there, ain't none. An' there was nobody home either.

IVAN. Oh, I wish I was dead. Did they ring for dinner?

MALASHKA. Yep, long ago. Here comes the master.

(*Enter* NIKOLAI IVANOVICH.)

SCENE 3

THE SAME *and* NIKOLAI IVANOVICH.

NIKOLAI IVANOVICH. Why did you come out here?

IVAN. Too many flies in there, an' too hot.

NIKOLAI IVANOVICH. So you've warmed up?

IVAN. It's like I'm on fire now.

NIKOLAI IVANOVICH. And where's Pyotr, is he at home?

IVAN. How can he be at home, at this time? He's gone t'the field t'get the sheaves.

NIKOLAI IVANOVICH. What's this they tell me about him going to prison?

IVAN. That's right, the policeman's gone t'the field t'get 'im.

(*Enter a pregnant woman carrying a sheaf of oats and a rake. She imme-diately hits* MALASHKA *on the back of the head.*)

SCENE 4

THE SAME *and the* WOMAN.

WOMAN. Whatcha leavin' the kid alone for? Don't yuh hear 'im howlin'? Yuh only know how t'run out on the street.

MALASHKA (*crying*). I just came out. Dad wanted a drink.

WOMAN. I'll teach yuh. (*Sees the master.*) Hello, Nikolai Ivanovich, sir. It's nothin' but trouble with 'em. I hafta take care of everythin' all by my-self, they're takin' my last worker t'prison, an' here's this deadbeat just lyin' aroun'.

NIKOLAI IVANOVICH. What are you talking about, he's sick.

WOMAN. Right, he's sick, an' I'm not? He's sick when it comes t'workin'. But he ain't too sick t'booze an' beat on me. Let 'im croak like a dog. I don't care!

NIKOLAI IVANOVICH. It's a sin to talk like that.

WOMAN. I know it's a sin, but I can't stop myself. Here I'm pregnant an' hafta work for two. The others already got their crops in, an' we still got two quarter sections t'cut. I should finish it up, but I can't; had t'come home an' take care o' the kids.

NIKOLAI IVANOVICH. The oats will be cut, I'll hire someone, and they'll bind them too.

WOMAN. Bindin's nothin', I'll do it myself; if only it's cut quickly. So, Nikolai Ivanovich, he's probably dyin', d'ya think so? He's really bad.

NIKOLAI IVANOVICH. I don't know. Ah, that's right, he's bad. I think we should take him to the hospital.

WOMAN. Oh. Lord! (*Begins to wail.*) Don't take 'im away. Let 'im die here. (*To her husband.*) What's wrong with yuh?

IVAN. I wanna go t'the hospital. Here I'm worse off 'an a dog.

WOMAN. I just donno. I'm goin' crazy. Malashka, get dinner.

NIKOLAI IVANOVICH. What do you have for dinner?

WOMAN. Potatoes an' bread, what else. There ain't no other food. (*Goes into the cottage. The sounds of a pig squealing and children screaming can be heard.*)

SCENE 5

THE SAME *without the* WOMAN.

IVAN (*groans*). Oh, Lord, I wish I was dead.

(*Enter* BORIS.)

THE SAME *and* BORIS.

BORIS. Can I be of any help to you?

NIKOLAI IVANOVICH. You can't be of help to anyone here. The evil is too deep rooted. You can only be of help to yourself by seeing what we build our happiness on. Here's this family: five children, the wife pregnant, the husband sick, and there's nothing to eat but some potatoes, and now the question of them having enough food for next year is at stake. And there's no help for them. How can you help? I'll hire a hand for her. But who's this hand? Just another peasant who has quit farming his own land because of drinking and poverty.

BORIS. Excuse me, but then what are you doing here?

NIKOLAI IVANOVICH. I'm getting to know my situation, getting to know who takes care of our garden, builds our houses, makes our clothes, feeds and dresses us.

(PEASANT MEN *with scythes and* PEASANT WOMEN *with rakes pass by and bow.*)

SCENE 7

THE SAME *and* PEASANT MEN AND WOMEN.

NIKOLAI IVANOVICH (*stopping one of them*). Yermil, won't you hire on to cut and bind for them?

YERMIL (*shaking his head*). I'd be mighty glad t', but I can't nohow. We ain't done wid our own yet, just hurryin' now t'do it. What's up, Ivan dyin'?

OTHER PEASANT. Maybe Pa Sevastyan here 'ill hire on. Pa Sevastyan, they're hirin' cutters.

SEVASTYAN. Go yerself. Now every day counts.

SCENE 8

THE SAME *without the* PEASANT MEN AND WOMEN.

NIKOLAI IVANOVICH. They're all half starved, only have bread and water, they're sick, often old. That old man over there, he's ruptured and
he's in pain, but he works from four in the morning till ten at night, and
is barely alive. And we? Once you understand this, how can you go on
living calmly and consider yourself a Christian? Well, forget about a
Christian, just not a beast?

BORIS. But what's there to do?

NIKOLAI IVANOVICH. Don't take part in this evil, don't own land, don't
feed on their toil. But I don't know how to bring this about. The main
thing here is... at least that's how it was with me. I lived and didn't understand how I was living, didn't understand that I'm a son of God, and
that we're all sons of God, and brothers. But when I understood this,
when I understood that we all have an equal right to live, my whole life
changed. However, I can't explain it to you now. I'll only say one thing:
I was blind then, just as my family at home is, but now my eyes have
opened, and I can't help seeing. And now that I see, I can't go on living
like this. Anyway, we'll talk later. Now I have to do what I can.

(*Enter the* POLICEMAN, PYOTR, *his wife, and son.*)

SCENE 9

THE SAME, *the* POLICEMAN, PYOTR, *his* WIFE, *and* SON.

PYOTR (*falls at* NIKOLAI IVANOVICH*'s feet*). Forgive me, for God's sake,
I'm done for now. The wife can't take care o' things. Maybe out on bail
or somethin'.

NIKOLAI IVANOVICH. I'll go and sign. (*To the* POLICEMAN.) Can't you
let him go now?

POLICEMAN. I have orders to take him to the station.

NIKOLAI IVANOVICH. Go on then, I'll hire a hand, and do what I can. This is all my fault. How can I live like this? (*Exits.*)

Curtain.

Change of scene. In the same country home as before.

SCENE 1

TONYA *has just finished playing a Schumann sonata and is sitting at the piano.* STYOPA *is standing by the piano.* LYUBA, BORIS, LIZANKA, MITROFAN YERMILOVICH, *and the* PRIEST *are seated. Everyone except* BORIS *is moved by the music.*

LYUBA. The andante is just lovely.
STYOPA. No, the scherzo. Actually all of it is lovely.
LIZANKA. Very nice.
STYOPA. I never imagined that you were such a virtuosa. That was a real, masterful performance. Obviously, no difficulties remain for you. You think only of the expression, and express it in an amazingly subtle way.
LYUBA. And majestic, too.
TONYA. But I feel it's not exactly what I want... Much is still lacking.
LIZANKA. It couldn't be better. It's amazing.
LYUBA. Schumann is fine, but Chopin still touches your heart more.
STYOPA. He's more lyrical.
TONYA. You can't compare them.
LYUBA. Do you remember his *prélude?*
TONYA. The one called George Sand's? (*Plays the beginning.*)
LYUBA. No, not that one. That's beautiful, but it's trite. But please, finish playing it.

(TONYA *plays the parts she knows, stopping from time to time.*)

LYUBA. No, it's in *ré mineur.*

TONYA. Oh, that one, it's a wonderful piece. It's somehow primordial, older than creation.

STYOPA (*laughs*). Yes, yes... Please, play it. But then again, don't, you're tired. We've already had a wonderful morning, thanks to you.

TONYA (*rises and looks out of the window*). The peasants are here again.

LYUBA. That's what's so precious about music. I understand Saul. I'm not tormented by an evil spirit, but I can understand him.[16] Music is the only art that can make you forget about everything. (*Goes to the window.*) What do you want?

PEASANTS. We were told t'see Nikolai Ivanovich.

LYUBA. He's not in, you'll have to wait.

TONYA. And you're marrying a man who understands nothing about music.

LYUBA. Of course he does.

BORIS (*inattentively*). Music. No, I like music, or rather I don't dislike it. But I prefer something simpler—I like songs.

TONYA. But isn't this sonata lovely?

BORIS. The main thing is that this isn't important, and I feel somewhat sorry for the other life because importance is ascribed to this.

(*They all eat candies that are on the table.*)

LIZANKA. How nice it is to have a fiancé around and candies.

BORIS. Well I had nothing to do with that. It's Mamá.

TONYA. And she's doing the right thing.

LYUBA. Music is precious because it grips you, possesses you, and carries you away from reality. Everything was so gloomy, and then you began to play, and suddenly everything brightened. It really did.

LIZANKA. Chopin's waltzes are stale, but still...

TONYA. How about this one?... (*Plays.*)

(*Enter* NIKOLAI IVANOVICH. *He greets* TONYA, STYOPA, LIZANKA, LYUBA, MITROFAN YERMILOVICH, *and the* PRIEST.)

SCENE 2

THE SAME *and* NIKOLAI IVANOVICH

NIKOLAI IVANOVICH. Where's Mamá?
LYUBA. In the nursery, I think.

(STYOPA *calls the* FOOTMAN.)

LYUBA. Papá, Tonya plays so marvelously. Where have you been?
NIKOLAI IVANOVICH. In the village.

(*Enter the* FOOTMAN.)

SCENE 3

THE SAME *and the* FOOTMAN.

STYOPA. Bring another samovar.
NIKOLAI IVANOVICH (*also greets the* FOOTMAN, *and shakes his hand*).
Hello!

(*The* FOOTMAN *is nervous and exits.* NIKOLAI IVANOVICH *exits.*)

SCENE 4

THE SAME *without the* FOOTMAN *and* NIKOLAI IVANOVICH.

STYOPA. Poor Afanasy. He got so confused. I don't understand. It's as if we
were to blame for something.

(*Enter again* NIKOLAI IVANOVICH.)

SCENE 5

THE SAME, *and* NIKOLAI IVANOVICH.

NIKOLAI IVANOVICH. I was about to go to my room without telling you
how I feel. But I don't think that's right. (*To* TONYA.) If you, as a guest,
are offended by what I'll say, forgive me, but I can't help saying it. Lyuba,
you say that the young princess plays well. All of you seven or eight
healthy, young men and women here slept till ten o'clock, drank, ate,
and are still eating, and playing and discussing music, while at the place
from where I've just returned with Boris Aleksandrovich they've been
up since three o'clock in the morning—and others pastured horses all
night and didn't sleep at all. And the old, the sick, the weak, children,
nursing mothers and pregnant women are working as hard as they can
so that we here can live on the fruits of their toil. As if that weren't
enough, one of them, the one and only breadwinner in the family, is now
being hauled off to jail because in the spring he cut down one of the
hundred thousand fir trees that grow in what's called *my* forest. And we
here are washed and dressed, after leaving a mess in the bedrooms for
our slaves to take care of, and we eat and drink, and discuss Schumann
and Chopin, and which of them touches us the most, and chases away
the blahs. I was thinking about this as I walked by you, and so I said what
I did. Just think, can you really go on living like this! (*Getting upset.*)
LIZANKA. It's true, really true.
LYUBA. If you think like this, you can't live.
STYOPA. Why not? I don't see why you can't talk about Schumann because
the peasants are poor. The one doesn't exclude the other. If people...
NIKOLAI IVANOVICH (*malevolently*). If someone has no heart, is made
of wood...
STYOPA. All right, I'll shut up.
TONYA. It's a terrible problem, a problem of our time, and we shouldn't
be afraid of it. We should look straight in the eye of reality in order to
solve it.
NIKOLAI IVANOVICH. There's no time to wait for the problem to be
solved by general measures. Everyone of us will die, if not today—tomorrow. How can I live without suffering from this inner conflict?

BORIS. There's only one way, of course: take no part in it.

NIKOLAI IVANOVICH. Well, forgive me if I've hurt you. I couldn't help saying what I felt. (*Exits.*)

SCENE 6

THE SAME *without* NIKOLAI IVANOVICH.

STYOPA. How can you not take part in it? Our entire life is linked to it.

BORIS. That's why he says that in the first place, don't have property, change your entire way of life: don't live to be served by others, live to serve others.

TONYA. I see that you've completely gone over to Nikolai Ivanovich's side.

BORIS. Yes, I've just understood it for the first time—and then the things I saw in the village. You just have to take off those would-be glasses through which we look at peasant life to understand the link between their sufferings and our joys, and it's all over.

MITROFAN YERMILOVICH. Yes, but the remedy shouldn't ruin your own life.

STYOPA. It's amazing how Mitrofan Yermilovich and I, though polar opposites, can agree: these are my very words—don't ruin your own life.

BORIS. That's understandable. You both want to live a pleasant life and, therefore, want life arranged so as to secure this for you. (*To* STYOPA.) You want to retain the present arrangement, while Mitrofan Yermilovich wants a new one.

(LYUBA *and* TONYA *talk in a whisper.* TONYA *goes to the piano and plays a Chopin nocturne. All become silent.*)

STYOPA. That is beautiful. That solves everything.

BORIS. It obscures and postpones everything.

(*While she is playing,* MARYA IVANOVNA *and the* PRINCESS *enter quietly, sit down and listen. Before the end of the nocturne there is the sound of bells.*)

SCENE 7

THE SAME, MARYA IVANOVNA, *and the* PRINCESS.

LYUBA. It's aunt Alina. (*Goes to meet her, as does* MARYA IVANOVNA.)

(*The music continues. Enter* ALEKSANDRA IVANOVNA *and* FATHER GERASIM, *a priest with a cross on his chest, and the* LAWYER. *All rise.*)

SCENE 8

THE SAME, ALEKSANDRA IVANOVNA, FATHER GERASIM, *and the* LAWYER.

GERASIM. Please go on. It's very nice.

(*The* PRINCESS *goes to receive his blessing, as does the* PRIEST.)

ALEKSANDRA IVANOVNA. I did exactly what I told myself I would. I found Father Gerasim, and then persuaded him to stop by. He's on his way to Kursk, and I've done my job. And the lawyer is here also. He has the papers ready. Just need to be signed.
MARYA IVANOVNA. How about having some lunch?

(*The* LAWYER *puts the papers on the table and exits.*)

SCENE 9

THE SAME *without the* LAWYER.

MARYA IVANOVNA. I'm very grateful to you, Father Gerasim.
GERASIM. What was there to do, it was out of my way, but I thought it my Christian duty to visit you.

(ALEKSANDRA IVANOVNA *whispers to the youngsters. They talk it over, and all go out on the terrace except* BORIS. *The* PRIEST *also wants to leave.*)

SCENE 10

MARYA IVANOVNA, ALEKSANDRA IVANOVNA, *the* PRINCESS, FATHER GERASIM, *the* PRIEST, *and* BORIS.

GERASIM. Why don't you stay. As his pastor and spiritual father, it will be good for him and for yourself. Stay, if Marya Ivanovna doesn't mind.

MARYA IVANOVNA. I don't. For me Father Vasily is like one of the family. I've also asked him for advice, but because of his age he doesn't have very much authority.

GERASIM. Of course, of course.

ALEKSANDRA IVANOVNA (*approaching him*). So you see, Father Gerasim, you're the only one that can help and straighten him out. He's an intelligent, educated man but, you know, education can only do harm. Something has come over him. He claims that according to the principles of Christianity a person should not own any property. But can that be right?

GERASIM. It's delusion, intellectual arrogance, willfulness. The Fathers of the Church have clarified that question well enough. But how did this all come about?

MARYA IVANOVNA. To tell you everything, when we got married he was completely indifferent to religion, and that's how we lived, and lived very well, for the first twenty years, our best years. Then he began to think about things. Perhaps his sister influenced him, or his reading, anyhow he began to think and read the Gospel, and then, all of a sudden, he became extremely religious, began going to church and visiting monks. And then, he suddenly stopped all this, and changed his way of life entirely. He started to work, would not allow the servants to wait on him, and what's more, he's now giving away his property. Yesterday he gave away a forest along with the land. I'm frightened, I have six children,[17] please talk to him. I'll go and ask him whether he wants to see you. (*Exits.*)

THE SAME *without* MARYA IVANOVNA.

GERASIM. Nowadays many are forsaking their religion. Well, is the property his or his wife's?

PRINCESS. His. That's the problem.

GERASIM. And what's his rank?

PRINCESS. It's not a high one. Captain, I think. He was in the military.

GERASIM. Many go astray like that. There was a lady in Odessa who was captivated by spiritualism, and began to do much harm. But God helped us bring her back to the Church.

PRINCESS. Please, understand the main thing: my son is about to marry his daughter. I consented, but the girl is used to living in luxury, and must have her own means so as not to put the entire burden on my son. Though I must say he's a hardworking, remarkable young man.

(*Enter* MARYA IVANOVNA *and* NIKOLAI IVANOVICH.)

SCENE 12

THE SAME *and* MARYA IVANOVNA *and* NIKOLAI IVANOVICH.

NIKOLAI IVANOVICH. Hello, Princess. Hello... [*To* FATHER GERASIM.] Excuse me, what's your name?[18]

GERASIM. Don't you want my blessing?

NIKOLAI IVANOVICH. No, I don't.

GERASIM. My name is Gerasim Fyodorov. Pleased to meet you.

(*The* FOOTMAN *brings lunch and wine.*)

GERASIM. Nice weather. Also good for harvesting.

NIKOLAI IVANOVICH. I suppose you've come here at the invitation of Aleksandra Ivanovna to steer me away from my errors and direct me to the path of truth. If that's so, let's not beat about the bush, and get right down to business. I don't deny that I disagree with the teachings of the Church; I used to agree, but I don't anymore. Yet I do wish with all my heart to know the truth, and I'll accept it immediately if you show it to me.

GERASIM. How can you say you don't believe the teachings of the Church? What's there to believe if not the Church.

NIKOLAI IVANOVICH. God and His law, given to us in the Gospel.

GERASIM. That's the law the Church teaches.

NIKOLAI IVANOVICH. If it did, I would believe it, but actually it teaches the contrary.

GERASIM. The Church cannot teach the contrary, because it was established by the Lord Himself. It is said: "I give you power... and the gates of hell shall not prevail against it."[19]

NIKOLAI IVANOVICH. That was not said in this context at all. But even if I were to acknowledge that Christ established the Church, how do I know that it is your church.

GERASIM. Because it is said: "For where two or three are gathered together in my name..."[20]

NIKOLAI IVANOVICH. And that too was not said in this context, and it doesn't prove anything.

GERASIM. How can you disavow the Church? It alone is the way to salvation.

NIKOLAI IVANOVICH. I didn't disavow the Church until I became convinced that it supports all that is contrary to Christianity.

GERASIM. The Church cannot be mistaken because it alone possesses the truth. Those who leave it lose their way, but the Church is sacred.

NIKOLAI IVANOVICH. But I've already told you that I don't acknowledge this. And I don't acknowledge it because in the Gospel it says, you shall know them by their deeds, you shall know them by their fruits.[21] I've learned that the Church sanctions oaths,[22] murder, and executions.

GERASIM. The Church acknowledges and sanctifies the powers[23] that God ordained.

(*During the conversation,* STYOPA, LYUBA, LIZANKA, TONYA, BORIS, *and* ALEKSANDRA IVANOVNA *enter, one at a time, and find seats or stand around listening.*)

NIKOLAI IVANOVICH. I know that the Gospel says not only do not kill, but do not be angry,[24] yet the Church sanctions the army. The Gospel says: "Swear not at all,"[25] yet the Church administers oaths. The Gospel says...

GERASIM. Excuse me, when Pilate said: "I adjure thee by the living God,"[26] Christ acknowledged the oath, saying: "Yes, it is I."[27]

NIKOLAI IVANOVICH. Well, what are you saying! That's simply ridiculous!

GERASIM. The reason the Church does not authorize individuals to interpret the Gospel on their own is to keep them from going astray, and like a mother who cares for her children, gives them an interpretation in keeping with their abilities. No, let me finish. The Church does not lay burdens on its children that are too heavy to bear, but demands that they obey the commandments: love, do not kill, do not steal, do not commit adultery.

NIKOLAI IVANOVICH. Yes, do not kill me, do not steal from me what I've stolen. We have all robbed the people, we have stolen their land, and then we enacted a law—a law against stealing. And the Church sanctions all this.

GERASIM. It's delusion and intellectual arrogance speaking in you. You should quell your arrogant intellect.

NIKOLAI IVANOVICH. No, that's not it, I'm asking you what should I do according to the principles of Christianity when I've recognized my sin in robbing the people and enslaving them by means of the land, what should I do? Continue owning the land, living off the toil of the starving—like this (*points to the* FOOTMAN *bringing in lunch and wine*), or return the land to those from whom my forefathers have robbed it?

GERASIM. You must act as is proper for a son of the Church. You have a family, children; you must see to it that they are kept and reared befitting their station in life.

NIKOLAI IVANOVICH. Why?

GERASIM. Because God has put you in that position. If you wish to be charitable, be charitable by giving away a part of your property, and by visiting the poor.

NIKOLAI IVANOVICH. But then why was the rich young man told that a rich man cannot enter the kingdom of heaven?[28]

GERASIM. It says, if you want to be perfect.[29]

NIKOLAI IVANOVICH. But I do want to be perfect. It says in the Gospel, be perfect as your Father in heaven.[30]

GERASIM. You should also understand the context.

NIKOLAI IVANOVICH. That's what I'm trying to understand, and everything that is said in the Sermon on the Mount is simple and clear.

GERASIM. Intellectual arrogance.

NIKOLAI IVANOVICH. Where's the arrogance, if it says what is hidden from the wise is revealed to babes.[31]

GERASIM. It is revealed to the meek, not to the arrogant.

NIKOLAI IVANOVICH. But who's arrogant? I, who consider myself a person like everyone else, and thus who, like everyone else, must live by the sweat of my brow and in the same poverty as my brethren, or those who consider themselves designated, sacred people, who know the whole truth, cannot err, and interpret the words of Christ in their own way?

GERASIM (*offended*). Excuse me, Nikolai Ivanovich, I didn't come here to settle the question of who is right with you, nor to listen to a sermon, I stopped by to talk at the request of Aleksandra Ivanovna. But you know everything better than I do, so I think it best to end this conversation. For the last time I only ask you in the name of God, come to your senses. You are going grievously astray and are ruining yourself. (*Rises.*)

MARYA IVANOVNA. Won't you have a bite to eat?

GERASIM. No, thank you. (*Exits with* ALEKSANDRA IVANOVNA.)

SCENE 13

MARYA IVANOVNA, *the* PRINCESS, NIKOLAI IVANOVICH, *the* PRIEST, *and* BORIS.

MARYA IVANOVNA (*to the* PRIEST). So what now?

PRIEST. Well, in my opinion Nikolai Ivanovich was right, and Father Gerasim didn't offer any proof.

PRINCESS. He wasn't allowed to speak, and what's more, he didn't like that it was made into some kind of competition. Everybody was listening. He withdrew out of modesty.

BORIS. It wasn't modesty at all. Everything that he said was simply wrong. It was so obvious, he had nothing to say.

PRINCESS. Yes, I see already, with your usual impetuousness you're beginning to agree with Nikolai Ivanovich about everything. If that's how you think, you shouldn't get married.

BORIS. I'm only saying, what's true is true, and I can't help it.

PRINCESS. You're the last person who should talk like that.

BORIS. Why?

PRINCESS. Because you're poor, and have nothing to give away. Anyway, it's none of our business. (*Exits, followed by everyone except* NIKOLAI IVANOVICH *and* MARYA IVANOVNA.)

SCENE 14

NIKOLAI IVANOVICH *and* MARYA IVANOVNA.

NIKOLAI IVANOVICH (*sits thoughtfully, then smiles at his own thoughts*). Masha, why are you doing this? Why did you invite that pitiful, misguided man? Why are that loud woman and that priest playing a part in our personal lives? Can't we sort out our own affairs?

MARYA IVANOVNA. But what am I to do if you want to leave our children with nothing? I can't take this calmly. You know very well that I'm not greedy, and that I don't need anything for myself.

NIKOLAI IVANOVICH. I know that, I do, and I believe you. But the trouble is that you neither believe the truth—I know you see it, but you can't bring yourself to believe it—you neither believe the truth nor me. But you do believe all sorts of people, the princess, and others.

MARYA IVANOVNA. I believe you, I've always believed you, but when you want to let the children go begging...

NIKOLAI IVANOVICH. Then that means you don't believe me. You think I haven't wrestled with that, haven't had my fears. But after that I became convinced not only that it can be done, but has to be done, that it is the only thing which should be done that is good for the children. You always say that if it were not for the children you would follow me; and

I say that if it were not for the children we could go on living the way we do—we would only ruin ourselves, but now we are ruining them.

MARYA IVANOVNA. But what can I do if I don't understand?

NIKOLAI IVANOVICH. And what can I do? I know very well why you sent for that pitiful man dressed up with his cassock and cross, and why Alina brought the lawyer. You want me to transfer the estate to you. I can't do it. You know that I love you after twenty years of life together—I love you and wish you well, and that's why I can't sign it over to you.[32] If I do sign it over, it will be to those from whom it was taken—the peasants. And I can't do otherwise. I have to give it to them. I'm glad the lawyer's here, and I have to do it.

MARYA IVANOVNA. No, that's terrible. Why are you so cruel? All right, you think it's a sin. Give it to me then. (*Cries.*)

NIKOLAI IVANOVICH. You don't know what you're saying. If I give it to you, I cannot go on living with you, I'll have to leave. I cannot go on living under these conditions. I cannot look on while the peasants are bled white and put into prison, though not in my name but in yours. Make your choice.

MARYA IVANOVNA. How cruel you are—is this Christianity? It's evil. You see, I cannot live the way you want me to. I cannot take away from my children and give to strangers: and that's why you want to leave me. Well go ahead, leave. I can see you don't love me anymore, and I even know why.

NIKOLAI IVANOVICH. All right, I'll sign. But Masha, you demand the impossible of me. (*Goes to the table and signs.*) You wanted it. I cannot live like this. (*Exits.*)

Curtain.

ACT III

The action takes place in Moscow. A large room with a carpenter's bench, a table with papers, a bookcase, mirror, picture, and many boards.

SCENE 1

NIKOLAI IVANOVICH, *wearing an apron, is at work planing a board on the bench.* CARPENTER.

NIKOLAI IVANOVICH (*takes the board out of the vise*). Is this good?

CARPENTER (*adjusting the setting on his plane*). Not so hot. Don't be 'fraid of it—like this.

NIKOLAI IVANOVICH. I wish I could. I just don't seem to get it right.

CARPENTER. Whacha wanna be a carpenter for anyways, sir? There're so many of us as is that yuh can't make a go of it.

NIKOLAI IVANOVICH (*returns to work*). I feel guilty not working: it's not...

CARPENTER. Yuh're not supposed t'work. God gave yuh property.

NIKOLAI IVANOVICH. That's just the point, I don't think God gave anything to anyone, it's people themselves who took everything, took everything away from their brethren.

CARPENTER (*at a loss*). That's right. But still, yuh don't hafta.

NIKOLAI IVANOVICH. I understand that it seems strange to you that in this house of plenty, I want to earn my living.

CARPENTER (*laughs*). It's aw right, rich folk, yuh know... They wanna try everythin'. Now run the jack plane over it.

NIKOLAI IVANOVICH. You won't believe it, you'll laugh, but I'll say it anyway, I used to live that way, I wasn't ashamed of it, but now I believe in the principles of Christianity that we're all brothers, and I am ashamed to live like this.

CARPENTER. If yuh're ashamed, give it all away.

NIKOLAI IVANOVICH. I wanted to, but couldn't; I turned it over to my wife.

CARPENTER. Oh well, yuh can't anyways. Yuh're used to it.

VOICE (*from outside*). Papá, may I come in?

NIKOLAI IVANOVICH. Of course you may, come in, come in.

SCENE 2

THE SAME *and* LYUBA.

LYUBA (*enters*). Hello, Yakov.

CARPENTER. How d' yuh do, miss.

LYUBA. Boris has gone to his regiment. I'm afraid he'll do or say something there. What do you think?

NIKOLAI IVANOVICH. What can I think? He'll do what he thinks is right.

LYUBA. But that's horrible. He doesn't have that long to serve, and what if he ruins his life.

NIKOLAI IVANOVICH. It's good he didn't stop by to see me. He knows that I can't tell him anything that he doesn't already know. He once told me himself that he's retiring, because he understands that there isn't a more unlawful, cruel and brutal activity than that which is entirely focused on murder alone; also, that there isn't a more degrading and vile one than to obey without question anyone who happens to be of higher rank. He knows all that.

LYUBA. That's just why I'm afraid. He knows that, and will want to do something.

NIKOLAI IVANOVICH. That's a matter for his conscience, for the God within him. If he had come to me, I would've given him one piece of advice: do nothing for reason's sake, but only when your whole being demands it. Otherwise you'll be the worse for it. Here, I wanted to do as Christ commands—to forsake father, wife, and children, and to follow Him[33]—and I almost did. But how did it end? It ended in my returning, and living in luxury with you in town. That's because I was trying to do something for which I wasn't strong enough. And so I find myself in this humiliating, senseless situation. I want to live a simple life, to work, but in these surroundings with footmen and doormen it becomes a kind of farce. There, I can see Yakov Nikanorovich laughing at me now...

CARPENTER. Why should I laugh? Yuh pay me, yuh gimme tea. I'm grateful.

LYUBA. I wonder if I shouldn't go to him.

NIKOLAI IVANOVICH. My dear, dear Lyuba, I know it's hard on you, you're frightened, though you shouldn't be. After all, I'm a person who understands life. Nothing bad can happen. Everything that seems bad just gladdens the heart. But understand one thing, a person who has started along this path has to make a choice. There are situations when God and Devil weigh in so evenly that the scales waver indecisively. And there God's greatest work is taking place—and there any outside interference is terribly dangerous and harmful. It is as though a man was to strain so hard under a heavy weight that just the touch of a finger could break his back.

LYUBA. But why suffer?

NIKOLAI IVANOVICH. It's the same as a mother asking, why suffer? There are no childbirths without suffering. It's the same in spiritual life. I can tell you one thing: Boris is a true Christian, and that's why he's free. And if you cannot as yet be what he is, if you cannot believe in God as he does, then believe in him, believe in God through him.

MARYA IVANOVNA (*from outside*). May I come in?

NIKOLAI IVANOVICH. Of course you may. What a gathering I'm having here today!

SCENE 3

THE SAME *and* MARYA IVANOVNA.

MARYA IVANOVNA. Our priest has come, our Vasily Nikanorovich. He's left his parish, and is on his way to see the bishop.

NIKOLAI IVANOVICH. That can't be!

MARYA IVANOVNA. He's here. Lyuba, ask him in. He wants to see you.

(*Exit* LYUBA.)

SCENE 4

THE SAME *without* LYUBA.

MARYA IVANOVNA. I also wanted to tell you about Vanya. He's behaving terribly, and the way he studies he'll never be promoted. I tried to talk to him, he talks back.

NIKOLAI IVANOVICH. Masha, you know I disagree with the kind of life you lead, and the education you give the children. The horrible problem for me is whether it's right of me to stand by and see how they perish before my eyes...

MARYA IVANOVNA. Then something else is necessary, something specific. And what do you suggest?

NIKOLAI IVANOVICH. I don't know. I can only say the first thing we have to do is rid ourselves of this corrupting luxury.

MARYA IVANOVNA. And make peasants of them—I can't agree to that.

NIKOLAI IVANOVICH. Then don't ask me. The things that upset you should do just that.

(*Enter the* PRIEST *and* LYUBA. *The* PRIEST *and* NIKOLAI IVANOVICH *kiss one another.*)

SCENE 5

THE SAME, *the* PRIEST *and* LYUBA.

NIKOLAI IVANOVICH. Are you really finished with it?

PRIEST. I couldn't go on.

NIKOLAI IVANOVICH. I didn't expect it so soon.

PRIEST. Just couldn't any more. In our circumstances you cannot be indifferent. You have to hear confession, administer communion; but when you know all this is false...

NIKOLAI IVANOVICH. So what now?

PRIEST. Now I'm going to the bishop for a hearing. I'm afraid I'll be banished to the Solovets monastery.[34] At one time I thought of fleeing abroad, I wanted to ask you for help, but then I changed my mind—it's cowardice. There is one thing—my wife.

NIKOLAI IVANOVICH. Where is she?

PRIEST. She's gone to her father. My mother-in-law came and took my little boy away. That hurt. I wanted so much... (*Pauses, holding back tears.*)

NIKOLAI IVANOVICH. Well, may God help you. So, are you staying with us?

SCENE 6

THE SAME *and the* PRINCESS.

PRINCESS (*running into the room*). So there, it's happened. He refused to serve and is now under arrest. I've just been there and they wouldn't let me in. Nikolai Ivanovich, please go.

LYUBA. What do you mean refused? How do you know?

PRINCESS. I myself was there. Vasily Andreyevich told me everything. He's a member of the military commission. Boris walked right in and announced that he would not serve and would not take the oath. And he also said all those things Nikolai Ivanovich taught him.

NIKOLAI IVANOVICH. Princess, can you teach such things?

PRINCESS. I don't know, but it has nothing to do with Christianity. Does it have to do with Christianity? Now you tell him, Father.

PRIEST. I'm no longer Father.

PRINCESS. It doesn't matter. You're just like him. It's all right for you, but I won't leave things as they are, no I won't. And what a cursed sort of Christianity it is that causes people to suffer and die. I hate this Christianity of yours. It's all right for you, since you know you won't be touched. But I have only one son, and you've ruined him.

NIKOLAI IVANOVICH. Please calm down, Princess.

PRINCESS. Yes, you've ruined him. You've ruined him, now you have to save him. Go and talk him out of all this nonsense. It's all right for rich people, but not for us.

LYUBA (crying). Papá, what can we do?

NIKOLAI IVANOVICH. I'll go. Maybe I can help. (*Takes off his apron.*)

PRINCESS (*helps him with his coat*). They wouldn't let me in, but we'll go together and I'll get through now. (*Exits with* NIKOLAI IVANOVICH.)

Curtain.

Change of scene. An office. A CLERK *sits [at a desk], and opposite him a* SENTRY *walks back and forth by the door. Enter the* GENERAL *and the* ADJUTANT. *The* CLERK *jumps to attention, the* SENTRY *salutes.*

SCENE 1

THE GENERAL, ADJUTANT, *and* CLERK.

GENERAL. Where's the colonel?
CLERK. With the inductee, Your Excellency.
GENERAL. Ah, very good. Have him come here.
CLERK. Yes, Your Excellency.
GENERAL. What are you copying there, the inductee's deposition?
CLERK. Yes, sir.
GENERAL. Give it here.

(*The* CLERK *hands it over and exits.*)

SCENE 2

THE SAME *without the* CLERK.

GENERAL (*hands the deposition to the* ADJUTANT). Please read it.
ADJUTANT (*reading*). "In regard to the questions put to me concerning: (1) Why I do not take the oath; and (2) Why I refuse to carry out the Government's orders; and [3] What prompted me to use language offensive not only to the military service but also to the highest authorities, my reply to the first question is: I do not take the oath, because I profess the teachings of Christ. In the teachings of Christ the taking of

oaths is openly and specifically forbidden, as in the Gospel according to Saint Matthew 5:34–37, and in the Epistle of James 5:12."

GENERAL. The way they rationalize, and give their own interpretations!

ADJUTANT (*continues to read*). "The Gospel says: 'Swear not at all. But let your communication be, Yea, yea; Nay, nay: for whatsoever is more than these cometh of evil.' The Epistle of James says: 'But above all things, my brethren, swear not, neither by heaven, neither by the earth, neither by any other oath: but let your yea be yea; and your nay, nay; lest ye fall into condemnation.' But it is not only the Gospel's explicit admonition against taking an oath. Even if there were no such admonition, I would still not be able to swear that I will carry out the will of men, since I, according to the principles of Christianity, must always carry out the will of God, which may not coincide with the will of men."

GENERAL. The way they rationalize! If it were up to me, there'd be none of this.

ADJUTANT (*reads on*). "I refuse to carry out the orders of men who call themselves the government, because..."

GENERAL. What insolence!

ADJUTANT. "...because those orders are criminal and evil. They order me to enter the army, and to learn and prepare to commit murder, which is forbidden by both the Old and New Testaments, and, moreover, by my conscience. As to the last question..."

(*Enter* COLONEL *and* CLERK. *The* GENERAL *shakes the* COLONEL's *hand.*)

SCENE 3

THE SAME, COLONEL, *and* CLERK.

COLONEL. You reading the deposition?

GENERAL. Yes. Unpardonably insolent language! Well, go on.

ADJUTANT. "As to the last question, what prompted me to use offensive language before the military commission, my reply is: I was prompted by the desire to serve God, and to expose the delusion that is perpetrated in His name. I hope to preserve this desire until the day I die. And therefore..."

GENERAL. That'll do. Who can listen to all that rubbish. The point is to root it out, and prevent the men from being corrupted by it. (*To the* COLONEL.) Have you talked with him?

COLONEL. I talk with him all the time. I tried to caution him, to convince him that he'll only hurt himself, and will achieve nothing by it. I talked about his family. He's very agitated, but sticks to his views.

GENERAL. You wasted your time talking. We're soldiers, we don't reason, we obey. Get him in here.

(*Exit* ADJUTANT *and* CLERK.)

SCENE 4

GENERAL *and* COLONEL.

GENERAL (*sits down*). No, Colonel, that's wrong. That's not the way to treat such characters. You need firm measures to remove a diseased limb. One rotten apple spoils the whole barrel. You can't be soft. That he's a prince and has a mother and a finacée is of no concern to us at all. For us he's a soldier. And we must obey the tsar's will.

COLONEL. I just thought it'd be easier to get to him by counseling.

GENERAL. Not at all. By firmness, only firmness. I know these characters. He has to be made to feel that he's nothing, that he's dirt under a wheel, and he can't stop it from turning.

COLONEL. Yes, we can try.

GENERAL (*becoming angry*). Try nothing. I don't have to try. I've served my sovereign for forty-four years. I've given, and am still giving, my life to his service, and here comes this brat, and begins lecturing me and quoting Scripture to me. Let him pull that stunt with the chaplains, but with me there's just one thing: he's a soldier or he's a prisoner. And that's all.

(*Enter* BORIS *guarded by* TWO SOLDIERS, *the* ADJUTANT, *and* CLERK.)

SCENE 5

THE SAME, BORIS, TWO SOLDIERS, ADJUTANT, *and* CLERK.

GENERAL (*pointing*). Stand him here.

BORIS. You don't stand me anywhere. I'll stand or sit down wherever I like, because I don't recognize your authority over...

GENERAL. Silence! So you don't recognize authority. I'll make you recognize it, sonny.

BORIS (*sits down on a chair*). It's wrong of you to shout like that.

GENERAL. Stand him up on his feet.

(*The* SOLDIERS *raise* BORIS.)

BORIS. You can do that. You can even kill me, but you cannot make me obey...

GENERAL. Silence, I said. Listen to what I have to say, sonny.

BORIS. I don't at all care to listen to what you, yes you, *sonny,* have to say.[35]

GENERAL. He's crazy. He should be taken to the hospital for observation. There's nothing else to do.

COLONEL. We have orders to turn him over to the Political Section for interrogation.

GENERAL. Very well, off with him. Just get his uniform on.

COLONEL. He won't let us.

GENERAL. Put him in irons. (*To* BORIS.) Now you listen to me. I don't care what happens to you, but for your own good I'll give you a piece of advice—wise up. You'll rot in a dungeon, and be of no use to anyone. Drop it. So, you got a little pissed off, I did too. (*Slaps him on the shoulder.*) Go on, take the oath and just drop it. (*To the* ADJUTANT.) Is the chaplain here? (*To* BORIS.) So, how about it? (BORIS *is silent.*) Why don't you answer? Really, it's better that way. You can't fight city hall. You can keep these thoughts of yours to yourself, just serve your time. We won't force anything on you. So, how about it?

BORIS. I have nothing more to say, I've said it all.

GENERAL. Here you write that there's such and such a verse in the Gospel. Now that's something the chaplains know. Have a talk with the chaplain, and then think it over. That'll be better. Good-bye, I hope when I see you next time, I'll be welcoming you to His Majesty's service. Send the chaplain in. (*Exits, followed by the* COLONEL *and* ADJUTANT.)

SCENE 6

BORIS, CLERK, *and* [TWO] SOLDIERS.

BORIS (*to the* CLERK *and* SOLDIERS). So, you see how they talk. They know themselves that they're deluding you. Don't give in to them. Lay down your rifles and go away. Let them beat the life out of you in a disciplinary battalion, anything's better than serving these deluders.

CLERK. But how can you do without the military? No way.

BORIS. We don't have to think about that. We have to think about what God wants from us. And God wants us to...

SOLDIER. Then why does it say the "Christian army?..."

BORIS. That's not said anywhere. Deluders thought that up.

SOLDIER. How could that be? The bishops must know.

(*Enter* POLITICAL OFFICER *with* CLERK.)

SCENE 7

THE SAME, POLITICAL OFFICER, *and* CLERK.

POLITICAL OFFICER (*to the* CLERK). Is the inductee, Prince Cheremshanov, being held here?

CLERK. Yes, sir. Here he is.

POLITICAL OFFICER. Step this way, please. Are you the Prince Boris Aleksandrovich Cheremshanov who refused to take the oath?

BORIS. I am.

POLITICAL OFFICER (*sits down and motions to a seat opposite him*). Please take a seat.

BORIS. I think our conversation will be completely useless.

POLITICAL OFFICER. I don't think so. At least for you it won't be. You see, I've been informed that you refuse to enter the military service and take the oath, and therefore you are under suspicion of belonging to a revolutionary party. That is what I have to investigate. If it's true, we'll have to remove you from the military service and either imprison or exile you, depending on the extent of your involvement in revolutionary activities. If it's not, we'll leave you to the military authorities. You see, I'm being very frank with you, and I hope you'll treat us with the same trust.

BORIS. In the first place, I cannot trust men who wear uniforms; secondly, I do not respect your profession, indeed, I have the greatest aversion toward it. However, I do not refuse to answer your questions. What do you want to know?

POLITICAL OFFICER. First, if you please, what is you name, rank, and religion?

BORIS. You know all this, and I will not answer. There's just one thing that's of great importance to me: I'm not a so-called Orthodox Christian.

POLITICAL OFFICER. Then what's your religion?

BORIS. I don't define it.

POLITICAL OFFICER What is it anyway?

BORIS. Well, a Christian according to the Sermon on the Mount.

POLITICAL OFFICER. Write that down. (*The* CLERK *writes. To* BORIS.) Nevertheless, do you acknowledge that you belong to some state or class?

BORIS. No, I don't. I consider myself an individual, a servant of God.

POLITICAL OFFICER. Why don't you consider yourself a member of the Russian state?

BORIS. Because I don't acknowledge any states.

POLITICAL OFFICER. What do you mean by don't acknowledge? Do you want them destroyed?

BORIS. Absolutely. I want that, and work for it.

POLITICAL OFFICER (*to the* CLERK). Write that down. How do you work for it?

BORIS. By exposing delusion and lies, and by spreading the truth. Just now, before you came in, I was telling these soldiers not to believe the delusion in which they were involved.

POLITICAL OFFICER. Besides such means as exposing and persuading, do you acknowledge any others?

BORIS. No, I do not, moreover I consider all violence a great sin; not only violence, but all dissembling, cunning...

POLITICAL OFFICER (*writing*). All right. Now let's turn to your acquaintances. Do you know Ivashenkov?

BORIS. No.

POLITICAL OFFICER. Klein?

BORIS. I've heard of him, but never met him.

(*Enter* CHAPLAIN.)

SCENE 8

THE SAME *and* CHAPLAIN.

POLITICAL OFFICER. Well, I think that does it. I don't consider you dangerous or subject to our jurisdiction. I hope you're released soon. Take care. (*Shakes his hand.*)

BORIS. There is one thing I'd like to say to you. Pardon me, but I can't help saying it: why did you choose this evil, vile profession? I'd advise you to leave it.

POLITICAL OFFICER (*smiling*). Thanks for your advice; I have my reasons. Take care. Father, he's all yours. (*Exits with* CLERK.)

SCENE 9

THE SAME *without the* POLITICAL OFFICER *and his* CLERK.

CHAPLAIN. Why do you cause the authorities such grief by refusing to fulfill your Christian duty and serve your tsar and country?

BORIS (*smiling*). It's precisely because I want to fulfill my Christian duty that I don't want to be a soldier.

CHAPLAIN. Why not? It is said a true Christian will "lay down his life for his friends..."[36]

BORIS. Yes, lay down his life, but not take another's. That's just what I want, to lay down my life.

CHAPLAIN. Your thinking is wrong, young man. And what did John the Baptist say to the soldiers...

BORIS (*smiling*). That only proves that even then soldiers robbed, and he stopped them.

CHAPLAIN. Well, why don't you want to take the oath?

BORIS. You know it's forbidden in the Gospel.

CHAPLAIN. Not at all. Why is it when Pilate said: "I adjure thee by the living God, that thou tell us whether thou be the Christ?" the Lord Jesus Christ answered: "I am."[37] That means an oath isn't forbidden.

BORIS. Aren't you ashamed of yourself? You, an old man...

CHAPLAIN. Take my advice and don't be stubborn. We can't change the world. Just take the oath and be quiet. And leave it to the Church to know what is a sin and what isn't.

BORIS. To you? Aren't you afraid of taking so much sin upon yourself?

CHAPLAIN. What sin? There can be no sin upon my soul, since I've been true to the faith in which I was reared, and I've been a chaplain for thirty years.

BORIS. Then whose sin is it when you delude so many people? What do they have in their heads? (*Points to the* SENTRY.)

CHAPLAIN. That, young man, is not for us to judge. We have to obey our superiors.

BORIS. Leave me alone. I pity you and, I must confess, it disgusts me to listen to you. It's one thing if you were like that general, but you came here with a cross and the Gospel to persuade me in the name of Christ to deny Christ. Go away. (*Upset.*) Leave me alone. Go away. [*To the* SENTRY.] Take me out of her so I won't have to see anyone. I'm tired, awfully tired.

CHAPLAIN. If that's the case, good-bye.

(*Enter* ADJUTANT.)

SCENE 10

THE SAME, *and the* ADJUTANT. BORIS *is sitting in the rear of the stage.*

ADJUTANT. Well, what about it?

CHAPLAIN. He's extremely stubborn, and insubordinate.

ADJUTANT. So he didn't agree to take the oath and serve?

CHAPLAIN. Not for anything.

ADJUTANT. Then he must be taken to the hospital.

CHAPLAIN. You mean make him out to be sick? That's certainly easier, otherwise he'll set too tempting an example.

ADJUTANT. For observation in a ward for the mentally ill. Those are my orders.

CHAPLAIN. Certainly. Have a good day. (*Exits.*)

SCENE 11

THE SAME *without the* CHAPLAIN.

ADJUTANT (*walks up to* BORIS). Please come with me. My orders are to escort you.

BORIS. Where?

ADJUTANT. For the time being to the hospital where it'll be quieter for you, and where you'll have the time to think things over.

BORIS. I've already thought everything over. Anyway, let's go.

(*They exit.*)

Curtain.

Change of scene. Reception room in hospital.

SCENE 1

HEAD DOCTOR *and* STAFF DOCTOR. OFFICER-PATIENT *in a hospital gown.* GUARDS *in smocks.*

PATIENT. I'm telling you, you're only making me worse. I've already felt absolutely fine several times.

HEAD DOCTOR. Now don't get upset. I'm willing to discharge you, but you yourself know that release is dangerous for you. If I were sure that someone would take care of you.

PATIENT. You think I'll start drinking again. I won't, I've learned my lesson. But every extra day I spend here is ruining me. You're doing the opposite of what (*getting excited*) has to be done. You're cruel. It's all right for you.

HEAD DOCTOR. Calm down. (*Makes a motion to the* GUARDS, *who approach [the* PATIENT *] from behind.*)

PATIENT. That's easy for you to say since you're free, but how is it for us among lunatics? (*To the* GUARDS.) Don't come near me, get away.

HEAD DOCTOR. I'm asking you, please calm down.

PATIENT. And I'm asking you, I demand you release me. (*Shreiks and rushes at the* DOCTOR, *but the* GUARDS *seize him. After a struggle they lead him away.*)

SCENE 2

HEAD DOCTOR *and* STAFF DOCTOR.

STAFF DOCTOR. So, it started again. He almost got you.

HEAD DOCTOR. Alcoholic... and nothing can be done. Nevertheless there is some improvement.

(*Enter* ADJUTANT.)

THE SAME, *and* ADJUTANT.

ADJUTANT. Hello.

HEAD DOCTOR. Good morning.

ADJUTANT. I've brought you an interesting subject. A Prince Cherem-shanov, who's been inducted, but refuses to serve on religious grounds. They sent him to the political section, but he doesn't come under their jurisdiction—it isn't a matter of subversion. The chaplain also talked to him and tried to set him straight, but to no avail.

HEAD DOCTOR (*laughing*). And as always, you bring him to us as the last resort. All right, let's have him.

(*Exit* STAFF DOCTOR.)

SCENE 4

THE SAME *without the* STAFF DOCTOR.

ADJUTANT. They say he's a very educated young man, and he also has a rich fiancée. It just makes no sense. I'm certain this is where he belongs.

HEAD DOCTOR. Yes, a mania...

(BORIS *is brought in.*)

SCENE 5

THE SAME *and* BORIS.

HEAD DOCTOR. Welcome! Take a seat, please. Let's have a chat. [*To the* ADJUTANT.] Please leave us.

(*Exit* ADJUTANT.)

SCENE 6

THE SAME *without the* ADJUTANT.

BORIS. If you're going to lock me up somewhere, I'd like to ask you, if possible, to do so quickly, and let me rest.

HEAD DOCTOR. I'm sorry, we have to abide by the rules. Just a few questions. How do you feel? What's bothering you?

BORIS. Nothing, I'm absolutely fine.

HEAD DOCTOR. Yes, but you don't behave like others.

BORIS. I behave as my conscience dictates.

HEAD DOCTOR. Look, you've refused to fulfill your military duty. How do you explain that?

BORIS. I'm a Christian, and therefore cannot kill.

HEAD DOCTOR. But still you have to defend your country from its enemies, and keep offenders from doing evil.

BORIS. No one is attacking our country; and there are many more offenders among those who govern than among those whom they coerce.

HEAD DOCTOR. What do you mean?

BORIS. I mean, for example, liquor—a major cause of evil—is sold by the government; a false, delusionary religion is spread by the government; and military service—which I'm required to fulfill, and which is a major means of corruption—is required by the government.

HEAD DOCTOR. So in your opinion, the government and the state are unnecessary.

BORIS. I don't know about that, but I do know for certain that I must not participate in evil.

HEAD DOCTOR. But what'll happen to the world? We're given the power of reason in order to anticipate things.

BORIS. We're also given it in order to comprehend that the social order is not sustained by coercion, but by benevolence; also, one man's refusal to participate in evil is not at all dangerous.

HEAD DOCTOR. Now let me examine you a bit. Please lie down. (*Begins to touch him.*) Any pain here?

BORIS. No.

HEAD DOCTOR. And here?

BORIS. No.

HEAD DOCTOR. Take a deep breath. Hold it. Thank you. Now, if you will. (*Takes out an instrument and measures his forehead and nose.*) Now please close your eyes and walk straight ahead.

BORIS. Aren't you ashamed to do all this?

HEAD DOCTOR. What's that?

BORIS. All this nonsense. You know very well that I'm fine, and I've been sent here because I refused to participate in their evil, and because they have nothing with which to counter the truth. And that is why they're pretending and making me out to be abnormal, and you're helping them. That's despicable and shameful. Enough of this.

HEAD DOCTOR. So you don't want to walk?

BORIS. No, I don't. You can torment me any way you like, go on, but I'll not help you. (*Angrily.*) Enough of this.

(*The* DOCTOR *rings for the* GUARDS. *Enter two* GUARDS.)

SCENE 7

THE SAME, *and* GUARDS.

HEAD DOCTOR. Please calm down. I understand; your nerves are on edge. Wouldn't you like to go to your ward?

(*Enter* STAFF DOCTOR.)

SCENE 8

THE SAME, *and* STAFF DOCTOR.

STAFF DOCTOR. There are some visitors for Cheremshanov.

BORIS. Who is it?

STAFF DOCTOR. Mr. Saryntsev and his daughter.

BORIS. I'd like to see them.

HEAD DOCTOR. All right, ask them in. [*To* BORIS.] You can see them here. (*Exits, followed by the* STAFF DOCTOR *and* GUARDS.)

(*Enter* NIKOLAI IVANOVICH *and* LYUBA. *The* PRINCESS *looks in at the door and says:* "Go in, I'll come later.")

SCENE 9

BORIS, NIKOLAI IVANOVICH, *and* LYUBA.

LYUBA (*goes straight up to* BORIS, *grasps him by the head, and kisses him*). Poor Boris.

BORIS. No, don't be sorry for me. I really feel good; I'm so happy and re-laxed. [*To* NIKOLAI IVANOVICH.] How are you? (*Embraces* NIKOLAI IVANOVICH.)

NIKOLAI IVANOVICH. I came to tell you one thing, the most important thing: first of all, in such matters it's better to do less than too much; and, secondly, in this matter you must do what is said in the Gospel, and not think in advance, "I'll do this, I'll say that": "And ye shall be brought before governors, take no thought how or what ye shall speak, the Spirit of your Father [shall speak] in you."[38] That is, don't act on the dictates of your thoughts, but act only when you feel with your whole being that you cannot do otherwise.

BORIS. That's just what I've done. I didn't think I'd refuse to serve. But when I saw all that delusion—symbols of justice, and then documents, police, and officials smoking away—I couldn't help saying what I said. And I was frightened, but only till I began; after that it was so simple, so delightful.

(LYUBA *sits and cries.*)

NIKOLAI IVANOVICH. But the main thing is, don't do anything for the sake of worldly glory or to gain the approbation of those whose opin-ions you value. As for myself, I can say emphatically that if you would take the oath now and enter the service, my love and respect for you would not lessen but increase all the more, because it is not what happens in the world that matters, but what happens in the soul.

BORIS. Of course, because if it happens in the soul, there will also be a change in the world.

NIKOLAI IVANOVICH. Now I've had my say. Your mother's here. She's taking it very hard. If you can do what she asks—do it, that's what I wanted to tell you.

(*Hysterical cries are heard in the corridor. A* PATIENT *bursts into the room followed by* GUARDS *who drag him away.*)

LYUBA. That's terrible. And you're going to be here! (*Cries.*)

BORIS. That doesn't frighten me, nothing frightens me now. I really feel good. The only thing I fear is how you feel about it. Please help me; I'm sure you will.

LYUBA. Can I feel glad about it?

NIKOLAI IVANOVICH. Not glad, that you can't. I'm not glad either, I agonize over him, and would gladly take his place. But though I agonize, I know it's a good thing.

LYUBA. All right. But when will they let him go?

BORIS. No one knows. I don't think about the future. The present is so good. And you can make it still better.

(*Enter* PRINCESS.)

SCENE 10

THE SAME, *and* PRINCESS.

PRINCESS. No, I can't wait any longer. (*To* NIKOLAI IVANOVICH.) So, have you convinced him? Does he agree? Borya, my darling, please understand, I can't take it. For thirty years I've lived just for you. I brought you up, I was proud of you. And now that everything is done and ready—you just turn it all down! Prison, disgrace. You can't do this, Borya.

BORIS. Mamá, just listen to me.

PRINCESS [*to* NIKOLAI IVANOVICH]. Why don't you say something? You ruined him, so you have to convince him. It's all right for you. Lyuba, you talk to him.

LYUBA. What can I do?

BORIS. Mamá, try to understand, there are things that can't be done anymore than you can fly. And so I cannot serve in the army.

PRINCESS. You only think you can't. Nonsense. Everyone has served and is serving. You and Nikolai Ivanovich have concocted some sort of Christianity. It's not Christianity, it's a fiendish doctrine that makes everyone suffer.

BORIS. It's what the Gospel says.

PRINCESS. No it isn't; and if it is, then it's stupid. Borya, my darling, have pity on me. (*Throws her arms around his neck and cries.*) My whole life has been nothing but misery. My only glimmer of happiness—and you're turning it into agony. Borya, have pity on me!

BORIS. Mamá, it's terribly hard on me. But I can't tell you what you want to hear.

PRINCESS. Come on, don't refuse, say you'll think it over.

NIKOLAI IVANOVICH. Say you'll think it over, and think it over.

BORIS. All right. But Mamá, have pity on me also. It's hard on me as well. (*Cries are again heard in the corridor.*) You know I'm in an insane asylum, and may really go out of my mind.

(*Enter* HEAD DOCTOR.)

SCENE 11

THE SAME, *and* HEAD DOCTOR.

HEAD DOCTOR. Madam, this can have very bad consequences. Your son is in a highly emotional state. I think this visit has to end. Regular visiting days are on Thursday and Sunday. Please come before noon.

PRINCESS. All right, all right, I'll leave. Good-bye, Borya. Think it over, have pity on me, and meet me on Thursday happy. (*Kisses him.*)

NIKOLAI IVANOVICH (*shaking his hand*). May God be with you, think as if you knew you were to die tomorrow. Only then will you make the right decision. Good-bye.

BORIS (*goes up to* LYUBA). And what do you say to me?

LYUBA. I can't lie. I don't understand why you're tormenting yourself and everybody else. I don't understand it, and have nothing to say. (*Exits crying.*)

SCENE 12

BORIS *alone.*

BORIS. Oh, how hard it is, how hard! Lord help me. (*Prays.*)

(*Enter* GUARDS *with a hospital gown.*)

SCENE 13

BORIS *and* GUARDS.

GUARD. Please change.

(BORIS *puts on the hospital gown.*)

Curtain.

ACT IV

Moscow, one year later. A hall in the Saryntsevs' home is prepared for an evening of dancing to piano music. FOOTMEN *arrange flowers in front of the grand piano. Enter* MARYA IVANOVNA *in a stylish silk gown, accompanied by* ALEKSANDRA IVANOVNA.

SCENE 1

MARYA IVANOVNA, ALEKSANDRA IVANOVNA, *and* FOOTMEN.

MARYA IVANOVNA. A ball? No, just a little dance party, *une sauterie*, as they used to say for *adolescents*. I can't let my children go out all the time and never give a party myself. There was a play night at the Makovs, and they've been to dances everywhere.

ALEKSANDRA IVANOVNA. I'm afraid it's very unpleasant for Nicolas.

MARYA IVANOVNA. What can I do? (*To the* FOOTMEN.) Put it here. God knows how I hate doing anything to displease him. But I don't think he's that demanding anymore.

ALEKSANDRA IVANOVNA. Oh yes he is. He just doesn't show it. He was very upset when he went to his room after dinner.

MARYA IVANOVNA. So, what can I do? What can I do? We all have to live, you know. After all, we have eight children,[39] and if there is no entertainment for them at home, God knows what they'll do. Anyway, I'm so happy about Lyuba now.

ALEKSANDRA IVANOVNA. Has he proposed yet?

MARYA IVANOVNA. As good as proposed. He talked with her, and she said yes.

ALEKSANDRA IVANOVNA. That'll be another awful blow for him.

MARYA IVANOVNA. He knows already. He can't help knowing.

ALEKSANDRA IVANOVNA. He doesn't like him.

MARYA IVANOVNA (*to the* FOOTMEN). Put the fruit on the buffet. Whom? Aleksandr Mikhailovich? Of course he doesn't, because he's a living contradiction to all his theories: he's a man of the world, kind, pleasant and nice. Oh, that horrible nightmare with Boris Cherem-shanov. How is he?

ALEKSANDRA IVANOVNA. Lizanka went to visit him. He's still there. They say he's gotten horribly thin, and the doctors fear for his life or sanity.

MARYA IVANOVNA. Yes, now there's a frightful sacrifice to his ideas. Why did he have to ruin himself? I never wished it.

(*Enter* PIANIST.)

SCENE 2

THE SAME, *and* PIANIST.

MARYA IVANOVNA (*to* PIANIST). Are you playing the dance?

PIANIST. Yes, I'm the pianist.

MARYA IVANOVNA. Please take a seat and wait a moment. Would you like some tea?

PIANIST. No, thank you. (*Walks over to the piano.*)

MARYA IVANOVNA. I never wished it. I liked Boris, but still he wasn't a good match for Lyuba—especially after he got carried away by Nikolai Ivanovich's ideas.

ALEKSANDRA IVANOVNA. Still, the strength of his convictions is re-markable. The way he suffers! They tell him that if he won't agree to serve, he'll either remain where he is or be sent to prison. He keeps on giving them the same answer. And Lizanka says he's happy and even cheery.

MARYA IVANOVNA. They're fanatics. But here comes Aleksandr Mikhailovich.

(*Enter the dashing* ALEKSANDR MIKHAILOVICH STARKOVSKY, *wearing a tailcoat.*)

THE SAME, *and* STARKOVSKY.

STARKOVSKY. I've come early. (*Kisses the hands of both ladies.*)

MARYA IVANOVNA. So much the better.

STARKOVSKY. And where's Lyubov Nikolayevna? She was going to dance so many dances to make up for all she's missed. I volunteered to help her.

MARYA IVANOVNA. She's sorting favors for the cotillion.

STARKOVSKY. I'll go and help her—is that all right?

MARYA IVANOVNA. By all means.

(*As* STARKOVSKY *is going out he meets* LYUBA *carrying a cushion, stars, and ribbons.*)

SCENE 4

THE SAME, *and* LYUBA.

LYUBA (*in evening dress, but not low cut*). Ah, here you are. Great. Come on and help me. There are two more cushions in the living room. Bring them all here. Hi, how are you!

STARKOVSKY. I'm off. (*Exits.*)

SCENE 5

MARYA IVANOVNA, ALEKSANDRA IVANOVNA, *and* LYUBA.

MARYA IVANOVNA (*to* LYUBA). Listen, Lyuba. We're going to have friends here tonight; they'll hint and ask questions. Can I announce it?

LYUBA. No, Mamá, no. Why? Let them ask. Papá won't like it.

MARYA IVANOVNA. He knows anyway or suspects it; sooner or later he will have to be told. I think it's best to announce it tonight. After all, *c'est le secret de la comédie.*

LYUBA. No, Mamá, please don't. It'll spoil the whole party. No, don't do it.
MARYA IVANOVNA. Well, as you wish.
LYUBA. Then you know what: at the end of the party, right before supper.

(*Enter* STARKOVSKY.)

SCENE 6

THE SAME, *and* STARKOVSKY.

LYUBA [*to* STARKOVSKY]. Well, have you got them?
MARYA IVANOVNA. I'll go now and look in on Natasha. (*Exits with* ALEKSANDRA IVANOVNA.)

SCENE 7

LYUBA *and* STARKOVSKY.

STARKOVSKY (*carrying three cushions, which he holds down with his chin, and dropping them on the way*). Lyubov Nikolayevna, don't bother, I'll pick up. Boy, you've made a lot! You just have to know how to arrange things. Vanya, come here.

SCENE 8

THE SAME, *and* VANYA.

VANYA (*carrying more favors*). That's all of them now. Lyuba, Aleksandr Mikhailovich and I have a bet: who'll earn the most awards.
STARKOVSKY. It'll be easy for you, you know everyone and have already earned them in advance, but I have to charm the girls first, and only then get my rewards. That means I'm giving you a forty-point head start.
VANYA. But you're engaged, and I'm only a kid.

STARKOVSKY. Well, I'm not engaged either, and worse off than a kid.

LYUBA. Vanya, please go to my room and bring the glue and pincushion from the little étagère. (VANYA *starts to leave.*) Only for God's sake don't break anything there.

VANYA. I'll break everything. (*Runs off.*)

SCENE 9

LYUBA *and* STARKOVSKY.

STARKOVSKY (*takes her hand*). Lyuba, may I? I'm so happy. (*Kisses her hand.*) The mazurka's mine, but that isn't enough. There isn't enough time in the mazurka to talk. And I have to talk. Can I wire my family that I've been accepted and am happy?

LYUBA. Yes, tonight.

STARKOVSKY. One word more: how will Nikolai Ivanovich take it? Have you told him yet? Have you told him? Have you?

LYUBA. No, I haven't; but I will. He'll take it as he now takes everything concerning the family. He'll say: "Do as you know best." But in his heart he'll be distressed.

STARKOVSKY. Because I'm not Cheremshanov? Because I'm a gentleman of the bedchamber, a marshal of nobility?

LYUBA. Yes. But I've already struggled with myself and deceived myself for his sake. And it's not because I don't love him enough that I don't do what he wants, but because I can't lie. And he says so himself. I have too strong a desire to live.

STARKOVSKY. And life is the only truth. Well, what about him, Cheremshanov?

LYUBA. Don't speak to me about him. I feel like blaming him, blaming him even while he's suffering. And I recognize it's because I feel guilty towards him. One thing I do know: there's love, and, I think, there's real love, which I've never felt for him.

STARKOVSKY. Lyuba, is that true?

LYUBA. You want me to say that I love you with that real love—but I won't say it. Yes, I love you, Aleksandr Mikhailovich.

STARKOVSKY. Aleksandr Mikhailovich...

LYUBA. I love you, Alek,[40] with a different kind of love, but it's not that one. Neither was my love for Boris, nor is my love for you that real one: if only they could be combined.

STARKOVSKY. No, I'm satisfied with mine. (*Kisses her hand.*) Lyuba!

LYUBA (*moves him away*). No, let's sort all these. They're beginning to arrive now.

(*Enter the* PRINCESS *with* TONYA, *and a* LITTLE GIRL.)

SCENE 10

THE SAME, *and* PRINCESS *with* TONYA *and* LITTLE GIRL.

LYUBA. Mamá will be out in a moment.

PRINCESS. Are we the first?

STARKOVSKY. Someone has to be. I suggested making a manikin lady the first.

(*Enter* STYOPA, *and* VANYA *carrying the glue and pincushion.*)

SCENE 11

THE SAME, STYOPA *and* VANYA.

STYOPA [*to* TONYA]. I thought I would see you yesterday at the Italian opera.

TONYA. We were at my aunt's, sewing for the poor.

(*Enter* STUDENTS, LADIES, MARYA IVANOVNA, *and* COUNTESS.)

SCENE 12

THE SAME, MARYA IVANOVNA, COUNTESS, STUDENTS, *and* LADIES.

COUNTESS. Shall we not see Nikolai Ivanovich?
MARYA IVANOVNA. No, he never comes.
STARKOVSKY. Quadrille, please. (*Claps his hands.*)

(*The dancers take their places and the dance begins.*)

ALEKSANDRA IVANOVNA (*goes up to* MARYA IVANOVNA). He's awfully upset. He had visited Boris Aleksandrovich, and returned and saw there was a ball, and now he wants to leave. I went up to his door and heard him talking to Aleksandr Petrovich.
MARYA IVANOVNA. So?
STARKOVSKY. *Rond des dames. Les cavaliers en avant.*
ALEKSANDRA IVANOVNA. He's decided that he cannot possibly live here, and is leaving.
MARYA IVANOVNA. What agony that man is! (*Exits.*)

Change of scene. NIKOLAI IVANOVICH*'s room. Music is heard in the background.* NIKOLAI IVANOVICH, *wearing an overcoat, puts a letter on the table.* ALEKSANDR PETROVICH, *wearing ragged clothes, is with him.*

SCENE 1

NIKOLAI IVANOVICH *and* ALEKSANDR PETROVICH.

ALEKSANDR PETROVICH. Don't worry, we won't need any money to get to the Caucasus; and once there you arrange things.
NIKOLAI IVANOVICH. We'll go by train to Tula, and from there we'll walk. Well, everything's ready. (*Places the letter in the middle of the table and, as he is leaving, meets* MARYA IVANOVNA.)

SCENE 2

NIKOLAI IVANOVICH, ALEKSANDR PETROVICH, *and* MARYA IVA-
NOVNA.

NIKOLAI IVANOVICH. Now why have you come?
MARYA IVANOVNA. Why? To keep you from doing a cruel thing. Why are
you doing this? What have I done?
NIKOLAI IVANOVICH. Why? Because I can't go on living like this. I can't
bear this awful, depraved life.
MARYA IVANOVNA. That's really awful. My life, which I've completely de-
voted to you and the children, is all of a sudden depraved. (*Sees* ALEK-
SANDR PETROVICH.) *Renvoyez au moins cet homme. Je ne veux pas qu'il
soit temoin de cette conversation.*
ALEKSANDR PETROVICH. Comprene. Tuzher mua parte.
NIKOLAI IVANOVICH. Wait for me out there, Aleksandr Petrovich, I'll
come in a moment.

(*Exit* ALEKSANDR PETROVICH.)

SCENE 3

NIKOLAI IVANOVICH *and* MARYA IVANOVNA.

MARYA IVANOVNA. What can you possibly have in common with such a
man? And why is he closer to you than your own wife? That's beyond
comprehension. Where are you going?
NIKOLAI IVANOVICH. I've left a letter for you. I didn't want to talk. It's
too hard on me; but if you wish, I'll try to tell you calmly.
MARYA IVANOVNA. No, I cannot understand it. Why do you hate and
punish a wife who had been completely devoted to you? Tell me: have I
been out gallivanting at dances, have I been a clotheshorse, a flirt? My
whole life has been devoted to my family. I nursed and raised them all
myself, and this past year the entire burden of their education, and man-
aging our affairs has been wholly on me...

NIKOLAI IVANOVICH (*interrupting*). But this burden is on you only because you didn't want to live as I suggested.

MARYA IVANOVNA. But I simply couldn't do that. Ask anyone. I couldn't let the children grow up uneducated, as you wanted them to, nor could I do the laundry and cooking by myself.

NIKOLAI IVANOVICH. I never wanted that.

MARYA IVANOVNA. Well it makes no difference, it was something like that. No, you're a Christian, you want to do good, you say you love mankind, then why are you punishing the woman who has devoted her whole life to you?

NIKOLAI IVANOVICH. How am I punishing you? I really love you, but...

MARYA IVANOVNA. Of course you're punishing me by leaving me and going away. What will everyone say? One of two things, either I'm a bad woman, or you're a madman.

NIKOLAI IVANOVICH. So let me be a madman, only I can't live like this.

MARYA IVANOVNA. But what's there so terrible about me giving a party once over the whole winter... just once, because I was afraid it will displease you—and a very modest one at that, just ask Manya and Varvara Vasilyevna! Everyone told me I could do no less, that it was unavoidable. And that's a crime, for which I must endure shame. Yes, and not just shame. The main thing is that you no longer love me. You love the whole world and that drunken Aleksandr Petrovich; but I still love you and can't live without you. Why are you doing this? Why? (*Cries.*)

NIKOLAI IVANOVICH. But you don't really want to understand my life, my spiritual life.

MARYA IVANOVNA. I want to understand it, but I can't. I see that your Christianity has made you hate your family and me, but I don't understand why.

NIKOLAI IVANOVICH. But others do.

MARYA IVANOVNA. Who? Aleksandr Petrovich who worms money out of you?

NIKOLAI IVANOVICH. He and others: Tonya and Vasily Nikanorovich. Anyway, I don't care. Even if no one understood, it wouldn't change anything.

MARYA IVANOVNA. Vasily Nikanorovich has repented and joined his parish again. And Tonya is now dancing and flirting with Styopa.

NIKOLAI IVANOVICH. That's a pity, but it can't turn black into white, and it can't change my life either. Masha, you don't need me. Let me go. I've tried to share your life, to bring into it what comprises my whole life, but it doesn't work. The only result is agony for you and for me. And I'm not only in agony myself, but I'm damaging what I do. Everyone, even this Aleksandr Petrovich, has the right to say, and actually tells me, that I'm a hypocrite; that I talk but do not do; that I preach the Gospel of poverty but live in luxury, justifying that by giving everything to my wife.

MARYA IVANOVNA. And you're ashamed to face people. Can't you really rise above that?

NIKOLAI IVANOVICH. It's not that I'm ashamed, though I really am, but that I'm damaging God's work.

MARYA IVANOVNA. You yourself said that God's work goes on despite our resistance to it. But that's not the point. Tell me, what do you want from me?

NIKOLAI IVANOVICH. I've told you already.

MARYA IVANOVNA. But, Nicolas, you know that's not possible. Just think, Lyuba is getting married now; Vanya has entered the university; Misha and Katya are in school. How can you break all this up?

NIKOLAI IVANOVICH. But what about me?

MARYA IVANOVNA. Practice what you preach: be forbearing, loving. Why is it so difficult for you? Just bear with us, and don't cut yourself off from us. Now, what's distressing you?

(*Enter* VANYA *running.*)

SCENE 4

THE SAME, *and* VANYA.

VANYA. Mamá, they're calling you.

MARYA IVANOVNA. Tell them I can't come. Go on, go.

VANYA. Come on, will you. (*Exits.*)

NIKOLAI IVANOVICH *and* MARYA IVANOVNA.

NIKOLAI IVANOVICH. You don't want to see my point, and understand me.

MARYA IVANOVNA. It's not that I don't want to, I can't.

NIKOLAI IVANOVICH. No, you don't want to, and we're moving further and further apart. Come into my world, put yourself in my place for a moment, and you'll understand. First of all, life here is thoroughly depraved. You're angry at my choice of words, but no other expression will do for a life built entirely on robbery—because the money you live on comes from the land you've stolen from the peasants. Moreover, I see that this life is depraving the children: "But whoso shall offend one of these little ones;"[41] and I see how they are perishing and becoming depraved right before my eyes. I cannot bear to see grown men, decked out in dress coats, serving us like slaves. Every meal is agony for me.

MARYA IVANOVNA. But it has always been that way. Everyone does it, both abroad and everywhere else.

NIKOLAI IVANOVICH. But I haven't been able to, since I understood that we are all brothers, and I can no longer look at it without being distressed.

MARYA IVANOVNA. That's self-inflicted. You can concoct anything.

NIKOLAI IVANOVICH (*heatedly*). It's this here lack of understanding that's so awful. Just take today. I spent the morning among the vagrants at the Rzhanov Hospice,[42] where I saw a baby literally die of hunger, a boy that had become an alcoholic, and a consumptive washerwoman on her way to do laundry. Then I came home, where a footman in a white tie opens the door for me, and I see my son, who's just a kid, order the footman to bring him some water, and I see this army of servants working for us. Then I went to visit Boris, a man who is putting his life on the line for truth, and I see him, that pure, strong, determined man, being intentionally driven to insanity and death so that they can be rid of him. I know and they know that he has a bad heart, and they harass him and drag him to a ward for raging lunatics. No, that's just terrible, terrible. And when I came home, I find out that the one member of the family who understood—not me—but the truth, my daughter, in one fell swoop, has rejected both her fiancé, whom she promised to love, and the truth, and is going to marry a flunky, a liar...

MARYA IVANOVNA. How very Christian of you!

NIKOLAI IVANOVICH. Yes, it's nasty. I'm wrong, but I only want you to put yourself in my place. I'm only saying that she rejected the truth...

MARYA IVANOVNA. You say the truth, but others—in fact the majority—say a mistake. You know Vasily Nikanorovich once thought he was mistaken, but now he's come back to the Church.

NIKOLAI IVANOVICH. That can't be.

MARYA IVANOVNA. He's written to Lizanka, she'll show you the letter. All this is very precarious. It's the same with Tonya, not to mention Aleksandr Petrovich, who simply finds it profitable.

NIKOLAI IVANOVICH (*becoming angry*). Well I don't care. I only ask you to understand me. I still think the truth is the truth. So it hurts me. And here at home I walk in and see a Christmas tree, and a dance party—hundreds of roubles being wasted while people are dying of hunger. I cannot live like this. Have pity on me, it's killing me. Let me go. Goodbye.

MARYA IVANOVNA. If you go, I go with you. And if I can't go with you, I'll throw myself under the train you travel on. And let them all go to blazes—Misha and Katya... My God, my God, what agony! Why? Why? (*Cries*).

NIKOLAI IVANOVICH (*at the door*). Aleksandr Petrovich, go home. I'm not going. [*To* MARYA IVANOVNA.] All right, I'll stay. (*Takes off his coat.*)

MARYA IVANOVNA (*embracing him*). We don't have much longer to live. Let's not spoil it after twenty-eight years of life together. Fine, I won't give any parties, but please don't punish me.

[*Enter* VANYA *and* KATYA *running.*]

SCENE 6

THE SAME, VANYA *and* KATYA.

VANYA AND KATYA. Mamá, come, quick.

MARYA IVANOVNA. Coming, coming. [*To* NIKOLAI IVANOVICH.] So let's forgive each other. (*Exits [with the children].*)

SCENE 7

NIKOLAI IVANOVICH *alone.*

NICKOLAI IVANOVICH. A child, a regular child, or a cunning woman. No, a cunning child. Yes, that's it. I see, Thou wilt not have me as Thy servant in this work of Thine. Thou wilt have me humbled so that all may point a finger at me and say: "He preaches but practices not." Well, so be it. Thou knowest best what Thou wilt have: humility, zeal. Yes, if only I could raise myself to Him.

(*Enter* LIZANKA.)

SCENE 8

NIKOLAI IVANOVICH *and* LIZANKA.

LIZANKA. Excuse me. I've brought you a letter from Vasily Nikanorovich. It's addressed to me, but he asked me to inform you.

NIKOLAI IVANOVICH. Is it really true?

LIZANKA. Yes. Should I read it?

NIKOLAI IVANOVICH. Please do.

LIZANKA (*reading*). "I am writing to ask you to convey the following to Nikolai Ivanovich. I very much regret the mistake which made me openly forsake the Holy Orthodox Church, and I rejoice in my return to it. I wish you and Nikolai Ivanovich would do the same. Please forgive me."

NIKOLAI IVANOVICH. They wore him down, poor guy. But still, that's terrible.

LIZANKA. I also wanted to tell you that the princess is here. She came up to my room in a terrible state of mind, and absolutely insists on seeing you. She's just visited her son. I think you're better off not seeing her. What good could come from your meeting?

NIKOLAI IVANOVICH. No, have her come here. Apparently today is meant to be a horrible day of tribulation.

LIZANKA (*exiting*). Then I'll go and get her.

SCENE 9

NIKOLAI IVANOVICH *alone.*

NIKOLAI IVANOVICH. Yes, yes, I need just remember that there is only life in serving Thee. To remember, that if Thou sendest tribulation, it is because Thou hast considered me capable of enduring it, and that I am equal to the task, otherwise it would not be tribulation... Father, help me—help me to do not my but Thy will.

(*Enter* PRINCESS.)

SCENE 10

NIKOLAI IVANOVICH *and* PRINCESS.

PRINCESS. So you do me the honor of receiving me. Good evening. I won't give you my hand, because I hate and despise you.

NIKOLAI IVANOVICH. What's happened?

PRINCESS. He's being transferred to a disciplinary battalion, that's what. And it's your doing.

NIKOLAI IVANOVICH. Princess, if you want anything, say so; but if you've come just to be abusive to me, you're only harming yourself. You really cannot offend me, because I feel for you with all my heart, and pity you.

PRINCESS. What compassion, what Christian eminence! No, Mr. Saryntsev, you cannot fool me one bit. I know all about you now. You don't care that you've ruined my son, you're busy giving parties, and your daughter—my son's fiancée—is getting married to a man whom you like. And here you are pretending that you lead a simple life, and fool around with carpentry. How disgusting you are with this neo-pharisaism of yours.

NIKOLAI IVANOVICH. Calm down, Princess. Tell me what you want. You surely didn't come just to berate me.

PRINCESS. I did in part. I have to get all this pain out of my system. But this is what I want: he's being transferred to a disciplinary battalion, and I cannot bear it. And you brought him to this. You did it. You, you, you.

NIKOLAI IVANOVICH. Not I, but God. And God sees how sorry I am for you. Don't resist the will of God. He wants to test you. Bear it humbly.

PRINCESS. I cannot bear it humbly. My son was my whole life, he alone, and you've taken him from me and ruined him. I cannot be calm. I've come to you in a last attempt to tell you that you've ruined him, and you must save him. Go and get him released. Go to the authorities, to the tsar, to whomever. You just have to do it. If you don't, I know what I'll do. You'll answer to me for it.

NIKOLAI IVANOVICH. Tell me what to do. I'm ready to do anything.

PRINCESS. I repeat once again: you must save him. If you don't—remember my words. Good-bye. (*Exits.*)

SCENE 11

NIKOLAI IVANOVICH *alone. Lies down on the sofa. Silence. The doors open, and the music of the* Grossvater Tanz *becomes louder. Enter* STYOPA.

SCENE 12

NIKOLAI IVANOVICH *and* STYOPA.

STYOPA. Papá's not here. Come on.

(*Enter* DANCING COUPLES, *young and old.*)

SCENE 13

NIKOLAI IVANOVICH, STYOPA *and* DANCING COUPLES.

LYUBA (*noticing* NIKOLAI IVANOVICH). Oh, you're here, excuse me.
NIKOLAI IVANOVICH (*rising*). That's all right.

(*The* DANCING COUPLES *exit.*)

SCENE 14

NIKOLAI IVANOVICH *alone.*

NIKOLAI IVANOVICH. Vasily Nikanorovich has returned to the Church.
   I've ruined Boris. Lyuba is getting married. Am I really mistaken, mistaken in believing in Thee? No. Father, help me.

Curtain.

ACT V

Disciplinary battalion. Barracks. Prisoners are sitting and lying about. BORIS *is reading the Gospel and explicating.*

A prisoner who has been punished is brought in. "Ah, Pugachëv[43] would show yuh." The princess bursts in; she is chased out. Altercation with an officer. At prayers. Boris is sent to the punishment cell. "We'll flog him."

Change of scene.

The tsar's study. Cigarettes, jokes, compliments. The princess is announced. Told to wait. Petitioners enter, flattery, then the princess. Refusal. Exits.

Change of scene.

Marya Ivanovna and doctor talk about [Nikolai Ivanovich's] illness. "He's changed, is meek, but depressed." Nikolai Ivanovich enters, talks with doctor. Uselessness of treatment—*ardor* more important. But he agrees to it for his wife's sake.

Enter Tonya, Styopa, Lyuba with Stakhovich.[44] Conversation about land. He [Nikolai Ivanovich] tries not to offend them. All exit. He with Lizanka. "I'm never sure whether I did right. I've accomplished nothing. I've ruined Boris, Vasily Nikanorovich returned to the Church. I'm an example of weakness. Evidently God doesn't want me to be His servant. He has many other servants and will do without me. And after I clearly understood this—I was at peace." She exits. He prays.

The princess bursts in, shoots him. Everyone comes running. He says he accidently did it himself, writes a petition to the tsar. Enter Vasily Nikanorovich with Dukhobors.[45] He dies, happy that the delusion of the Church has begun to show, and for him his life is now meaningful.

The Living Corpse

A Drama in Six Acts (Twelve Vignettes) 1900

Fyodor Vasilyevich Protasov
    (Fedya, Fyodor Vasilych)
Elizaveta Andreyevna Protasova
    (Liza) [Lizaveta, Liza
    Rakhmanova, Lizanka]
    his wife
Misha [Mishechka, Mika]
    their young son
Anna Pavlovna
    Liza's mother
Sasha
    Liza's sister
Viktor Mikhailovich Karenin
    [Victòr]
Anna Dmitrievna Karenina
    his mother
Marya Vasilyevna Kryukova
    [Masha]
    Liza's friend
Prince Sergey Dmitrievich
    Abrezkov
Masha [Mashka, Mashenka]
    a Gypsy girl
Ivan Makarovich
    an old Gypsy, Masha's father
Nastasya Ivanovna
    *an old Gypsy woman, Masha's
    mother*
Mikhail Andreyevich Afremov
Stakhovich
Butkevich
Korotkov
    Fedya's friends
Ivan Petrovich Aleksandrov
Petushkov
    an artist

Artemyev
Voznesensky
    Karenin's secretary
Pretrial investigator[1]
Clerk of the pretrial investigator
Melnikov
Petrushin
    a lawyer
Young lawyer
Doctor
Officer at the Gypsies'
Musician
Katya
Gasha
    Gypsy girls
Gypsy girl
First Gypsy
Second Gypsy
Lady in court
Officer in court
Court Official
Nannie of the Protasovs
    [Trifonovna]
Dunyasha
    the Protasov's maid
Footman of the Protasovs
Footman of the Karenins
Woman in tavern
Waiter in tavern
Policeman
Attendant
Owner of tavern
Gentleman in court
Judges, spectators, witnesses
Gypsy band of men and women

ACT I

VIGNETTE 1

SCENE 1

ANNA PAVLOVNA, *a stout, corseted, gray-haired lady, is sitting alone at a table set for tea.*

SCENE 2

ANNA PAVLOVNA *and* NANNIE *carrying a teapot.*

NANNIE. Can I get a little water from you?

ANNA PAVLOVNA. Yes. How's Mishechka?

NANNIE. Oh, restless. It's really bad when the mistress nurses 'im. She's got 'er troubles an' the poor kid suffers. How good can 'er milk be when she don't sleep nights an' cries.

ANNA PAVLOVNA. But it seems she's calmed down now.

NANNIE. Some calm! It makes me sick t'look at 'er. She was writin' somethin' and cryin'.

SCENE 3

THE SAME, *and* SASHA (*enters*).

SASHA (*to* NANNIE). Liza's looking for you in the nursery.

NANNIE. I'm on my way. (*Exits.*)

SCENE 4

ANNA PAVLOVNA *and* SHASHA.

ANNA PAVLOVNA. Nannie says she cries all the time. How come she can't calm down?

SASHA. You're really amazing, Mamá. She's left her husband, the father of her child, and you want her to be calm.

ANNA PAVLOVNA. Well, not calm—but what's done is done. If I, her own mother, not only allowed my daughter to leave her husband, but am glad of it, then he deserves it. You shouldn't be sad, but glad that you can be free of such a bad person—free of such a gem.

SASHA. Mamá, why do you talk like that? You know very well that's not true. He's not bad; on the contrary, he's a wonderful, wonderful person, despite his faults.

ANNA PAVLOVNA. Yes, really a wonderful person—as soon as he gets his hands on some money, his own or somebody else's...

SASHA. Mamá, he's never taken anyone else's money.

ANNA PAVLOVNA. His wife's, it's just as bad.

SASHA. But after all he gave his entire estate to his wife.

ANNA PAVLOVNA. Of course he did, since he himself knew he'd squander it all.

SASHA. Squander it or not, I only know that you shouldn't separate from a husband, especially from one like Fedya.

ANNA PAVLOVNA. So you think you should wait till he squanders everything and brings his Gypsy mistresses home with him?

SASHA. He doesn't have any mistresses.

ANNA PAVLOVNA. That's the trouble, he's charmed all of you somehow. But not me, no way; I can see through him, and he knows it. If I were in Liza's place, I wouldn't have left him now but a year ago.

SASHA. You make it sound easy.

ANNA PAVLOVNA. No, it's not easy. For me, as a mother, it's not easy to see my daughter divorced. Believe me, it's not at all easy. Still it's better than ruining her life. No, I thank God that she's decided to do it and it's over with now.

SASHA. Maybe it's not over with.

ANNA PAVLOVNA. If only he'd give her a divorce.

SASHA. What good will that be?

ANNA PAVLOVNA. She's young, and she can still be happy, that's what.

SASHA. Oh Mamá, that's terrible what you're saying; Liza couldn't love anyone else.

ANNA PAVLOVNA. Why not, if she were free? There are men a thousand times better than your Fedya who'll be happy to marry Liza.

SASHA. Mamá, that's bad. I know you're thinking of Victòr Karenin.

ANNA PAVLOVNA. And why shouldn't I think of him? He's been in love with her for ten years, and she loves him.

SASHA. Yes she does, but not the way she loves her husband. They've been friends since childhood.

ANNA PAVLOVNA. We know all about that kind of friendship. If only there were no obstacles.

SCENE 5

THE SAME. *Enter* MAID.

ANNA PAVLOVNA. What is it?

MAID. The mistress sent the yardman to Viktor Mikhailovich with a note.

ANNA PAVLOVNA. What mistress?

MAID. Our mistress, Lizaveta Andreyevna.

ANNA PAVLOVNA. Well, what of it?

MAID. Viktor Mikhailovich told me to say that he'll come right over.

ANNA PAVLOVNA (*surprised*). We were just speaking about him. Only I can't understand why. (*To* SASHA.) Do you know?

SASHA. Maybe I do, and maybe I don't.

ANNA PAVLOVNA. You and your secrets.

SASHA. When Liza comes, she'll tell you.

ANNA PAVLOVNA (*nodding her head, to the* MAID). The samovar needs to be heated up. Take it, Dunyasha.

(*The* MAID *takes the samovar and exits.*)

SCENE 6

ANNA PAVLOVNA *and* SASHA.

ANNA PAVLOVNA (*to* SASHA, *who has risen and wants to leave*). So it has turned out just as I said. She immediately sent for him.

SASHA. Maybe she sent for him for an entirely different reason.

ANNA PAVLOVNA. For what reason, then?

SASHA. Now, at this moment, Karenin is just like Nannie Trifonovna to her.

ANNA PAVLOVNA. You wait and see. I know her. She sent for him looking for consolation.

SASHA. Oh, Mamá, you don't know her very well if you can think that.

ANNA PAVLOVNA. Just wait and see, and I'm very, very glad.

SASHA. We'll see. (*Exits, humming.*)

SCENE 7

ANNA PAVLOVNA *alone.*

ANNA PAVLOVNA (*shaking her head and mumbling*). Good. Let her do it... Good, let her do it... Yes...

SCENE 8

ANNA PAVLOVNA *and the* MAID.

MAID (*enters*). Viktor Mikhailovich has come.

ANNA PAVLOVNA. Well, show him in, and go tell your mistress.

(*The* MAID *exits through an inner door.*)

SCENE 9

ANNA PAVLOVNA *and* VIKTOR KARENIN.

KARENIN (*enters and greets* ANNA PAVLOVNA). Lizaveta Andreyevna sent a note asking me to come. I was going to stop by tonight anyway, so I'm very glad... Is Lizaveta Andreyevna feeling all right?

ANNA PAVLOVNA. She's all right. The baby's a little restless. She'll be here in a minute. (*Sorrowfully.*) Yes, yes it's a difficult time. But you know all that...

KARENIN. I do. You know I was here the other day when she got his letter. But is this matter really irrevocably settled?

ANNA PAVLOVNA. Of course, certainly. It would be terrible to go through it all over again.

KARENIN. Yes, but this is where you have to look before you leap. It's hard to cut the cord.

ANNA PAVLOVNA. Of course it is. But their marriage was strained long ago, so for it to break apart was easier than you think. He himself understands that he can't possibly come back after all that's happened.

KARENIN. Why not?

ANNA PAVLOVNA. How can he after all his nasty stunts, after he swore he'd never do it again, and if he did, he would voluntarily forfeit all his rights as a husband, and grant her complete freedom.

KARENIN. Yes, but what freedom is there for a married woman?

ANNA PAVLOVNA. Divorce. He promised a divorce, and we'll insist on it.

KARENIN. Yes, but Lizaveta Andreyevna loved him so.

ANNA PAVLOVNA. Oh, her love has been put to the *n*th test, so there's hardly anything left of it. His drunkenness, and lies, and infidelities. How can you love such as husband?

KARENIN. Love makes everything possible.

ANNA PAVLOVNA. Love, you say, but how can you love such a person— a rag, someone totally unreliable? Here's what happened now... (*Looks around at the door and hurries to finish what she was saying.*) Their affairs are a mess, everything's mortgaged, they've no money. Finally an uncle sends two thousand to pay the interest. He goes off to pay up and...

disappears. His wife's left with a sick baby, waiting for him, and, finally, there's a note—send him his clothes and things...

KARENIN. Yes, yes, I know.

SCENE 10

THE SAME. *Enter* SASHA *and* LIZA.

ANNA PAVLOVNA. Well, here's Viktor Mikhailovich, you called and he came.

KARENIN. Yes, I was slightly detained. (*Greets the sisters.*)

LIZA. Thank you. I have to ask you to do me a big favor. You're the only person I can turn to.

KARENIN. I'll do all I can.

LIZA. After all, you know all about it.

KARENIN. Yes, I do.

ANNA PAVLOVNA. Then I'll leave you. (*To* SASHA.) Let's go, we'll leave them alone. (*Exits with* SASHA.)

SCENE 11

LIZA *and* KARENIN.

LIZA. Yes, he wrote me a letter saying that as far as he's concerned it's all over. I... (*holding back her tears*) was so offended, so... well, in short, I agreed to break up. And I answered that I accept his rejection.

KARENIN. But then?...

LIZA. Then? Then I felt it was wrong of me, that I can't do this. Anything is better than parting with him. Well, in short, give him this letter. Please, Victòr, give him this letter and tell him... and bring him back.

KARENIN. All right. (*Bewildered.*) Yes, but how can I?

LIZA. Tell him I'm asking him to forget about everything, forget about everything and come back. I could just send him the letter. But I know him: his initial impulse will be good, as always, but then someone will influence him, and he'll change his mind and won't do what he really wants to...

KARENIN. I'll do what I can.

LIZA. Are you surprised that I'm asking you of all people?

KARENIN. No... But to tell you the truth—yes, I am surprised...

LIZA. You're not angry, are you?

KARENIN. How can I be angry with you?

LIZA. I asked you because I know you care for him.

KARENIN. For him and for you. You know that. And I do so not for my sake but for yours. Thank you for believing in me. I'll do what I can.

LIZA. I knew you would. I'll tell you everything: I went to Afremov's today to find out where he is. They told me that the two of them went to the Gypsies. And that's what I am afraid of. I'm afraid of this passion of his. I know he'll get carried away if he's not stopped in time. And that's what has to be done. So will you go?

KARENIN. Of course, immediately.

LIZA. Go, find him and tell him everything is forgotten and I'm waiting for him.

KARENIN (*rising*). But where should I look for him?

LIZA. He's at the Gypsies'. I went there myself. I was by the porch, I wanted to have the letter passed to him, then I changed my mind and decided to ask you... Here's the address. So just tell him to come back, tell him nothing has happened, everything's forgotten. Do this out of concern for him, and friendship for us both.

KARENIN. I'll do all I can. (*Lingers, bows, and exits.*)

SCENE 12

LIZA *alone.*

LIZA. I can't, I can't. Anything's better than... I can't.

SCENE 13

LIZA. *Enter* SASHA.

SASHA. So, did you send him?

(LIZA *nods her head.*)

SASHA. And he agreed?
LIZA. Of course.
SASHA. Why him—I don't understand...
LIZA. Who else?
SASHA. But don't you know he's in love with you?
LIZA. That's all over and done with. So whom do you want me to ask? Do you think he'll come back?
SASHA. I'm sure, because...

SCENE 14

THE SAME *and* ANNA PAVLOVNA. ANNA PAVLOVNA *enters,* SASHA *stops speaking.*

ANNA PAVLOVNA. Where's Viktor Mikhailovich?
LIZA. He's left.
ANNA PAVLOVNA. Why?
LIZA. I asked him to do me a favor.
ANNA PAVLOVNA. What favor? Again secrets?
LIZA. It's no secret, I just asked him to hand a letter to Fedya.
ANNA PAVLOVNA. Fedya? Fyodor Vasilyevich?
LIZA. Yes, Fedya.
ANNA PAVLOVNA. I thought everything was over between you.
LIZA. I can't part with him.
ANNA PAVLOVNA. So it starts all over again?
LIZA. I wanted to. I tried, but I can't. I'll do anything you want, but I can't part with him.

ANNA PAVLOVNA. So what is it, you want him back?

LIZA. Yes.

ANNA PAVLOVNA. Let that snake into the house again?

LIZA. Mamá, please don't speak like that about my husband.

ANNA PAVLOVNA. He was your husband.

LIZA. No, he's still my husband.

ANNA PAVLOVNA. A bum, a drunkard, a womanizer, and you can't part with him?

LIZA. Why are you tormenting me? It's hard enough for me as it is, and it's as if you purposely want to...

ANNA PAVLOVNA. If I'm tormenting you, I'll leave. I just can't look at this anymore.

(LIZA *is silent.*)

ANNA PAVLOVNA. I see that's what you want, I'm in your way. I can't live like this. I just don't understand any of you. This is all the new way. First you decide to break up, then suddenly you call on a man who's in love with you...

LIZA. That's not at all true.

ANNA PAVLOVNA. Karenin proposed to you once... and you send him to get your husband. Why? To make him jealous?

LIZA. Mamá, you're saying terrible things. Leave me alone.

ANNA PAVLOVNA. Right, drive your mother out of the house, and let your wretch of a husband back in. No, I won't wait for that. Good-bye, and may God help you all, do as you please. (*Exits, slamming the door.*)

SCENE 15

LIZA *and* SASHA.

LIZA (*drops into a chair*). Just what I needed.

SASHA. Don't worry. Everything will be all right. We'll work on Mamá.

SCENE 16

THE SAME *and* ANNA PAVLOVNA.

ANNA PAVLOVNA (*crossing the room in silence*). Dunyasha, my trunk!
SASHA. Mamá, listen to me! (*Winks to her sister and exits after her*).

Curtain.

VIGNETTE 2

SCENE 1

A room at the Gypsies'. The band is singing. FEDYA, *with his jacket off, is lying facedown on a sofa.* AFREMOV *sits astride a chair opposite the lead singer. An* OFFICER *stands by a table on which there are bottles of champagne and glasses. At the same table a* MUSICIAN *is writing down the notes.*

AFREMOV. Fedya, you asleep?

FEDYA (*rises*). Don't talk. The steppe, the tenth century, not freedom but free will. And now do "Not the Glow of Evening."[2]

GYPSY LEAD SINGER. We can't, Fyodor Vasilyevich. Let Masha sing a solo now.

FEDYA. Well, okay. And then do "Not the Glow of Evening." (*Lies down again.*)

OFFICER. Sing "Fatal Moment." Agreed?

AFREMOV. Fine.

OFFICER (*to the* MUSICIAN). So, have you got it down?

MUSICIAN. I can't. It's different every time. And the scale somehow isn't the same. Now here. (*Addresses a* GYPSY WOMAN *who is watching.*) How's this? (*Hums.*)

GYPSY WOMAN. That's how it goes. It's marvelous.

FEDYA (*rising*). He won't get it down. And even if he does and shoves it into an opera, he'll screw it all up. All right, Masha, go on, let's have that

"Moment" song. Get your guitar. (*Gets up, sits down in front of her, and looks into her eyes.*)

(MASHA *sings.*)

FEDYA. That's also good. Atta girl, Masha. And now do "Not the Glow of Evening."

AFREMOV. No, wait. First my song, the dirge.

OFFICER. Why a dirge?

AFREMOV. Because when I'm dead... get it, dead and in my coffin, the Gypsies'll come... get it? I'll leave instructions for my wife. And they'll sing "Gypsy Caravan"—and I'll jump right out of my coffin—get it? (*To the* MUSICIAN.) Get this one down. [*To the* GYPSIES.] Well, hit it.

(*The* GYPSIES *sing.*)

AFREMOV. Ah, great. Now do—"Big Brave Hearts."

(*The* GYPSIES *sing.* AFREMOV *dances several steps. The* GYPSIES *smile and continue to sing, clapping their hands.* AFREMOV *sits down. The song ends.*)

GYPSY. Bravo, Mikhail Andeyevich, he's a real Gypsy.

FEDYA. And now do—"Not the Glow of Evening."

SCENE 2

THE SAME, *enter a* GYPSY.

GYPSY (*to* FEDYA). A gentleman is asking for you.

FEDYA. What gentleman?

GYPSY. I don't know. Well dressed, sable coat.

FEDYA. A gent? All right, show him in.

[*Exit* GYPSY.]

SCENE 3

THE SAME *without the* GYPSY.

AFREMOV. Who's looking for you here?

FEDYA. How the hell should I know. Who can want me? (*Rises, staggering.*)

(MASHA *says something to the other* GYPSIES *and exits.*)

SCENE 4

THE SAME *without* MASHA. *Enter* KARENIN. *He looks around.*

FEDYA. Ah, Victòr. I sure didn't expect you. Take off your coat. What brings you here? Come, sit down. Victòr, listen to "Not the Glow of Evening."

(*The* GYPSIES *sing.*)

FEDYA. Now this song... this song. It's wonderful. And where does all that it says ever happen? Ah, it's great. And why is it that a man can reach such ecstasy, but can't prolong it?

MUSICIAN (*writing down the song*). Yes, it's very original.

FEDYA. Not original, it's genuine...

AFREMOV. Hey, Gypsies, take a break. (*Takes a guitar and sits down next to* KATYA.)

MUSICIAN. Actually it's simple, except for the rhythm.

KARENIN. *Je voudrais vous parler sans témoins.*

FEDYA. What about?

KARENIN. *Je viens de chez vous. Votre femme m'a chargé de cette lettre et puis...*

FEDYA (*takes the letter, reads, frowns, then smiles kindly*). Listen, Karenin, you know what's in this letter, right?

KARENIN. Yes. And I want to say...

FEDYA. Wait, wait. Please don't think I'm drunk and my words irresponsible, I mean I'm irresponsible. I am drunk, but I see very clearly through this business. So, what were you told to say?

KARENIN. I was asked to find you and tell you that she's... waiting for you. She asks you to forget everything and come back.

FEDYA (*listens silently while looking at him*). I still don't understand, why you?

KARENIN. Lizaveta Andreyevna sent for me and asked me...

FEDYA. Oh?...

KARENIN. But I ask you not so much on behalf of your wife as on my own behalf—come home with me.

FEDYA. You're a better man than I am. What nonsense! It's not at all hard to be better than me. I'm worthless, and you're really a good man. And that's exactly why I won't change my mind. And not only because of that, but simply because I can't and won't. How can I go back?

KARENIN. Let's go to my place. I'll say that you'll come back, and tomorrow...

FEDYA. What's tomorrow? I'll still be the same, and so will she. No. (*Walks over to the table and takes a drink.*) It's better to pull a tooth with a single yank. You know, I said if I broke my word again, she should leave me. I broke it, and it's all over.

KARENIN. For you, but not for her.

FEDYA. It's amazing that you should care that we stay married.

(KARENIN *wants to say something.* MASHA *enters.*)

SCENE 5

THE SAME, *and* MASHA. *Then the* GYPSIES.

FEDYA (*interrupts him*). You just listen, just listen. Masha, sing.

(*The* GYPSIES *assemble.*)

MASHA (*in a whisper*). We should sing in his honor.[3] What's his name?

FEDYA (*laughs*). Go ahead, it's Viktor Mikhailovich...

(*The* GYPSIES *sing.*)

KARENIN (*listens in embarrassment, then asks*). How much should I give
them?
FEDYA. Well, give them twenty-five.

(KARENIN *gives them the money, [and exits].*)

SCENE 6

THE SAME *without* KARENIN.

FEDYA. Marvelous! Now do "Flax in Bloom." Karenin took off. Well, the
hell with him.

(*The* GYPSIES *disperse.*)

FEDYA (*waves his arm in disgust, goes to* MASHA *and sits down beside her
on the sofa.*) Oh, Masha, Masha, how you just turn me inside out.
MASHA. And how 'bout what I asked you for...
FEDYA. What? The money? (*Takes money out of his pants' pocket.*) All right,
take it.

(MASHA *laughs, takes the money and hides it in her bosom.*)

FEDYA (*to the* GYPSIES). Go ahead, figure it out. She opens heaven for me,
and all she asks for is money for some cheap perfume. [*To* MASHA.] You
don't understand what the hell you're doing.
MASHA. What do you mean I don't. I understand that for the one I love I
try hard and sing the best I can.
FEDYA. And do you love me?
MASHA. Sure I do.
FEDYA. Wonderful. (*Kisses her.*)

(*The* GYPSY MEN AND WOMEN *exit. Some couples remain:* FEDYA *with* MASHA, AFREMOV *with* KATYA, *the* OFFICER *with* GASHA. *The* MUSICIAN *writes, and a* GYPSY *strums a waltz on the guitar.*)

FEDYA. You know I'm married, and your troupe won't let you stay with me. Are you all right?

MASHA. Sure, when the guests are nice. We have our fun too.

FEDYA. Do you know who that man was?

MASHA. I've heard his name.

FEDYA. He's a wonderful person. He came to take me back home to my wife. She loves me, fool that I am, and look what I'm doing.

MASHA. Well, it's not right. You should go back to her. You should feel sorry for her.

FEDYA. You think I should? But I think I shouldn't.

MASHA. Sure, if you don't love her you shouldn't. Love is all that matters.

FEDYA. And how do you know?

MASHA. I just know.

FEDYA. Then kiss me. Gypsies! One more time "Flax in Bloom," and then quit.

(*The* GYPSIES *begin to sing.*)

FEDYA. Ah, great. If only I could go on this way, never to wake up, and die.

[*Curtain.*]

ACT II

VIGNETTE 1

Two weeks have passed since Act I. LIZA*'s home.* KARENIN *and* ANNA PAVLOVNA *are sitting in the dining room. Enter* SASHA.

SCENE 1

KARENIN. So, how is he?

SASHA. The doctor says he's out of danger now. He just mustn't catch a cold.

ANNA PAVLOVNA. Well, thank God. But Liza's completely exhausted.

SASHA. He says it's either something like croup or a mild case of it... What's that? (*Pointing to a basket.*)

ANNA PAVLOVNA. That's the grapes Victòr brought.

KARENIN. Do you want some?

SASHA. Yes, she likes them. She's become very nervous.

KARENIN. No wonder, she hasn't slept or eaten for two days.

SASHA (*smiling*). Neither have you.

KARENIN. I'm another matter.

SCENE 2

THE SAME. *Enter the* DOCTOR *and* LIZA.

DOCTOR (*with authority*). So that's it. Change it every half hour if he's not asleep. If he is, don't disturb him. You don't have to swab his throat. And keep the temperature in the room as it is...

LIZA. And what if he begins to wheeze again?

DOCTOR. It's not likely. But if he should, use the spray. And also give him the powders—one in the morning, and the other at night. I'll give you a prescription now.

ANNA PAVLOVNA. Would you like some tea, Doctor?

DOCTOR. No, thank you. I have patients waiting. (*Sits down at the table.*)

(SASHA *brings him paper and ink.*)

LIZA. So you're sure it's not the croup.
DOCTOR (*smiling*). Absolutely. (*Writes.*)

(ANNA PAVLOVNA *stands over the* DOCTOR.)

KARENIN [*to* LIZA]. Well now have some tea, or better yet, go take a nap—
you should see what you look like.
LIZA. I'm fine now. Thank you. There's a true friend. (*Squeezes his hand.*)

(*Angrily* SASHA *walks over to the* DOCTOR.)

LIZA. I'm so thankful, dear friend. It's at times like these that you appreciate help.
KARENIN. What have I done? There's nothing to thank me for.
LIZA. And who didn't sleep nights, who brought this specialist? It's all your doing...
KARENIN. I'm already rewarded by Mika's being out of danger, and above all by your kindness. (*Squeezes her hand again and laughs, revealing the money that she has in her hand.*)
LIZA (*smiling*). That's for the doctor. I just never know how to give it.
KARENIN. Well I can't either.
ANNA PAVLOVNA (*walking up*). You can't what?
LIZA. Give money to the doctor. He's saved something dearer to me than life, and I just give him money. Something's not right here.
ANNA PAVLOVNA. Give it to me. I know how. It's very simple...
DOCTOR (*rises and hands over the prescription*). Now these powders are to be carefully dissolved in a table spoon of boiled water and... (*continues his directions*).

(KARENIN *sits at the table drinking tea.* ANNA PAVLOVNA *and* SASHA *come forward.*)

SASHA. I can't look at how they treat each other. It's as if she's in love with him.

ANNA PAVLOVNA. And what's so surprising?

SASHA. It's disgusting...

(*The* DOCTOR *takes leave of everyone and exits.* ANNA PAVLOVNA *accompanies him.*)

SCENE 3

LIZA, KARENIN, *and* SASHA.

LIZA (*to* KARENIN). He's so sweet now. As soon as he felt better he was all smiles and bubbly. I have to go to him, but I don't like leaving you.

KARENIN. First have some tea, and eat something.

LIZA. I don't need anything now. I feel so good after all that worry. (*Sobs.*)

KARENIN. Just look at how run down you are.

LIZA. I'm happy. Do you want to take a look at him?

KARENIN. Of course I do.

LIZA. Come with me. (*They exit.*)

SCENE 4

SASHA *and* ANNA PAVLOVNA.

ANNA PAVLOVNA (*returns*). I gave him the money nice and easy, and he took it. Why are you pouting?

SASHA. It's sickening. She took him with her to the nursery. It's as though he were her fiancé or husband.

ANNA PAVLOVNA. What's it to you? Why are you all steamed up? Maybe you intend to marry him yourself?

SASHA. Me, marry that beanpole? I'd sooner marry anyone, but not him. The thought never entered my mind. I just find it disgusting that, after Fedya, Liza could become so intimate with another man.

ANNA PAVLOVNA. He's not just another man—he's been a friend since childhood.

SASHA. I can see by the way they smile and look at one another that they're in love.

ANNA PAVLOVNA. What's so surprising about that? The man took an interest in the child's illness, sympathized and helped, and she's grateful. And besides, why shouldn't she fall in love with Victòr and marry him?

SASHA. That would be horrible; it's sickening, sickening.

SCENE 5

KARENIN *and* LIZA *enter.*

(KARENIN *silently takes his leave.* SASHA *exits angrily.*)

SCENE 6

ANNA PAVLOVNA *and* LIZA.

LIZA (*to her mother*). What's with her.

ANNA PAVLOVNA. I really don't know.

(LIZA *quietly sighs.*)

Curtain.

VIGNETTE 2

AFREMOV*'s study. Glasses of wine are on the table.* GUESTS.

SCENE 1

AFREMOV, FEDYA, STAKHOVICH, *a man with a shaggy head of hair,* BUTKEVICH, *a clean-shaven man, and* KOROTKOV, *a hanger-on.*

KOROTKOV. I'm telling you he'll be left behind: La Belle-Bois is the best horse in Europe. I'll bet you.

STAKHOVICH. Cut the crap. You know nobody believes you, and nobody will take your bet.

KOROTKOV. I'm telling you your Cartouche will be left behind.

AFREMOV. Stop arguing. I'll settle this for you. Ask Fedya. He'll set you straight.

FEDYA. Both horses are good. It all depends on the jockey.

STAKHOVICH. Gusev's a rogue. You got to keep him under your thumb.

KOROTKOV (*shouts*). No!

FEDYA. Now wait. I'll settle this for you. So who took the Derby?

KOROTKOV. He did, but that was a piece of cake. It was a fluke. If Crown Prince hadn't been scratched—he wouldn't have.

(*Enter* FOOTMAN.)

SCENE 2

THE SAME, *and* FOOTMAN.

AFREMOV. What is it?

FOOTMAN. A lady is here, asking for Fyodor Vasilyevich.

AFREMOV. Who is she? A real lady?

FOOTMAN. I don't know who, but a real lady.

AFREMOV. Fedya, a lady's asking for you!

FEDYA (*uneasy*). Who is it?

AFREMOV. He doesn't know. (*To the* FOOTMAN.) Show her into the hall.

FEDYA. Wait, I'll go and have a look. (*Exits.*)

THE SAME *without* FEDYA *and the* FOOTMAN.

KOROTKOV. Who came to him? Must be Mashka.

STAKHOVICH. What Mashka?

KOROTKOV. The Gypsy girl, Masha. She's after him like a cat on the prowl.

STAKHOVICH. She's nice. And sings, too.

AFREMOV. She's beautiful! Tanyusha and she. They sang with Pyotr yesterday.

STAKHOVICH. That's one lucky guy...

AFREMOV. Because the women fall for him? He can have them.

KOROTKOV. I can't stand Gypsy women. They've got no class.

BUTKEVICH. You can say that again.

KOROTKOV. I'd let you have them all for one French woman.

AFREMOV. Well, we all know what fine taste you have. I'll go and see who's come. (*Exits.*)

SCENE 4

THE SAME *without* AFREMOV.

STAKHOVICH. If it's Masha, bring her here. Let her sing for us. No, Gypsies aren't what they used to be. Now there was Tanyusha!... Ah, one hell of a girl.

BUTKEVICH. Well, I think they're just the same.

STAKHOVICH. How can they be the same when they sing conventional ballads instead of Gypsy songs?

BUTKEVICH. There are some good ballads.

KOROTKOV. I'll have them sing: you want to bet that you won't know whether it's a song or a ballad?

STAKHOVICH. Korotkov's always betting.

THE SAME, *and* AFREMOV.

AFREMOV (*enters*). It's not Masha, gentlemen. And there's no place to receive her except here. Let's go to the billiard room.

KOROTKOV [*to* STAKHOVICH]. Let's bet: so, did you chicken out?

STAKHOVICH. All right, all right.

KOROTKOV. And now you're going to lose a bottle.

STAKHOVICH. That's okay. Just grab the wine.

(*They exit, talking.*)

SCENE 6

Enter FEDYA *and* SASHA.

FEDYA. Come in here. Ah, ah, why are you... Yes, yes.

SASHA (*embarrassed*). Fedya, forgive me if this bothers you, but for God's sake listen to me. (*Her voice falters.*)

FEDYA (*paces around the room.* SASHA *sits down and looks at him*). I'm listening.

SASHA. Fedya, come home.

FEDYA. I do understand you, Sasha dear, and if I were you I'd do the same thing: somehow I'd try to get things back to where they were before. But if you were me, if you—strange as it may sound—my dear, sensitive girl, were in my place, you would've certainly done what I did, that is, you would've left, and stopped messing up someone else's life.

SASHA. What do you mean messing up? How can Liza live without you?

FEDYA. Oh, Sasha dear, sweetheart, she can, yes she can. And she'll be happy, too, much happier than with me.

SASHA. Never.

FEDYA. That's what you think. (*Folds the letter he is holding in his hand.*) But that's not the point, that is, not that it's not the point, but the main thing is, I just can't. You know, take a thick piece of paper and fold it back and forth. Do it a hundred times, and it still remains intact; but then do it for the hundred and first time, and it comes apart. That's how it was with Liza and me. It hurts me too much to look her in the eyes. And believe me, it's also the same for her.

SASHA. No, no it isn't.

FEDYA. You say it isn't, but you yourself know it is.

SASHA. I can only judge by myself; but if I were in her place and you told me what you just said, it would be awful for me.

FEDYA. Yes, for you it would be.

(Silence. Both are embarrassed.)

SASHA *(rises)*. Must things really remain as they are?

FEDYA. I guess so.

SASHA. Fedya, come back.

FEDYA. Thank you, Sasha dear. You'll always be a lovely memory to me... Well, good-bye, sweetheart. Let me kiss you. *(Kisses her on the forehead.)*

SASHA *(upset)*. No, I'm not saying good-bye and I don't believe, I don't want to believe... Fedya...

FEDYA. Well then, listen to me. Only give me your word you won't tell anyone what I tell you. Will you give me your word?

SASHA. Certainly.

FEDYA. Well then, listen, Sasha. I may be her husband and father of her child, but I'm in her way. Wait, wait, don't argue. You think I'm jealous? Not one bit. First of all, I have no right; secondly, I have no reason. Victòr Karenin is her old friend and mine too. He loves her, and she loves him.

SASHA. No.

FEDYA. She loves him as an honest, moral woman who doesn't allow herself to love anyone except her husband can. But she loves him and will love him when this obstacle *(points to himself)* is removed. And I'll remove it, and they will be happy. *(His voice falters.)*

SASHA. Fedya, don't talk like that.

FEDYA. Now you know that's the truth. And I'll be happy for them, and

it's the best thing I can do. I'm not coming back, I'll give them their freedom, please tell them that. Don't answer, don't; good-bye. (*Kisses her on
the head and opens the door.*)
SASHA. Fedya, I admire you.
FEDYA. Good-bye, good-bye.

(SASHA *exits.*)

SCENE 7

FEDYA *alone.*

FEDYA. Yes, yes, it's fantastic, it's great. (*Rings.*)

SCENE 8

FEDYA *and* FOOTMAN.

FEDYA. Call your master.

(*The* FOOTMAN *exits.*)

SCENE 9

FEDYA *alone.*

FEDYA. And it's true, it's true.

SCENE 10

Enter AFREMOV.

AFREMOV. So how did you work things out?

FEDYA. Fantastic. [*Sings.*] "She swore and did vow..." Fantastic. Where's everyone?

AFREMOV. Over there, playing.

FEDYA. Fine. Let's go... [*Sings.*] "she'd come to me now."

Curtain.

ACT III

VIGNETTE 1

PRINCE ABREZKOV, *a sixty-year-old refined bachelor, with a moustache but no beard, a former military man, very dignified, has a sad expression on his face.* ANNA DMITRIEVNA KARENINA, VICTÒR'*s mother, a fifty-year old* grande dame *who tries to appear younger, and punctuates her speech with French words.* LIZA, VICTÒR, *and* FOOTMAN. ANNA DMITRIEVNA'*s study, a modest, well-appointed room filled with knickknacks.*

SCENE 1

ANNA DMITRIEVNA *is writing a letter.*

SCENE 2

ANNA DMITRIEVNA *and* FOOTMAN.

FOOTMAN. Prince Sergey Dmitrievich.
ANNA DMITRIEVNA. Well, certainly. (*She turns and primps before a mirror.*)

(*The* FOOTMAN *exits.*)

SCENE 3

ANNA DMITRIEVNA *and* PRINCE ABREZKOV.

PRINCE ABREZKOV (*enters*). *J'espère que je ne force pas la consigne.* (*Kisses her hand.*)
ANNA DMITRIEVNA. You know that *vous êtes toujours le bienvenu.* And especially today. Did you get my note?
PRINCE ABREZKOV. I did, and being here is my answer.

ANNA DMITRIEVNA. Ah, my friend, I'm really beginning to lose hope. *Il est ensorcelé, positivement ensorcelé.* I have never seen such determination in him, such persistence, and such harshness and indifference towards me. He's completely changed since that woman left her husband.

PRINCE ABREZKOV. But what's going on, how do things stand?

ANNA DMITRIEVNA. He wants to marry her come what may, that's how.

PRINCE ABREZKOV. But how about her husband?

ANNA DMITRIEVNA. He's giving her a divorce.

PRINCE ABREZKOV. I see!

ANNA DMITRIEVNA. And he, Victòr, is going along with it, with all the dirt—lawyers, evidence of guilt. *Tout ça est dégoutant.* And that doesn't deter him. I don't understand him. He used to be so sensitive, so shy...

PRINCE ABREZKOV. He's in love. Ah, when a man is really in love...

ANNA DMITRIEVNA. Yes, but how come in our day love could be pure, a loving friendship that lasted for life? That's the kind of love I understand and value.

PRINCE ABREZKOV. Nowadays the younger generation is no longer satisfied with an ideal relationship. *La possession de l'âme ne leur suffit plus.* That's how it is. But what's there to do about him?

ANNA DMITRIEVNA. No, don't even talk about him. It's some kind of spell. He's been completely transformed. You know, I paid her a call. He begged me to. I went there, she wasn't in, and I left my card. *Elle m'a fait demander quand je pourrai la recevoir.* And today (*looks at her watch*), after one, which means now, she should be here. I promised Victòr to receive her, but you can understand how I feel. I'm not myself. And by force of habit, I sent for you. I need your help.

PRINCE ABREZKOV. Thank you.

ANNA DMITRIEVNA. Please understand, this meeting will decide the whole matter—Victòr's fate. I have to either disapprove or... But how can I?...

PRINCE ABREZKOV. Do you know her at all?

ANNA DMITRIEVNA. I've never seen her. But I'm afraid of her. A good woman can't just go and leave her husband, and such a good man, too. He's a friend of Victòr's, you know, and used to come here often. He was very nice. Not that it matters. *Quels que soient les torts qu'il a eus vis-à-vis d'elle,* you can't leave your husband. You have to bear your cross. The thing I don't understand is how Victòr, with his convictions, can agree to marrying a divorced woman. How many times—just recently in my presence—has he argued heatedly with Spitsyn that divorce is incompatible with true Christianity, and now he's going along with it himself. *Si elle a pu le charmer à un tel point,* I'm afraid of her. Anyway, I sent for you to hear what you have to say, and I just go on talking instead. What do you think? Tell me. What's your opinion? What should I do? Have you spoken with Victòr?

PRINCE ABREZKOV. Yes, I talked to him. I think he loves her, he's used to loving her, and this love has gained power over him—for he's a man who doesn't make decisions quickly, but sticks to them firmly. What has once entered his heart is there to stay. And he won't love anyone but her, and won't be happy without her, or with anyone else.

ANNA DMITRIEVNA. And Varya Kazantseva would've married him gladly. What a nice girl, and loves him so...

PRINCE ABREZKOV (*smiling*). *C'est compter sans son hôte.* That's completely out of the question now. I think it's best to give in and help him get married.

ANNA DMITRIEVNA. To a divorced woman, and then have him run into his wife's husband? I can't understand how you can speak about this so calmly. Is she the woman whom a mother could wish as a wife for her only son, and such a son?

PRINCE ABREZKOV. It can't be helped, my dear friend. Of course it would be better if he married a girl whom you knew and liked. But since that can't be... And after all, he's not marrying a Gypsy girl, or God knows whom. Liza Rakhmanova is a very fine, nice woman; I know her through my niece Nelly. She's a gentle, kind, affectionate, and moral woman.

ANNA DMITRIEVNA. A moral woman who's decided to leave her husband.

PRINCE ABREZKOV. I don't recognize you. You're being unkind, cruel. Her husband is one of those men of whom they say that he's his own worst enemy. But he's even more of an enemy to his wife. He's a weak man, depraved and a drunk. He's squandered his entire estate, and hers as well—and she has a child. How can you condemn a woman for leaving such a man? Besides, she didn't leave, he left her.

ANNA DMITRIEVNA. Oh, what dirt, what dirt. And I have to soil myself with it.

PRINCE ABREZKOV. And what about your religion?

ANNA DMITRIEVNA. Yes, yes, forgive. "As we forgive our debtors."[4] *Mais c'est plus fort que moi.*

PRINCE ABREZKOV. But how could she live with such a person? Even if she didn't love anyone else she would've had to do this. She had to for her child. The husband himself—an intelligent and kind person when he's in his right mind—urges her to do it.

SCENE 4

ANNA DMITRIEVNA *and* PRINCE ABREZKOV. *Enter* KARENIN, *who kisses his mother's hand and greets* PRINCE ABREZKOV.

KARENIN. Mamá, I just dropped by to tell you one thing: Lizaveta Andreyevna will be here at any moment, and I ask just one thing, I implore you, if you still disapprove of my marriage...

ANNA DMITRIEVNA (*interrupting him*). Of course I still disapprove.

KARENIN (*continues, frowning*). ...I ask one thing, I implore you, don't speak about your disapproval, don't resolve matters negatively.

ANNA DMITRIEVNA. I don't think we'll talk about anything like that. At least I won't initiate it.

KARENIN. Neither will she. I only want you to get to know her.

ANNA DMITRIEVNA. The one thing I can't understand is how you reconcile your desire to marry Mrs. Protasova, whose husband is still living, with your religious conviction that divorce is contrary to Christianity?

KARENIN. Mamá, that is cruel of you. Are we all really so infallible that we can't deviate from our convictions in this complex life? Mamá, why are you so cruel to me?

ANNA DMITRIEVNA. I love you, and I want you to be happy.

KARENIN (*to* PRINCE ABREZKOV). Sergey Dmitrievich, please!

PRINCE ABREZKOV. Of course you want him to be happy, but it's hard for us older folks to understand young people. And it's especially hard for a mother who has her own fixed ideas about her son's happiness. All women are like that.

ANNA DMITRIEVNA. So that's it. you're all against me. Of course you can do this, *vous êtes majeur,* but you'll be the death of me.

KARENIN. I don't recognize you. This is worse than cruelty.

PRINCE ABREZKOV (*to* VICTÒR). Stop it, Victòr. Mamá's words are always worse that her actions.

ANNA DMITRIEVNA. I'll tell her what I think and feel, but I'll do it without offending her.

PRINCE ABREZKOV. I'm sure of that.

SCENE 5

ANNA DMITRIEVNA, PRINCE ABREZKOV, *and* KARENIN. *Enter* FOOTMAN.

PRINCE ABREZKOV. Here she is.

KARENIN. I'm leaving.

FOOTMAN. Lizaveta Andreyevna Protasova.

KARENIN. I'm leaving, Mamá. Please...

(PRINCE ABREZKOV *also rises.*)

ANNA DMITRIEVNA. Ask her in. (*to* PRINCE ABREZKOV) No, you stay.

SCENE 6

ANNA DMITRIEVNA *and* PRINCE ABREZKOV.

PRINCE ABREZKOV. I thought *tête-à-tête* would be easier for you.

ANNA DMITRIEVNA. No, I'm afraid. (*Anxious.*) If I want to be left *tête-à-tête,* I'll nod. *Ça dépendra...* Being alone with her might make me uncomfortable. If not, I'll do like this for you to leave. [*Nods.*]

PRINCE ABREZKOV. I'll understand. I'm certain you'll like her. Just be fair.

ANNA DMITRIEVNA. Oh how you're all against me!

SCENE 7

THE SAME. *Enter* LIZA *wearing a hat and a dress for a formal visit.*

ANNA DMITRIEVNA (*half rising*). I was sorry not to find you in, but it's very kind of you to come here yourself.

LIZA. I never expected you. I'm so grateful that you wanted to see me.

ANNA DMITRIEVNA. Are you acquainted? (*Indicating* PRINCE ABREZ-KOV.)

PRINCE ABREZKOV. Why yes, I've had the honor of being introduced. (*They shake hands and sit down.*) My niece Nelly often speaks about you.

LIZA. Yes, we were very good friends. (*Looking back at* ANNA DMITRIEVNA *timidly.*) And we are still friends. I never expected that you would want to see me.

ANNA DMITRIEVNA. I knew your husband well. He and Victòr were friends, and he used to come often to our house before he moved to Tambov. Wasn't it there that he married you?

LIZA. Yes, we got married there.

ANNA DMITRIEVNA. But after he returned to Moscow later, he stopped coming.

LIZA. Yes, he hardly went anywhere.

ANNA DMITRIEVNA. And he didn't introduce us. (*An awkward silence.*)

PRINCE ABREZKOV. The last time I met you was at play night at the Denisovs. Do you remember? It was very nice. You were in the play.

LIZA. No... yes... of course... I remember. Yes I was. (*Silence again.*) Anna Dmitrievna, forgive me if what I'm going to say displeases you, but I can't, I'm unable to pretend. I came because Viktor Mikhailovich said... because he, that is because you wanted to see me... But it's best to get it all out... (*Sobs.*) It's very hard for me... and you're so kind.

PRINCE ABREZKOV. Well, I better leave.

ANNA DMITRIEVNA. Yes, do.

PRINCE ABREZKOV. Good-bye. (*Takes leave of both women, and exits.*)

SCENE 8

ANNA DMITRIEVNA *and* LIZA.

ANNA DMITRIEVNA. Listen, Liza, I don't know your full name, and I don't want to know it.

LIZA. It's Elizaveta Andreyevna.

ANNA DMITRIEVNA. Well, no matter—Liza will do. I feel sorry for you, and I like you. But I love Victòr. He's the only one I love in the world. I know his heart as I do my own. It's a proud heart. Even as a boy of seven he was proud. Proud not of his name nor wealth, but proud of his high morals, of his innocence, and he has guarded it. He's as innocent as a virgin.

LIZA. I know.

ANNA DMITRIEVNA. He has never loved a woman. You're the first. I can't say I'm not jealous of you. I am. But we mothers—your son is still a baby so it's too early for you—prepare for it. I was prepared to relinquish him to his wife and not be jealous; but to a wife as innocent as he.

LIZA. I... Don't you think I...

ANNA DMITRIEVNA. Forgive me, I know it's not your fault, but you are unhappy. And I know him. Now he's prepared to take on anything, and he will without ever saying a word, but he'll suffer. His wounded pride will suffer, and he won't be happy.

LIZA. I've thought about that.

ANNA DMITRIEVNA. Liza, dear. You're an intelligent, a fine woman. If you love him you want his happiness more than your own. And if that's so, you won't want to tie him down and make him regret it—though he will never ever say a word.

LIZA. I know he won't. I've thought about that and asked myself that question. I have, and I've talked to him. But what can I do when he says he doesn't want to live without me? I told him: "Let's be friends, but make a life for yourself; don't tie your innocent life to my unhappy one." He doesn't want to hear that.

ANNA DMITRIEVNA. No, now he doesn't.

LIZA. Please, convince him to leave me. I fully agree to that. My love for him longs only for his happiness, not for mine. Just help me, don't hate me. United in our love for him, let's seek his well-being.

ANNA DMITRIEVNA. Yes, yes, I'm beginning to like you. (*Kisses her.* LIZA *cries.*) But still, still, it's awful. If only he had fallen in love with you before you got married.

LIZA. He says he had even then, but didn't want to spoil a friend's happiness.

ANNA DMITRIEVNA. Ah, how hard all this is. But still let's become good friends, and God will help us find what we want.

SCENE 9

THE SAME, *and* KARENIN.

KARENIN (*entering*). Mamá, dear. I heard everything. It's just as I expected: you like her. Now everything is going to be fine.

LIZA. I'm really sorry you heard. I wouldn't have said...

ANNA DMITRIEVNA. Nothing is settled yet. I can only say that if not for these trying circumstances, I would be very happy. (*Kisses her.*)

KARENIN. Just don't change your mind, please.

Curtain.

VIGNETTE 2

A plain apartment: a bed, desk, and sofa.

SCENE 1

FEDYA *is alone. There is a knock on the door, and a woman's voice from outside says: "Why have you locked yourself in, Fyodor Vasilych? Fedya, open up."*

SCENE 2

FEDYA *and* MASHA.

FEDYA (*gets up and opens the door.* MASHA *enters*). Boy, I'm glad you came. I'm down, really down.

MASHA. So why didn't you come to us? Drinkin' again? Eh, and you promised...

FEDYA. You know I don't have any money.

MASHA. Why did I ever fall in love with you?

FEDYA. Masha!

MASHA. What "Masha, Masha." If you loved me, you'd've divorced her long ago. And they asked you to, too. And you say you don't love 'er. But you hold on to her. Means, you don't wanna.

FEDYA. But you know why I don't want to.

MASHA. That's all nonsense. What they say is right—you're a good-for-nothin'.

FEDYA. What can I tell you? Tell you what you say hurts me? You know that yourself.

MASHA. Nothin' hurts you...

FEDYA. You know very well your love is my only joy in life.

MASHA. My love yes! But what about yours?

FEDYA. Well, I'm not going to try to convince you. There's no need to—you know it yourself.

MASHA. Fedya, what are you tormentin' me for?

FEDYA. Who's tormenting whom?

MASHA (*crying*). You're no good.

FEDYA (*goes up to her and hugs her*). Masha! What are you doing? Stop. You have to live and not spend your time crying. That's not like you. You're the most beautiful woman I know.

MASHA. But do you love me?

FEDYA. Who else is there for me?

MASHA. Only me? Well read me what you've written.

FEDYA. It'll just bore you.

MASHA. If you wrote it, I'll listen.

FEDYA. All right listen. (*Reads.*) "Late in the fall my friend and I agreed to meet at Murygin Field. This field was a firm strip of land with a healthy number of hatchlings. It was a gloomy, warm, calm day. The mist..."

SCENE 3

FEDYA *and* MASHA. *Enter an old Gypsy man,* IVAN MAKAROVICH, *and an old Gypsy woman,* NASTASYA IVANOVNA—*Masha's parents.*

NASTASYA IVANOVNA (*walking up to her daughter*). Here she is, that damn stray sheep. My respects to you, sir. (*To her daughter.*) Just what do you think you're doin', eh?

IVAN MAKAROVICH (*to* FEDYA). It's not right, sir. You're ruinin' the girl. No, not right. You're doin' 'er dirt.

NASTASYA IVANOVNA. Put on your kerchief and get a move on, right now. Look at her, ran away. What'll I tell the band? Messin' aroun' with a deadbeat. What can you get from him?

MASHA. I'm not messin' around. I love the man, and that's all. And I'm not leavin' the band. I'll sing, and as to...

IVAN MAKAROVICH. Say another word and I'll pull all your hair out. Tramp! Who're you takin' after? Not your father, or your mother, or your aunt. It's nasty, sir. We liked you; how many times did we sing for you for nothin'—we felt sorry for you. And look what you've done.

NASTASYA IVANOVNA. You've ruined our daughter for nothin', our flesh an' blood, our only beloved, precious, dear daughter—you've dragged her into the mud, that's what you've done. You've got no conscience.

FEDYA. You do me an injustice, Nastasya Ivanovna. Your daughter is like a sister to me. I guard her honor. And don't think otherwise. I love her. I can't help it.

IVAN MAKAROVICH. But you didn't love 'er when you had money. If you would've then paid the band ten thousand roubles, you could've had her fair and square. And now that you've squandered everythin', you've stolen her away. For shame, sir, for shame!

MASHA. He didn't steal me; I came to him myself. And if you take me away now, I'll come back. I love him and that's that. My love is stronger than all your locks... I won't leave.

NASTASYA IVANOVNA. Now Mashenka, darlin', don't get all worked up. You didn't do right, so let's go.

IVAN MAKAROVICH. Enough of this talk. Get a move on (*takes her by the hand*). Forgive us, sir. (*All three exit*).

SCENE 4

FEDYA. *Enter* PRINCE ABREZKOV.

PRINCE ABREZKOV. Excuse me. I was an involuntary eavesdropper on an unpleasant scene.

FEDYA. Whom do I have the honor of...? (*Recognizes him.*) Oh, Prince Sergey Dmitrievich. (*They shake hands.*)

PRINCE ABREZKOV. I was an involuntary eavesdropper on an unpleasant scene. I wish I hadn't been. But as I have, I considered it my duty to tell you so. I was told I would find you here and had to wait by the door for your guests to leave. All the more so since my knocking on the door went unheard over the raised voices inside.

FEDYA. Yes, yes. Please come in. Thank you for telling me this. It gives me the opportunity to explain what took place. I don't care what you may think of me, but I'd like you to know that the reproaches you overhead, which were directed at the Gypsy girl, the singer, were undeserved. This girl is morally as pure as a dove. And my relationship to her is that of a friend. Even though there might be a poetic touch to it, this in no way impairs the purity and honor of this girl. That's what I wanted to tell you. Now, what can I do for you? How can I be of service?

PRINCE ABREZKOV. First of all, I...

FEDYA. Excuse me, Prince. My present social standing is such that my superficial acquaintance with you of long past does not warrant a visit from you unless it's on business—what is it?

PRINCE ABREZKOV. I won't deny it, you guessed right. I've come on business. But still let me assure you that your change of circumstances does not in any way affect my attitude toward you.

FEDYA. I'm sure it doesn't.

PRINCE ABREZKOV. The fact of the matter is that the son of my old friend, Anna Dmitrievna Karenina, and she herself, have asked me to find out directly from you what your relationship... May I speak about your relationship with your wife, Lizaveta Andreyevna Protasova?

FEDYA. My relationship with my wife, I should say my former wife, is completely over.

PRINCE ABREZKOV. That's how I understood it, and that's the only reason I undertook this delicate mission.

FEDYA. It's over and, let me say immediately, through no fault of hers but mine, or rather my innumerable faults. As for her, she is, as she always has been, an entirely irreproachable woman.

PRINCE ABREZKOV. So Victòr Karenin, and especially his mother, asked me to find out what your intentions are.

FEDYA (angrily). What intentions? I don't have any. I leave her perfectly free. Moreover, I'll never disturb her peace of mind. I know she loves Victòr Karenin. Fine, let her. I consider him very dull, but a very nice, upright man, and I think she'll be, as the saying goes, very happy with him. And *que le bon dieu les bénisse.* That's all.

PRINCE ABREZKOV. Yes, but we'd...

FEDYA (interrupting). And don't think that I'm in the least bit jealous. If I said Victòr is dull, I take that back. He's a fine, upright, moral man, almost my exact opposite. And he's loved her since childhood. Maybe she also loved him when she married me. These things happen. The truest love may be the one you're not conscious of. I think she's always loved him. But as an honorable woman she didn't admit it even to herself, though it cast kind of a shadow over our family life... but why am I opening up to you?

PRINCE ABREZKOV. Please go on. Believe me, more important to me than my mission is my feeling of friendship for you, and my wish to understand this relationship fully. I understand you, I understand that this shadow, as you so aptly put it, could've...

FEDYA. Yes, it did, and maybe that's why I couldn't be happy with the family life she gave me, and went looking for something else, and kept getting carried away. However, it's as though I'm justifying myself. I don't want to, and I can't justify myself. I *was,* I can outrightly say *was,* a bad husband; I *was* because I've long since stopped thinking of myself as her husband, and consider her completely free. So, there you have my answer to your mission.

PRINCE ABREZKOV. Yes, but you know Victòr's family and him too. His relationship to Lizaveta Andreyevna has always been, and still is, one of utmost respect and propriety. He helped her when she had problems.

FEDYA. Yes, I helped bring them together by my depravity. What can you do, that's what was meant to be.

PRINCE ABREZKOV. You know his and his family's strict Christian convictions. I don't share them, since I take a broader view of things. However, I respect and understand them. I understand that for him, and especially for his mother, intimacy with a woman is unthinkable without a church wedding.

FEDYA. Yes, I know his stu... his rectitude and conservatism in this respect. So what do they want of me? A divorce? I told them long ago that I was ready to grant it, but my having to acknowledge adultery and perjure myself in doing so is very hard.[5]

PRINCE ABREZKOV. I understand, and completely share your feelings. But what can you do? I think that's the only way. Of course, you're right. This is terrible, and I understand you.

FEDYA (*shakes the* PRINCE'*s hand*). Thank you, my dear Prince. I always thought of you as a kind, honest man. But tell me, how should I act? What should I do? Put yourself in my place. I'm not trying to make myself look good. I'm worthless; but there are things I cannot do casually. I cannot lie casually.

PRINCE ABREZKOV. Now, there's also something I don't understand about you. You, a capable, intelligent man with such sensitivity for what's good, how can you let yourself get so carried away, how can you forget what you demand of yourself? How did you come to this and ruin your life?

FEDYA (*moved, holds back his tears*). I've been leading a dissipated life now for ten years, and this is the first time that a man like you has felt sorry for me. Friends have felt sorry for me, and so have carousers and women, but a sensible, kind man like you... Thank you. How did I come to ruin? First of all, liquor. It's not that I like the taste of liquor, you know. But whatever I do, I always feel I'm doing the wrong thing, and I feel ashamed. I'm speaking with you now, and I'm ashamed. And the thought of being an official, of having a position in a bank—is so shameful, so shameful... It's only when I drink that I stop being ashamed. And music, not operas or Beethoven, but the Gypsies... That's the life; you're energized·and vibrant. And then those enchanting dark eyes, and the smile. And the more alluring it is, the more ashamed you feel afterwards.

PRINCE ABREZKOV. And what about work?

FEDYA. I've tried it. It's no good. I don't like anything. But why talk about myself. Thank you.

PRINCE ABREZKOV. Then what should I tell them?

FEDYA. Tell them I'll do what they want. Obviously they want to get married, and don't want anything to stand in their way.

PRINCE ABREZKOV. Of course.

FEDYA. I'll do it. Tell them, I'll certainly do it.

PRINCE ABREZKOV. But when?

FEDYA. Wait a minute. Well, let's say in two weeks. Will that do?

PRINCE ABREZKOV (*rising*). Then can I tell them this?

FEDYA. You can. Good-bye, Prince. Once again, thank you.

(PRINCE ABREZKOV *exits.*)

SCENE 5

FEDYA, *alone.*

FEDYA (*sits for a long time in silence, smiling to himself*). Good. Very good. That's how it should be. That's how it should be. That's how it should be. Great!

Curtain.

ACT IV

VIGNETTE 1

A private room in a tavern. A WAITER *shows in* FEDYA *and* IVAN
PETROVICH ALEKSANDROV.

SCENE 1

FEDYA, IVAN PETROVICH, *and* WAITER.

WAITER [*to* FEDYA]. This way, please. No one'll disturb you here, and I'll
bring some paper right away.

IVAN PETROVICH. Protasov, I'm coming in with you.

FEDYA (*preoccupied*). All right, come in, but I'm busy and... Come in, if
you want to.

IVAN PETROVICH. You want to reply to their demands? I'll tell you how. I
wouldn't do it that way. I always come right to the point and act resolutely.

FEDYA (*to the* WAITER). Bring a bottle of champagne.

(WAITER *exits.*)

SCENE 2

FEDYA *and* IVAN PETROVICH

FEDYA (*takes out a revolver and puts it on the table*). Wait a minute.

IVAN PETROVICH. What now, you're going to shoot yourself? You can,
yeah. I understand you. They want to humiliate you, and you'll show
them who you really are. You'll kill yourself with the revolver and them
with high-mindedness. I understand you. I understand it all, genius that
I am.

FEDYA. Yes, yes. Only...

(*Enter* WAITER *with paper, inkwell [and a bottle of champagne].*)

SCENE 3

THE SAME, *and* WAITER.

FEDYA (*covers the gun with a napkin*). Open it. Let's have a drink. (*They drink.* FEDYA *writes.*) Wait a bit.

IVAN PETROVICH. Here's to your... big trip. You know, I'm above all this. I'm not going to try to stop you. Life and death are the same for a genius. I die in life and live in death. You're going to kill yourself so that they, those two people, should feel sorry for you. But I—I'm going to kill myself so that the whole world should understand what it's lost. And I won't hesitate or think twice. I'll just take it (*grabs the revolver*)—bang and finished. But it's not yet time (*puts down the revolver*). And I don't have to write anything, they should understand themselves... Oh, you...

FEDYA (*writing*). Just wait a minute.

IVAN PETROVICH. Pathetic people. You putter and fuss, and don't understand, don't understand a thing... I'm not talking to you—I'm just thinking out loud. And what does mankind need? Very little: simply to appreciate its geniuses. But they are always executed, persecuted and tortured. No. I won't be your plaything. I'll blow the whistle on you. No-o-o! Hypocrites!

FEDYA (*finishes writing, empties his glass, and reads*). Go away, please.

IVAN PETROVICH. Go away? Well then, good-bye. I'm not going to try to stop you. I'll do the same thing. But it's not yet time. I just want to tell you...

FEDYA. All right. You'll tell me afterwards, but now here's what, my friend. Please give this to my landlord (*gives him money*) and ask whether there's a letter and a parcel for me. Please.

IVAN PETROVICH. All right. Then you'll wait for me? I still have something important to tell you—something you won't otherwise hear either in this world or in the next, at least not until I get there. Should I give it all to him?

FEDYA. Whatever's necessary.

(IVAN PETROVICH *exits.*)

SCENE 4

FEDYA *alone.*

FEDYA (*gives a sigh of relief, locks the door behind* IVAN PETROVICH, *takes the revolver, cocks it, puts it up to his temple, shudders, and carefully lowers it. Mumbles*). No, I can't, I can't, I can't.

(*There is a knock at the door.*)

FEDYA. Who's there?

(MASHA's *voice from outside:* "It's me.")

FEDYA. Who's me? Oh, Masha... (*Opens the door.*)

SCENE 5

FEDYA *and* MASHA.

MASHA. I've been to your place, to Popov's, to Afremov's, and finally guessed you must be here. (*Sees the revolver.*) Now that's nice! What a fool! A regular fool! Are you really gonna?

FEDYA. No, I can't.

MASHA. Don't I mean somethin'? You heathen! You didn't feel sorry for me. Oh, Fyodor Vasilyevich, it's a sin, a sin. After all my love...

FEDYA. I wanted to liberate them, I promised. And I can't lie.

MASHA. But what about me?

FEDYA. What about you? I'd set you free as well. Are you better off suffering with me?

MASHA. Certainly I am. I can't live without you.

FEDYA. What kind of life could you have with me? You would've cried a little and gone on with your life.

MASHA. I wouldn't cry at all, the hell with you if you don't feel sorry for me. (*Cries.*)

FEDYA. Masha, dear, I wanted to do what's best.

MASHA. Best for you.

FEDYA (*smiling*). How can it be best for me if I'd kill myself?

MASHA. Sure it can. Just what is it you want? Tell me.

FEDYA. What do I want? I want a lot of things.

MASHA. Well what? What?

FEDYA. First of all, to keep my promise. That's the first thing, and it's enough. I can't lie and do all those nasty things you have to do to get a divorce. I can't.

MASHA. All right, they're nasty. I myself...

FEDYA. Then, I absolutely have to free them, both my wife and him. Why, they're good people. Why should they suffer? That's the second thing.

MASHA. Well, there ain't much good about 'er if she dumped you.

FEDYA. She didn't—I dumped her.

MASHA. All right, all right. You did everythin'. She's an angel. So what else?

FEDYA. So there's you, a nice, sweet girl—I love you, and if I go on living, I'll ruin you.

MASHA. That's none of your business. I know all by myself where I'll be ruined...

FEDYA (*sighing*). But the main thing, the main thing... What good is my life? Don't I see that I'm finished and of no use? I'm a burden to everyone and to myself, as your father said. I'm a good-for-nothing...

MASHA. What nonsense! I won't let you go. I'm stuck to you, and that's it. And as to your leadin' a bad life, drinkin' and carousin'... You're a livin' being—cut it out, and that's it.

FEDYA. That's easy to say.

MASHA. Just do it.

FEDYA. Yes, when I look at you, it seems I can do anything.

MASHA. And you will, too. You'll do it all. (*Sees the letter.*) What's that? You wrote them? What did you write?

FEDYA. What did I write? (*Takes the letter and is about to tear it up.*) There's no need for it now.

MASHA (*grabbing the letter*). You wrote that you killed yourself, right? You didn't write about the gun—just that you killed yourself?

FEDYA. Yes, that I'll be no more.

MASHA. All right, all right, all right. Did you ever read *What Is to Be Done?*[6]

FEDYA. I think so.

MASHA. It's a boring novel, but there's one very, very good thing there. He, that, what's his name, Rakhmanov,[7] goes and pretends that he drowned himself. You can't swim, can you?

FEDYA. No.

MASHA. Good. Gimme your clothes. Everythin', your wallet too.

FEDYA. What for?

MASHA. Wait, wait, wait. Let's go home. You'll change there.

FEDYA. But that's fraud.

MASHA. It's great. You went swimming, your clothes were left on the bank. In a pocket is your wallet and this letter.

FEDYA. And what then?

MASHA. And then, then we'll go away and live happily ever after.

SCENE 6

THE SAME. *Enter* IVAN PETROVICH.

IVAN PETROVICH. Good Lord! And what about the revolver? I'll take it.

MASHA. Take it, take it. And off we go.

Curtain.

VIGNETTE 2

The PROTASOVS' *parlor.*

SCENE 1

KARENIN *and* LIZA.

KARENIN. He promised so emphatically that I'm certain he'll keep his word.

LIZA. I'm ashamed to admit it, but what I found out about that Gypsy girl freed me completely. Don't think it's jealousy. It's not at all jealousy, you know, it's liberation. How shall I put it, Viktor Mikhailovich...

KARENIN. Again Viktor Mikhailovich.

LIZA. Vitya.[8] Don't interrupt me, Viktor Mikhailovich, I mean, Vitya, let me say what I feel. The main thing that tormented me was that I felt I loved two men. And that meant I was an immoral woman.

KARENIN. You, an immoral woman?

LIZA. But since I found out that he had another woman and therefore didn't need me, I was free, and felt I could honestly say that I love you, Viktor Mikhailovich, I mean, Vitya. Now all is clear in my heart, and the only thing that troubles me is my situation. This divorce! This is all so painful. This waiting!

KARENIN. It'll soon be over, very soon. He promised; besides, I asked my secretary to take a petition to him, and not to leave until he signs it. If I didn't know him as well as I do, I'd think he's doing this on purpose.

LIZA. On purpose? No, it's just that he's so weak and honest. He doesn't want to lie. Only you shouldn't have sent him money.

KARENIN. I had to. That could've been the reason for the delay.

LIZA. No, the money part isn't good.

KARENIN. Well, he doesn't have to be so *pointilleux*.

LIZA. What egotists we're turning out to be!

KARENIN. Yes, I'm sorry. It's all your fault. After all that waiting, that hopelessness, I'm so happy now. And happiness turns you into an egotist. It's your fault.

LIZA. You think it's only you. I am too. I'm filled with happiness, I revel in it. I have everything: Mika has recovered, and your mother loves me, and you do, and, the main thing, I'm, I'm in love.

KARENIN. You are? No regrets? No turning back?

LIZA. Since that day everything suddenly changed in me.

KARENIN. And there's no going back?

LIZA. Never. My only wish is that it should be as final for you as it is for me.

THE SAME, *and* NANNIE *with a child.*

(*Enter* NANNIE *with a little boy. The boy goes to his mother. She picks him up and puts him on her lap.*)

KARENIN. We're a miserable lot.

LIZA. Why? (*Kisses the child.*)

KARENIN. When you married, and I heard about it—after my return from abroad—I felt I had lost you forever and was unhappy. I was then pleased to learn that you still remembered me. That was enough for me. Then, when we had become friends, I felt you were affectionate toward me, that in our friendship there was a tiny spark of something more than just friendship, and I was almost happy. Only, I was troubled and concerned over being dishonest towards Fedya. On the other hand, I never conceived of any other relationship than one of proper friendship with the wife of my friend—and I knew you too—so I was not overly troubled by it, and was content. Then, when Fedya began causing you trouble, and I felt that I was your support and that my friendship was making you uneasy, I sensed a sort of vague hope, and was rather happy. Then... he became utterly impossible and you decided to leave him; I bared my soul for the first time, and you didn't say no, but went away in tears, I was thoroughly happy. And if anyone had asked me what else do I want, I would've said, nothing! But then there was a possibility of uniting our lives. *Maman* had taken a liking to you, this possibility was becoming a reality, you told me that you had loved me and still loved me, and—as you said just now—that he no longer exists for you, and that you love only me—what more could I possibly wish for? But no, now, now I'm tormented by the past; I'd wish there was no past, that there was nothing to remind me of him.

LIZA (*reproachfully*). Victòr!

KARENIN. Please forgive me, Liza. I'm telling you this only because I don't want a single thought of mine about you hidden from you. I've purposely told you all this to show how bad I am, and how well I know that this is as bad as it could be, and that I must fight to overcome myself. And I've done that now. I like him.

LIZA. That's how it should be. I did all I could. Not I but my heart has done all you could wish for: everything has vanished from it but you.

KARENIN. Everything?

LIZA. Yes, everything—or else I wouldn't say so.

SCENE 3

THE SAME, *and* FOOTMAN.

FOOTMAN. Mr. Voznesensky.

KARENIN. He's back with Fedya's answer.

LIZA (*to* KARENIN). Have him come here.

KARENIN (*rising and walking to the door*). Well, here comes the answer.

LIZA (*gives the child to the* NANNIE). Will this really settle everything, Victòr? (*Kisses him.*)

[NANNIE *and child exit.*]

SCENE 4

KARENIN, LIZA, *and enter* VOZNESENSKY.

KARENIN. Well?

VOZNESENSKY. He wasn't in.

KARENIN. He wasn't? And he hasn't signed the petition?

VOZNESENSKY. The petition isn't signed, but a letter was left for you and Lizaveta Andreyevna. (*Takes the letter out of his pocket and gives it to* KARENIN.) I went to his apartment. They told me he was in the restaurant. I went there. Then Fyodor Vasilyevich told me to come back in an hour and I'll have his answer. I went back and here it is...

KARENIN. Does this really mean another delay? More excuses? No, that's really bad. How low he's fallen!

LIZA. Now read the letter, what does it say?

(KARENIN *opens the letter.*)

VOZNESENSKY. You don't need me anymore, do you?

KARENIN. No, good-bye, thank you... (*Stops, amazed by what he reads.*)

(VOZNESENSKY *exits.*)

SCENE 5

KARENIN *and* LIZA.

LIZA. What, what is it?

KARENIN. This is terrible!

LIZA (*grasps the letter*). Read it!

KARENIN (*reads*). "Liza and Viktor, I am addressing myself to both of you. I am not going to lie and call you 'my dears' or 'my dear friends.' I cannot overcome a feeling of bitterness and blame—I blame myself, but all the same it is painful when I think of you, of your love, of your happiness. I know everything. I know, as circumstances would have it, that though I was the husband, I have been in your way. *C'est moi qui suis l'intrus.* But all the same, I cannot refrain from feeling bitter and cold toward you. In theory I love you both, especially Liza, dear Lizanka, but in reality I feel more than cold toward you. I know I am wrong and I cannot change."

LIZA. How can he...

KARENIN (*continues reading*). "But let's get down to business. It is precisely this ambivalent feeling that forces me to fulfill your desire in a way different from what you wanted. Lying, taking part in a disgusting farce, bribing officials at the Church Tribunal, and all this dirty trickery is unbearable and repulsive to me. I may be dirty myself, but I'm dirty in a different way, and I cannot take part in this kind of dirty trickery—I simply *cannot.* I have found another way out, a very simple one. To be happy you have to get married. I'm in the way, therefore I have to do away with myself..."

LIZA (*seizes* KARENIN's hand). Victòr!

KARENIN (*reads*). "Have to do away with myself. And I shall. When you receive this letter, I shall be no more.

"P.S. I very much regret that you sent me money for the divorce proceedings. This is offensive, and unlike you. But what can you do? I have made so many mistakes, you have the right to make one too. The money is being returned. My way out is faster, cheaper, and surer. I have one request: don't be angry with me; think kindly of me. And one more thing: there is a watchmaker here, Yevgenyev. Would you help him and straighten out his affairs? He's weak, but a good man. Good-bye. Fedya."

LIZA. He killed himself. Has he?

KARENIN (*rings and runs into the anteroom*). Get Mr. Voznesensky back.

LIZA. I knew it, I knew it. Fedya, my dear Fedya.

KARENIN. Liza!

LIZA. It's not true, it's not true that I didn't love him, that I don't love him. He's the only one, the only one I love. And I destroyed him. Leave me alone.

(*Enter* VOZNESENSKY.)

SCENE 6

THE SAME, *and* VOZNESENSKY.

KARENIN. Where's Fyodor Vasilyevich? What did they tell you?

VOZNESENSKY. They told me he went out in the morning, left this letter, and didn't come back again.

KARENIN. We have to look into this. Liza, I'm going out.

LIZA. Forgive me, but I can't lie either. Leave me alone now. Go, go and find out...

Curtain.

ACT V

VIGNETTE 1

A dirty room in a tavern. A table with people drinking tea and vodka. In the foreground is a small table at which sits FEDYA, *run down and ragged, and* PETUSHKOV, *a considerate, gentle man with long hair, who resembles a cleric. Both are slightly drunk.*

SCENE 1

FEDYA *and* PETUSHKOV.

PETUSHKOV. I understand, I understand. That's genuine love. So what of it?

FEDYA. Well, you know, it's one thing if a woman of high station displayed such feelings and sacrificed everything for the man she loved, but here's a Gypsy girl, thoroughly trained in moneygrubbing, with this pure, selfless love. She gives everything and asks for nothing in return. The contrast is really striking.

PETUSHKOV. Yes, we artists call this "value." You can only get an absolutely bright red when around it... But that's not the point. I understand, I understand...

FEDYA. Yes, and this, I think, is the only good thing I did in my life—I didn't take advantage of her love. And do you know why?

PETUSHKOV. You felt sorry...

FEDYA. On no. I didn't feel sorry for her. I always felt elated in her presence, and when she sang—ah, how she would sing, and perhaps still does now—I always looked up to her. I didn't ruin her simply because I loved her. I really loved her. And now this is a sweet, sweet memory. (*Drinks.*)

PETUSHKOV. I understand, I understand. It's ideal.

FEDYA. I'll tell you something: I've had my passions. I was in love once— there was this beautiful woman–and I was in love in a filthy, animal fashion, and she arranged a rendezvous with me. I didn't show up, because I felt it was a rotten stunt to pull on her husband. And even now, strangely enough, whenever I look back at this I want to feel glad and praise myself for having acted honorably, but instead... I repent as if I had sinned. Now with Masha it's just the opposite. I'm always glad, glad that I didn't defile this feeling of mine... I may fall lower still, I may hit bottom, I may sell everything I own, and become covered with lice and scabs, but this diamond, no, not diamond, but ray of sunlight, yes, will always be in me, with me.

PETUSHKOV. I understand, I understand. So where is she now?

FEDYA. I don't know. And I'd rather not know. That was all part of another life, and I don't want to mix it with this one.

(*A woman's scream is heard from the table behind them. The* OWNER *and a* POLICEMAN *come and take her away.* FEDYA *and* PETUSHKOV *look, listen, and remain silent.*)

PETUSHKOV (*after all is quiet again*). Yes, your life is remarkable.

FEDYA. No, it's very simple. You know, for everyone of the station into which I was born there are three choices—only three: The first is to go into government service, earn money, and add to the abuse which surrounds us. To me that was repulsive. Perhaps I was unfit for it, but the main thing, it was repulsive. The second is to eradicate this abuse; but for this one has to be a hero, and I'm not a hero. And the third is to be oblivious—drink, have a good time, and sing. That's what I've been doing. And this is where it's brought me. (*Drinks.*)

PETUSHKOV. And what about family life? I'd be happy if I had a wife. My wife ruined me.

FEDYA. Family life? Yes, my wife was an ideal woman. She's still alive. But how should I put it? There was no sparkle in it—you know, the sparkle in champagne?[9] There was no fun in our life. And I had to be oblivious. You can't be that when there's no fun. Then I began doing nasty things. And you know we like people for the good we do them, and dislike them for the wrong we do them. And I have really done her wrong. She seemed to love me.

PETUSHKOV. Why do you say "seemed"?

FEDYA. Because there was never anything about her that got to my heart as Masha did. But that's not the point. When she was pregnant or nursing, I'd disappear and come back drunk. And of course, I loved her less and less because of that. Yes, yes (*ecstatically*), the thought just occurred to me now: the reason I love Masha is that I did her good and never wronged her. That's why I love her. The other one I made miserable, because... not that I didn't love her... No, I simply didn't love her. I used to be jealous, but I got over that as well.

SCENE 2

THE SAME, *and* ARTEMYEV, *who enters with a cockade on his cap, dyed moustaches, and wearing old, mended clothes.*

ARTEMYEV. Enjoy your meal. (*Bows to* FEDYA.) You're acquainted with our artist friend the painter?

FEDYA (*coldly*). Yes, we're acquainted.

ARTEMYEV (*to* PETUSHKOV). So have you finished the portrait?

PETUSHKOV. No, it didn't work out.

ARTEMYEV (*sits down*). Am I intruding?

(FEDYA *and* PETUSHKOV *remain silent.*)

PETUSHKOV. Fyodor Vasilyevich was telling me about his life.

ARTEMYEV. Secrets? Then I won't intrude, just go on. I certainly don't need you, you bastards. (*Goes off to the next table and orders a beer. He keeps on listening to the conversation between* FEDYA *and* PETUSHKOV *by leaning toward them.*)

FEDYA. I don't like that man.

PETUSHKOV. He was offended.

FEDYA. Well, the hell with him. I just can't, can't say a word with someone like him around. Now with you it's easy, and pleasant. So what was I saying?

PETUSHKOV. You were saying you used to be jealous. Well how did you part with your wife?

FEDYA. Ah! (*Becomes thoughtful.*) That's an incredible story. My wife is married.

PETUSHKOV. What do you mean? You got a divorce?

FEDYA. No. (*Smiles.*) She is my widow.

PETUSHKOV. Just what do you mean?

FEDYA. Just what I said: she is a widow. I don't exist.

PETUSHKOV. You don't?

FEDYA. No. I'm a corpse. Yes, I am. (ARTEMYEV *leans over and listens attentively.*) You see... I can tell you, since it happened a long time ago, and you don't know my last name. Here's how it happened. Just when I had made my wife's life completely miserable, squandered everything I could, and became insufferable, a protector showed up for her. Don't think that there was anything indecent or improper—no, he was my friend, a fine, fine man, and my direct opposite in every respect. And as there was much more bad in me than good, he really was and is a fine, very fine man: honest, firm, restrained, and, in short, virtuous. He had known my wife since childhood, had loved her, and when she married me he reconciled himself to his fate. But later, when I became nasty and began to make her miserable, he began to come more often to our house. That was just what I wanted. And they fell in love with one another, by which time I had gotten completely out of hand and left my wife. And what's more, there was Masha. I myself suggested that they marry. They didn't want to, but I just became more and more impossible, and finally they...

PETUSHKOV. As usual...

FEDYA. No. I'm certain, I know for sure they remained innocent. As a religious man he considered an unconsecrated marriage a sin. So they began to ask for a divorce and urged me to agree to it. I had to admit to adultery,[10] had to do a lot of lying... and I couldn't. Believe me, it would have been easier for me to commit suicide than to lie—and I was about to do it. And right then a nice person said, "Why?" and arranged everything. I sent a farewell letter, and the next day my clothes along with my wallet and some letters were found on the river bank. I can't swim.

PETUSHKOV. But what about the body? They didn't find one!

FEDYA. Yes, they did. Imagine that. A body was found a week later, and my wife was asked to identify it. It was decomposed. She took a look. "Is it he?"—"Yes, it is." And that settled it. I was buried, and they got married, live here in town, and are prospering. And as for me—here I am, alive and drinking. Yesterday I passed by their house. There was light in the windows, and someone's shadow cut across the blind. Sometimes it's bad, and sometimes it's not. It's bad when there's no money... (*Drinks.*)

ARTEMYEV (*comes up to* FEDYA). Excuse me, but I heard your story. It's a very good story and, above all, a useful one. You say it's bad when there's no money. There's nothing worse. In your situation you should always have money. You see, you're a corpse. Great.

FEDYA. Excuse me, I wasn't talking to you and I don't want your advice.

ARTEMYEV. But I want to give you some. You're a corpse, but if you should come back to life, then they—your wife and that gentleman who are prospering—they would be bigamists, and face banishment to distant places at best. So why should you be without money?

FEDYA. Please leave me alone.

ARTEMYEV. Just write a letter. If you want, I'll write it, only give me the address, and you'll thank me.

FEDYA. Beat it, I'm telling you. I've told you nothing.

ARTEMYEV. Yes, you have. Here's my witness. The waiter heard you say that you're a corpse.

WAITER. I don't know nothin'.

FEDYA. You swindler.

ARTEMYEV. I'm a swindler? Hey, officer. File a complaint.

(FEDYA *rises and starts to leave.* ARTEMEYEV *holds him back. Enter* POLICEMAN.)

Curtain.

VIGNETTE 2

The action takes place on an ivy-covered terrace in the country.

SCENE 1

ANNA DMITRIEVNA KARENINA, LIZA *pregnant,* NANNIE, *and* MISHA.[11]

LIZA. By now he's on his way from the station.

MISHA. Who's on his way?

LIZA. Papa.

MISHA. Papa's on his way from the station?

LIZA. *C'est étonnant comme il l'aime tout-à-fait comme son père.*

ANNA DMITRIEVNA. *Tant mieux. Se souvient-il de son père véritable?*

LIZA (*sighs*). I haven't told him. I think, why confuse him. And then I think, I have to tell him. What do you think, *maman?*

ANNA DMITRIEVNA. I think it depends on how you feel, Liza, and if you yield to your feelings, your heart will tell you what to say and when to say it. It's amazing how death conciliates. I admit there was a time when I found Fedya—and I've known him since he was a child—to be obnoxious; but now I only remember him as a nice kid, Victòr's friend, and as the passionate man who sacrificed himself—albeit illegally and irreligiously—but nevertheless sacrificed himself for the sake of those he loved. *On aura beau dire, l'action est belle...* I hope Victòr won't forget to bring some wool, I'll be all out soon. (*Knits.*)

LIZA. Here he comes. (*The sound of wheels and bells is heard.* LIZA *rises and walks to the edge of the terrace.*) There's someone with him, a woman. It's Masha! I haven't seen her for ages. (*Goes to the door.*)

SCENE 2

THE SAME. *Enter* KARENIN *and* MARYA VASILYEVNA.

MARYA VASILYEVNA (*kisses* LIZA *and* ANNA DMITRIEVNA). Victòr met me and brought me along.

ANNA DMITRIEVNA. He did well.

MARYA VASILYEVNA. Yes, of course. I thought, when will I have another chance to visit with you, and so I didn't postpone it. Well here I am, and if you don't kick me out, I'll stay till the evening train.

KARENIN (*kisses his wife, his mother, and* MISHA). I'm so happy, congratulate me. I get to stay home for two days. They'll manage it all without me tomorrow.

LIZA. Wonderful. Two days. It's long since that's happened. Let's take a trip to the monastery. Okay?

MARYA VASILYEVNA. What a resemblance! What a fine looking boy! I hope he doesn't inherit everything from his father: just his heart.

ANNA DMITRIEVNA. But not his weakness.

LIZA. Everything, everything. Victòr agrees with me, if only everything had been channeled into the right direction from the start...

MARYA VASILYEVNA. Well, I don't know anything about that. But I can't think of him without crying.

LIZA. Neither can we. How much more kindly we think of him now.

MARYA VASILYEVNA. Yes, I should think so.

LIZA. It all seemed so unsolvable at one time. And then suddenly everything was solved.

ANNA DMITRIEVNA. Well, Victòr, did you bring the wool?

KARENIN. Yes, I did. (*Taking things out of a bag.*) Here's the wool, the eau de cologne, and letters, and here's an official envelope addressed to you, Liza. (*Hands it to his wife.*) Well, Marya Vasilyevna, if you'd like to freshen up, I'll show you the way. I have to do the same myself, and then dinner straightaway. Liza, the corner room downstairs for Marya Vasilyevna, right?

(*Turning pale,* LIZA *holds the document with trembling hands, and reads.*)

KARENIN. What is it? Liza, what's the matter?

LIZA. He's alive. Oh, my God! When will he set me free? Victòr, how can this be? (*Sobs.*)

KARENIN (*takes the document and reads it*). This is terrible.

ANNA DMITRIEVNA. What is it, tell me.

KARENIN. This is terrible. He's alive. She's a bigamist and I'm a criminal. This is a subpoena from the pretrial investigator for Liza to appear before him.

ANNA DMITRIEVNA. What a terrible person... Why did he do this?

KARENIN. It was all lies, lies.

LIZA. Oh, how I hate him. I don't know what I'm saying. (*Exits in tears,* KARENIN *follows her.*)

SCENE 3

ANNA DMITRIEVNA *and* MARYA VASILYEVNA.

MARYA VASILYEVNA. How can he still be alive?

ANNA DMITRIEVNA. I always knew that as soon as Victòr came into contact with that dirty world, they would implicate him. And so they did. It's all deceit, all lies.

Curtain.

ACT VI

VIGNETTE 1

PRETRIAL INVESTIGATOR's *office.*

SCENE 1

PRETRIAL INVESTIGATOR, MELNIKOV, *and* CLERK.

PRETRIAL INVESTIGATOR (*sits at a table and talks with* MELNIKOV. *At one side the* CLERK *is looking over the documents*). I never said anything of the sort to her. She invented the whole thing, and now blames me.

MELNIKOV. She's not blaming you, she's just upset.

PRETRIAL INVESTIGATOR. All right, I'll come to dinner. But now I have a very interesting case here. (*To the* CLERK.) I'm ready.

CLERK. Call both of them?

PRETRIAL INVESTIGATOR (*finishes smoking and hides the cigarette*). No, only Mrs. Karenin, or rather, as she was first known, Mrs. Protasov.

MELNIKOV (*exiting*). Ah, it's the Karenin woman.

PRETRIAL INVESTIGATOR. Yes, it's a nasty case. Of course I'm only beginning the inquiry, but it looks bad. Well, good-bye.

(MELNIKOV *exits.*)

SCENE 2

PRETRIAL INVESTIGATOR, CLERK, *and* LIZA, *enters veiled and wearing black.*

PRETRIAL INVESTIGATOR. Please be seated. (*Points to a chair.*) Believe me, I deeply regret having to question you, but we are obliged to... Do relax, and remember you have the right not to answer my questions. But I think it's best for you, and for all concerned, that you tell the truth. It is always the best and most practical way.

LIZA. I have nothing to hide.

PRETRIAL INVESTIGATOR. Well then. (*Looks at the document.*) I have written down your name, social status, and religion—is everything correct?

LIZA. Yes.

PRETRIAL INVESTIGATOR. You are accused of marrying another man while knowing that your husband was still alive.

LIZA. I did not know that.

PRETRIAL INVESTIGATOR. And also of inducing your husband by bribing him with money to commit fraud—a fake suicide—in order to free yourself of him.

LIZA. That is all untrue.

PRETRIAL INVESTIGATOR. Well then, allow me to ask several questions. Did you send him twelve hundred roubles in July of last year?

LIZA. It was his own money; it came from the sale of his things. I sent him the money, since at the time I was separated from him and was expecting a divorce.

PRETRIAL INVESTIGATOR. All right. Very good. The money was sent on the seventeenth of July, that is, two days before his disappearance.

LIZA. I think it was on the seventeenth. I don't remember.

PRETRIAL INVESTIGATOR. And why were the divorce proceedings before the Church Tribunal discontinued at that very time, and the lawyer dismissed?

LIZA. I don't know.

PRETRIAL INVESTIGATOR. Well, when the police asked you to identify the dead body, how did you determine it was that of your husband?

LIZA. I was so flustered then that I did not look at the body. But I was so sure it was he, that when they asked me, I said I thought it was.

PRETRIAL INVESTIGATOR. Yes, you did not look closely because, quite understandably, you were upset. Fine. Well, and why, may I ask, were you sending money every month to Saratov, to the very town where your first husband was living?

LIZA. My husband sent that money, and I cannot say what it was for, because I would be betraying a secret. But it was not sent to Fyodor Vasilyevich.[12] We were firmly convinced that he was dead. I can definitely tell you that.

PRETRIAL INVESTIGATOR. Very well. Permit me to make one observation, madam: though we are servants of the law, that does not stop us from being human. Believe me, I fully understand your situation, and sympathize with you. You were tied to a man who squandered his wealth, was unfaithful, and who, in short, made you unhappy.

LIZA. I loved him.

PRETRIAL INVESTIGATOR. Yes, but nevertheless the desire to free yourself was natural, and you chose this simpler method, not realizing that it might lead you to what is considered a crime—bigamy. I understand that, and the jury[13] will understand it too. Therefore, I would advise you to reveal everything.

LIZA. I have nothing to reveal. I have never lied. (*Cries.*) Do you need me any longer?

PRETRIAL INVESTIGATOR. I would request that you stay a little longer. I will not trouble you with any more questions, none at all. Just, if you would, read and sign this here deposition. Check whether your answers have been taken down correctly. This way, please. (*Points to an armchair by the window. To the* CLERK.) Call in Mr. Karenin.

SCENE 3

THE SAME. *Enter* KARENIN *looking stern and solemn.*

PRETRIAL INVESTIGATOR. Please be seated.

KARENIN. Thank you. (*Remains standing.*) What can I do for you?

PRETRIAL INVESTIGATOR. I have to take your deposition.

KARENIN. In what capacity?

PRETRIAL INVESTIGATOR (*smiling*). I, as the pretrial investigator, must take your deposition as the defendant.

KARENIN. Is that so? And the charge?

PRETRIAL INVESTIGATOR. Party to bigamy. Anyway, let's proceed according to protocol. Please be seated.

KARENIN. Thank you.

PRETRIAL INVESTIGATOR. Your name?

KARENIN. Viktor Karenin.

PRETRIAL INVESTIGATOR. Station?

KARENIN. Chamberlain and councilor of state.

PRETRIAL INVESTIGATOR. Age?

KARENIN. Thirty-eight.

PRETRIAL INVESTIGATOR. Religion?

KARENIN. Russian Orthodox; and have never before had to appear before the law. Well, what now?

PRETRIAL INVESTIGATOR. Were you aware that Fyodor Vasilyevich Protasov was alive when you entered into marriage with his wife?

KARENIN. No, I was not; we were both convinced that he had drowned.

PRETRIAL INVESTIGATOR. To whom in Saratov did you send money every month after Protasov's purported death became known?

KARENIN. I do not wish to answer that question.

PRETRIAL INVESTIGATOR. Very well. Why did you send twelve hundred roubles to Mr. Protasov on the seventeenth of July, just prior to his feigned death?

KARENIN. That money was given to me by my wife.

PRETRIAL INVESTIGATOR. By Mrs. Protasov?

KARENIN. By my wife to send to her husband. She considered that money to be his property, and, after breaking all ties with him, considered it unfair to keep it.

PRETRIAL INVESTIGATOR. I have one more question: why did you discontinue the divorce proceedings?

KARENIN. Because Fyodor Vasilyevich took responsibility for the divorce proceedings, and wrote to me about it.

PRETRIAL INVESTIGATOR. Do you have this letter?

KARENIN. It has gotten lost.

PRETRIAL INVESTIGATOR. How strange, everything that might convince the court of the veracity of your testimony has been lost and is missing.

KARENIN. Is there anything else you need?

PRETRIAL INVESTIGATOR. All I need is to do my duty, but what you need is to exonerate yourself, and I would advise you what I have just advised Mrs. Protasov—do not conceal what is evident to all, but relate everything as it actually happened. All the more so since Mr. Protasov is in such a state that he has already admitted everything, and will most likely admit the same in court. I would advise...

KARENIN. I would ask you to stay within the confines of your duties, and desist from giving your advice. May we leave? (*Goes up to* LIZA, *who rises and takes his arm.*)

PRETRIAL INVESTIGATOR. I am very sorry but I must detain you...

(KARENIN *turns around in astonishment.*)

PRETRIAL INVESTIGATOR. Oh no, I don't mean arrest you. Though that would greatly facilitate my inquiry, I will not resort to this measure. Only I would like to take Protasov's deposition in your presence, and confront him with you so that it will be easier for you to expose any misrepresentation on his part. Please be seated. Call Mr. Protasov.

SCENE 4

THE SAME. *Enter* FEDYA, *grimy and rundown.*

FEDYA (*addresses* LIZA *and* KARENIN). Liza, Lizaveta Andreyevna, Victòr. It's not my fault. I wanted to do what's best. But if it is my fault... Forgive me, forgive me... (*Bows low before them.*)

PRETRIAL INVESTIGATOR. I request you answer my questions.

FEDYA. Go ahead, ask.

PRETRIAL INVESTIGATOR. Your name?

FEDYA. Well, you know it.

PRETRIAL INVESTIGATOR. I request you answer the question.

FEDYA. All right. Fyodor Protasov.

PRETRIAL INVESTIGATOR. Your station, age, and religion?

FEDYA (*is silent for a moment*). Aren't you ashamed to ask such nonsense? Ask what's important, and not this trash.

PRETRIAL INVESTIGATOR. I request that you be more cautious in what you say, and answer my questions.

FEDYA. Well, if you're not ashamed, all right. Station—university graduate; age—forty; religion—Russian Orthodox. Well, what next?

PRETRIAL INVESTIGATOR. Did Mr. Karenin and your wife know that you were alive when you left your clothes on the river bank and disappeared?

FEDYA. Certainly not. I actually wanted to kill myself, but then... Well, I don't have to go into that. The point is that they did not know a thing.

PRETRIAL INVESTIGATOR. Why then did you give a different account to the police officer?

FEDYA. What police officer? Oh, the one who came to the Rzhanov Shelter to see me? I was drunk and told him a bunch of lies—don't even remember what. That was all rubbish. I'm not drunk now, and I'm telling you the whole truth. They did not know a thing. They believed I was dead, and I was happy they did. And that's how it would have remained if not for that swindler, Artemyev. And if anyone is to blame, it is I alone.

PRETRIAL INVESTIGATOR. I understand your desire to be magnanimous, but the law demands the truth. Why was money sent to you?

(FEDYA *remains silent.*)

PRETRIAL INVESTIGATOR. Did you receive through Simonov[14] the money sent to you in Saratov?

(FEDYA *remains silent.*)

PRETRIAL INVESTIGATOR. Why don't you answer? It will be entered in the record that the defendant did not answer these questions, and that could be very damaging both to you and to them. So what will it be?

FEDYA (*after remaining silent for awhile*). Oh, Mr. Investigator, shame on you! Why do you poke your nose into other people's lives? You're glad you have power, and to show it you torment people, not physically but psychologically, people who are a thousand times better than you.

PRETRIAL INVESTIGATOR. I request...

FEDYA. There's nothing to request. I'll say whatever I think. (*To the* CLERK.) And you write it down. At least for once there will be sane, human words on record. (*Raises his voice.*) There are three people: I, he, and she. The relationship among them is tangled, a struggle between good and evil, a spiritual struggle the likes of which you cannot fathom. The struggle ends in a way that disentangles everything. Everyone is satisfied. They are happy—they think kindly of me. In my downfall I am happy that I did what I had to, and that I, a good-for-nothing, left this life so as not to be in the way of those who are good and full of life. And we all live happily. Suddenly a swindler appears, a blackmailer who demands that I take part in blackmail. I send him packing. He comes to you, the champion of justice, the custodian of morality. And you, who get a few coins a month for playing your dirty tricks, put on your uniform and, with an easy conscience, lord it over them, over people whose little finger you're not worth, and who wouldn't let you set foot in their house. But you got to them and you're happy...

PRETRIAL INVESTIGATOR. I'll have you taken away.

FEDYA. I'm not afraid of anyone, because I'm a corpse and you can't do anything to me. I couldn't be any worse off. So go ahead, take me away.

KARENIN. May we leave now?

PRETRIAL INVESTIGATOR. Just a moment, you have to sign the record.

FEDYA. You'd really be hilarious if you weren't so repulsive.

PRETRIAL INVESTIGATOR. Take him away. You're under arrest.

FEDYA (*to* KARENIN *and* LIZA). Please forgive me.

KARENIN (*comes up to him and offers him his hand*). Apparently it was meant to be so.

(LIZA *passes by,* FEDYA *bows low.*)

Curtain.

VIGNETTE 2

A corridor in the circuit court. In the background there is a glass door, next to which stands an ATTENDANT. *To the right is another door, through which the defendants are brought in.* IVAN PETROVICH, *ragged, comes to the first door and tries to enter.*

SCENE 1

A T T E N D A N T *and* I V A N P E T R O V I C H.

A T T E N D A N T. Where're yuh goin'? Whacha so pushy for. Yuh can't go in.
I V A N P E T R O V I C H. Why not? The law says sessions are public.

(*Applause is heard.*)

A T T E N D A N T. Yuh just cant, an' that's it. It's against orders.
I V A N P E T R O V I C H. You clown. You don't know whom you're talking to.

(*Enter* Y O U N G L A W Y E R *wearing a tailcoat.*)

SCENE 2

T H E S A M E, *and* Y O U N G L A W Y E R.

Y O U N G L A W Y E R. Are you involved in this case?
I V A N P E T R O V I C H. No, I'm the public. And this clown, this Cerberus,[15] won't let me in.
Y O U N G L A W Y E R. But this door is not for the public.
I V A N P E T R O V I C H. I know. They don't let me in over there either. And I'm someone who should be let in.
Y O U N G L A W Y E R. Wait a moment, there will be a recess shortly. (*Starts to leave when he meets* P R I N C E A B R E Z K O V.)

SCENE 3

T H E S A M E, *and* P R I N C E A B R E Z K O V.

P R I N C E A B R E Z K O V. Can you tell me how the case is going?
Y O U N G L A W Y E R. The lawyers are summing up. Petrushin is speaking.

(*Applause is heard again.*)

PRINCE ABREZKOV. And how are the defendants holding up?

YOUNG LAWYER. With great dignity, especially Karenin and Lizaveta Andreyevna. They are not being tried, rather they are trying society. That's the feeling, and that is what Petrushin is addressing.

PRINCE ABREZKOV. What about Protasov?

YOUNG LAWYER. He's awfully upset; sort of shaking all over. Well, that's understandable considering his lifestyle. But for some reason he's extremely irritable: he's interrupted the prosecutor and the lawyer several times. He's extremely excited.

PRINCE ABREZKOV. What do you think the verdict will be?

YOUNG LAWYER. It's difficult to say. The jury is mixed. In any event they won't be found guilty of premeditation, but still... (*A* GENTLEMAN *comes out of the courtroom and* PRINCE ABREZKOV *moves toward the door.*) Do you want to go in?

PRINCE ABREZKOV. Yes, I'd like to.

YOUNG LAWYER. Are you Prince Abrezkov?

PRINCE ABREZKOV. Yes.

YOUNG LAWYER (*to the* ATTENDANT). Let him in. There's an empty chair just to your left.

(*The* ATTENDANT *lets* PRINCE ABREZKOV *in. As the door opens the* LAWYER *is seen speaking.*)

SCENE 4

ATTENDANT, YOUNG LAWYER, *and* IVAN PETROVICH.

IVAN PETROVICH. Aristocrats! I'm a spiritual aristocrat, and that's much higher.

YOUNG LAWYER. Well, I'm sorry. (*Exits.*)

SCENE 5

ATTENDANT, IVAN PETROVICH, *and* PETUSHKOV *enters hurriedly.*

PETUSHKOV. Ah, how are you, Ivan Petrovich? How's it going?

IVAN PETROVICH. The lawyers are still summing up. And they won't let me in.

ATTENDANT. Don't make noise here. This ain't no tavern.

(*Applause is heard again; the doors open, and lawyers and spectators—men and women—come out.*)

SCENE 6

THE SAME, *a* LADY *and an* OFFICER.

LADY. Wonderful. He brought tears to my eyes.

OFFICER. Better than any novel. Only it's hard to understand how she could love him so. Such a dreadful type.

SCENE 7

THE SAME. *The other door opens and the defendants come out: first* LIZA *and* KARENIN—*who walk along the corridor—followed by* FEDYA *alone.*

LADY. Quiet. Here he is. Look how upset he is.

(*The* LADY *and* OFFICER *exit.*)

FEDYA (*goes up to* IVAN PETROVICH). Did you bring it?

IVAN PETROVICH. Here it is. (*Gives* FEDYA *something.*)

FEDYA (*hides it in his pocket and starts to go when he sees* PETUSHKOV). It's so stupid, so vulgar. And how boring, how boring. It's senseless. (*Starts to exit.*)

SCENE 8

THE SAME. *Enter* PETRUSHIN, *Fedya's lawyer, a stout, ruddy, lively person.*

PETRUSHIN (*approaching* FEDYA). Well, my friend, we're doing fine, just don't mess it up for me in your final statement.

FEDYA. I won't speak at all. What can I say to them? I just won't.

PETRUSHIN. But you have to. Only don't get unnerved. It's all in the bag now. You just tell them what you told me—that if you're being tried, it's only for *not* committing suicide; that is, for not doing what's considered a crime by both civil and ecclesiastical law.

FEDYA. I won't say a word.

PETRUSHIN. Why not?

FEDYA. I don't want to and I won't. Just tell me one thing: what's the most that can happen?

PETRUSHIN. I've already told you: the most is exile to Siberia.

FEDYA. Exile for whom?

PETRUSHIN. For you and your wife.

FEDYA. And what's the least?

PETRUSHIN. Church penance and, of course, annulment of the second marriage.

FEDYA. Then they'll tie me to her again, I mean, her to me?

PETRUSHIN. Yes, that's how it has to be. But don't worry. And please say what I tell you—just that. Above all, don't say anything unnecessary. Well, anyway... (*Noticing that they are surrounded by people listening.*) I'm tired, I'll go sit for a while, and you relax while the jury is deliberating. The main thing is, don't lose heart.

FEDYA. And there can't be another sentence?

PETRUSHIN (*exiting*). No, there cannot.

SCENE 9

THE SAME *without* PETRUSHIN. *Enter* COURT OFFICIAL.

COURT OFFICIAL. Move on, move on. No loitering in the corridor.
FEDYA. Just a minute. (*Takes out a pistol and shoots himself in the heart. Falls down. Everyone rushes to him.*) It's all right, it seems fine. Liza...

SCENE 10

Spectators, judges, defendants, and witnesses run out from all the doors. In front of all is LIZA *followed by* MASHA *and* KARENIN, IVAN PETROVICH, *and* PRINCE ABREZKOV.

LIZA. Fedya, what have you done? Why?
FEDYA. Forgive me, I couldn't... free you in another way. It's not for you... its better for me this way. You know... for a long time... I've been ready...
LIZA. You'll live.

(*The* DOCTOR *leans over* FEDYA *and listens.*)

FEDYA. I know without any doctor. Good-bye, Victòr. Ah, Masha, you're too late. (*Sobs.*) How good... How good... (*Dies.*)

Curtain.

The Wisdom of Children

1909–1910

BOY. Why's Nannie all dressed up today, and why did she put a new shirt on me?

MOTHER. Because it's a holiday today, and we're going to church.

BOY. What holiday?

MOTHER. Ascension Day.

BOY. What does ascension mean?

MOTHER. It means that the Lord Jesus Christ ascended to heaven.

BOY. What does ascended mean?

MOTHER. It means flew off.

BOY. How did he fly off, on wings?

MOTHER. No, not on wings, he just flew off, because he's God, and God can do anything.

BOY. But where did he fly off to? Daddy told me there isn't such a thing as heaven, and there's nothing there, just stars, and beyond the stars are more stars, and the sky never ends. So where did he fly off to?

MOTHER (*smiling*). You can't understand it all, you have to believe.

BOY. Believe what?

MOTHER. What those older than you tell you.

BOY. But you told me when I said somebody would die because salt was spilled, you told me I shouldn't believe such silly things.

MOTHER. Of course you shouldn't.

BOY. But how am I to know what's silly and what's not?

MOTHER. Believe the true faith, and not silly things, that's how.

BOY. But what's the true faith?

MOTHER. Our faith. (*Aside.*) I think I'm saying silly things myself. (*Aloud.*) Now go tell Daddy we're ready, and put on a scarf.

BOY. Will I get some chocolate after mass?

ON WARS

karlchen. Because our Prussia won't let the Russians take our land away.

petya. But we say it's our land because we conquered it first.

masha. Whose is ours?

petya. Oh, you're too little, you don't understand. Ours means our country's.

karlchen. All people live like that—some belong to one country, others to another.

masha. Who do I belong to?

petya. Same as everybody else—to Russia.

masha. And what if I don't want to?

petya. Want to or not, you're a Russian. Every nation has its own tsar or king.

karlchen (*interjecting*). Or parliament.

petya. Each one has its own army, and collects taxes from its own people.

masha. Why are they all separate?

petya. What do you mean why? Because each country is by itself.

masha. But why are they separate?

karlchen. What do you mean why? Because every man loves his own homeland.

masha. I don't understand why they're separate. Isn't it better to be all together?

petya. It's better to play games together, but these aren't games, they're important things.

masha. I don't understand.

karlchen. You will when you grow up.

masha. Then I don't want to grow up.

petya. You're a little girl, but stubborn already like all the rest of them.

ON THE FATHERLAND, THE STATE

GAVRILA, *a soldier in the reserves, a servant.* MISHA, *the young son of Gavrila's master.*

GAVRILA. Well, good-bye, Mishenka, my dear Master. Now God only knows if I'll see yuh again.

MISHA. So you're really leaving?

GAVRILA. Sure enough. There's war again, an' I'm in the reserves.

MISHA. War with who? Who's fighting who?

GAVRILA. God only knows. There's no makin' it out. I read somethin' 'bout it in the papers but don't understand what's what. They say the Austrian got mad at our tsar cuz he went along with those, what's their name...

MISHA. So why are you going? The tsars got into an argument, let them fight it out.

GAVRILA. What can I do? I gotta for the tsar, the fatherland, and the Orthodox Faith.

MISHA. But you don't want to go, do you?

GAVRILA. An' who does? Leavin yer wife an kids. Why would I wanna after such good livin'.

MISHA. So why are you going? Tell them "I don't want to," and don't go. What will they do to you?

GAVRILA (*laughs*). What'll they do? They'll haul me off.

MISHA. Who will?

GAVRILA. Oh, just men like me, those with no choice.

MISHA. Why would they haul you off? After all, they're just like you.

GAVRILA. Cuz o' their commanders. They'll get orders an' do it.

MISHA. And what if they won't want to?

GAVRILA. Never happen.

MISHA. Why not?

GAVRILA. Cuz... cuz that's not the law.

MISHA. What law?

GAVRILA. You're really talking funny, Master! I'm wasting too much time talking with you. I'd better go put the samovar on for the last time.

ON TAXES

VILLAGE ELDER *and* GRUSHKA.

The VILLAGE ELDER *enters a poor peasant cottage. No one is there except seven-year-old* GRUSHKA.[2] *He looks around.*

VILLAGE ELDER. Nobody else here?

GRUSHKA. Ma's gone for the cow, and Fedka's[3] at the master's place.

VILLAGE ELDER. Well, then tell yer mom the village elder stopped by. Tell 'er it's the third time I'm remindin' 'er; tell 'er I'm givin' 'er an order: bring the taxes widout fail by Sunday or I'll take the cow.

GRUSHKA. Whatcha mean take the cow? Are yuh some kinda crook? We won't let yuh.

VILLAGE ELDER (*smiling*). Look at 'er, what a smart girl! What's yer name?

GRUSHKA. Grushka.

VILLAGE ELDER. Hey, at-a-girl, Grushka. Listen now, you just tell yer mother that I ain't no crook, but I'll take the cow.

GRUSHKA. Why would yuh take the cow if yuh ain't no crook?

VILLAGE ELDER. Cuz yuh gotta pay what's due. I'll take the cow for the taxes.

GRUSHKA. What's taxes?

VILLAGE ELDER. That girl's a pill. What's taxes? It's what the tsar saw fit for folks t'pay.

GRUSHKA. T'who?

VILLAGE ELDER. T'the tsar of course. Then they'll know what t'do with it.

GRUSHKA. Is he poor? We're poor, the tsar's rich. So why's he takin' it from us?

VILLAGE ELDER. He don't take it for 'imself. He takes it for us, us fools, for our needs, for the authorities, for the army, for education. It's for our own good.

GRUSHKA. What good is it for us if yuh take the cow? That's no good at all.

VILLAGE ELDER. When you grow up, yuh'll catch on. So be sure t'tell yer mom.

GRUSHKA. I ain't about t'tell 'er such nonsense. You and the tsar look after your own needs, we'll look after our own.

VILLAGE ELDER. Just wait till that girl grows up, she'll be a firebrand.

JUDGMENT

MITYA, *10*, ILYUSHA, *9*, SONYA, *6*.

MITYA. I was telling Pyotr Semyonych that we could train ourselves to make do without clothes. And he said: "No, you can't." Then I told him what Mikhail Ivanovich told me, that we've trained our faces not to feel cold, and we can do the same with our whole body. And he said, "Your Mikhail Ivanovich is a fool." (*Laughs.*) But Mikhail Ivanovich said to me just yesterday: "Your Pyotr Semyonych," he says, "talks a lot of nonsense. Well," he says, "you can expect anything from a fool." (*Laughs.*)

ILYUSHA. I would've told him: you call him names and he calls you the same.

MITYA. No, seriously, I can't tell which of them is the fool.

SONYA. Both are fools. Whoever calls someone a fool is a fool himself.

ILYUSHA. Now you've gone and called both of them fools, so you must be a fool too.

MITYA. No, what I don't like is speaking about each other like that and not to one's face. When I grow up, I won't do that. I'm going to say what I think.

ILYUSHA. Me too.

SONYA. Well I'll do it my own way.

MITYA. What do you mean, your own way?

SONYA. Just that. When I want to, I will, when I don't, I won't.

ILYUSHA. See what a fool you are!

SONYA. You said you weren't going to call people names.

ILYUSHA. But I'm not doing it behind your back.

ON KINDNESS

The children, MASHA *and* MISHA, *are building a doll house in front of their home.*

MISHA (*to* MASHA *angrily*). Not that one. Give me the other stick. Stupid!

OLD WOMAN (*comes out on the porch, crosses herself, and exclaims*). God bless 'er! Has the soul of an angel. Takes pity on everyone.

(*The children stop playing and look at the* OLD WOMAN.)

MISHA. Who are you talking about?

OLD WOMAN. Yer mom. She's mindful o' God. Takes pity on us poor folk. Here she's given me a skirt, an' some tea, an' some money. Save 'er, O Lord, an' Queen o' Heaven! Not like that infidel over there: "Lots o' yer kind," he says, "hangin' 'round here." An' his dogs are as mean as him. I barely got away from 'em in one piece.

MISHA. Who's that?

OLD WOMAN. The one opposite the liquor stall. Oh, what a mean man. Well, never mind. I'm thankful to 'er, the dear heart, she favored an' conforted a miserable wretch. How could we live if there wasn't such people. (*Weeps.*)

MASHA (*to* MISHA). How kind she is.

OLD WOMAN. When you grow up, kiddies, don't forget the poor. And God won't forget you. (*The* OLD WOMAN *leaves.*)

MISHA. How pitiful she is.

MASHA. I'm glad Mama gave her something.

MISHA. I don't know why we shouldn't give if we have it. We don't need it, but she does.

MASHA. Do you remember what John the Baptist said: "He that hath two coats, let him give one away."[4]

MISHA. Yes, when I grow up, I'll give everything away.

MASHA. You can't give away everything.

MISHA. Why not?

MASHA. And what about yourself?

MISHA. I don't care. You always have to be kind. Then everybody will be happy.

And MISHA *stopped playing and went to the nursery, tore a sheet from a notebook, wrote something on it, and put it into his pocket. On the paper was written:*

"YU HAV TO BEE KYND."

ON COMPENSATION

FATHER *and* KATYA, *9, and* FEDYA, *8.*

KATYA. Daddy, our sled broke. Can you fix it?

FATHER. I can't, dear. I don't know how. You have to give it to Prokhor, he'll fix it for you.

KATYA. We went to see him. He says he doesn't have time. He's making a gate.

FATHER. Well, what can you do, just wait.

FEDYA. Are you sure you don't know how, Daddy?

FATHER (*smiling*). Absolutely, Sonny.

FEDYA. Don't you know how to do anything?

FATHER (*laughing*). No, I know how to do some things. But I don't know how to do what Prokhor does.

FEDYA. Do you know how to make samovars like Vasily?

FATHER. No, I don't.

FEDYA. How to harness horses?

FATHER. No, I don't.

FEDYA. I wonder why we don't know how to do anything and they do everything for us? Is that good?

FATHER. To each his own. You just pay attention, then you'll find out who has to know how to do what.

FEDYA. Don't we have to know how to cook meals and harness horses?

FATHER. There are more important things than that.

FEDYA. Yes, I know: to be kind, not to get angry, not to fight. But it's possible to cook meals and harness horses, and be good too. Isn't that true?

FATHER. Of course it is. Wait till you grow up, you'll understand.

FEDYA. And what if I don't grow up?

FATHER. You say such silly things.

KATYA. So may we tell Prokhor?

FATHER. Yes, yes. Go to Prokhor and tell him I said so.

ON DRINKING

Evening. Autumn.

MAKARKA, *12, and* MARFUTKA, *8, come out of their house into the street.* MARFUTKA *is crying.* PAVLUSHKA, *10,[5] is standing on the porch of the house next door.*

PAVLUSHKA. Where the hell are yuh off to this time o' night?

MAKARKA. He's hit the bottle again.

PAVLUSHKA. Who, Pa Prokhor?

MAKARKA. Who else?

MARFUTKA. He's beatin' Mom up...

MAKARKA. I ain't goin' back. He'll clobber me too. (*Sits down on the steps.*) I'll sleep here. I ain't goin' back.

(MARFUTKA *cries.*)

PAVLUSHKA (*to* MARFUTKA). Nuff o' that. It's aw right. What can yuh do? Nuff.

MARFUTKA (*through her tears*). If I was the tsar, I'd clobber the ones who let 'im have liquor. I wouldn't let no one keep that there liquor.

PAVLUSHKA. Fat chance! The tsar 'imself sells liquor. Only he don't let no one else do it so's not t'lose the profit.

MAKARKA. Bullshit.

PAVLUSHKA. Bullshit yuhself. Go an' ask. Why'd they toss Akulina into jail? Cuz yuh don't sell liquor an' make 'em lose the profit.

MAKARKA. For that? They was sayin' she did somethin' 'gainst the law.

PAVLUSHKA. Sellin' liquor, that's what's 'gainst the law.

MARFUTKA. I wouldn't let 'er either. It's all cuz o' this liquor. He ain't bad, but when drunk he beats everyone up for no reason.

MAKARKA (*to* PAVLUSHKA). Yuh're talkin' weird. I'll ask the teacher tomorrow. He must know.

PAVLUSHKA. Go 'head an' ask.

The following morning PROKHOR, MAKARKA*'s father, having slept it off, has gone out to get a drink in order to feel better.* MAKARKA*'s mother,* *with a swollen, black eye, has been kneading dough.* MAKARKA *has gone off to school. The children have not as yet assembled. The* TEACHER *is sitting on the stoop and smoking while letting the children enter the school.*

MAKARKA (*walking up to the* TEACHER). Tell me, Evgeny Semyonych, is it true what someone was tellin' me yesterday that the tsar sells liquor an' Akulina was tossed into jail for doin' the same thing?

TEACHER. That's a stupid question and the one who told you that is a fool. The tsar does not sell anything. That's why he is tsar. And Akulina was imprisoned because she was selling liquor without a license thereby causing a loss of revenue to the treasury.

MAKARKA. Why a loss?

TEACHER. Because there is an excise tax on liquor. It costs two roubles to produce a gallon, but it sells for eight roubles and forty kopecks. The difference is profit for the state. And this profit is very big—seven hundred million roubles.

MAKARKA. That means the more liquor that's drunk, the bigger the profit.

TEACHER. Of course. If it were not for this profit, there would not be the money to maintain the army, schools, or anything else that all of you need.

MAKARKA. But if everyone needs these things, why not take the money straight out, why through liquor?

TEACHER. Why through liquor? Because that's, you know, how it should be. Well, children, you're all here now, take your seats.

ON CAPITAL PUNISHMENT

PYOTR PETROVICH, *a professor.* MARYA IVANOVNA, *his wife (is sewing).* FEDYA, *their son, 9 (listens to his father's conversation).* IVAN VASILYEVICH, *military prosecutor.*

IVAN VASILYEVICH. But you cannot deny historical experience. We have seen this not only in postrevolutionary France and in other historical instances, but we see it now in our own country, that elimination, that is, removal of subversive and dangerous members of society achieves its end.

PYOTR PETROVICH. No, we cannot know this, we cannot know the ultimate consequences, and it does not justify exceptional procedures.

IVAN VASILYEVICH. But neither do we have the right to assume that exceptional measures will have harmful consequences, and even if they were to turn out harmful, that the cause of this was specifically the use of exceptional measures. That's number one. In the second place, intimidation cannot fail to have an effect on people who have lost all semblance to human beings, and have turned into beasts. What other than intimidation can work on people like the man who calmly butchered an old woman and three children so as to steal three hundred roubles?

PYOTR PETROVICH. But look here, I do not reject the use of capital punishment per se, I only reject trials by court-martial which impose it so frequently. If these frequent executions produced only intimidation, but along with intimidation they also produce depravity: they lead people to treat with indifference the killing of their fellow men.

IVAN VASILYEVICH. Here again we do not know the ultimate consequences, but knowing the beneficial nature...

PYOTR PETROVICH. Beneficial?!

IVAN VASILYEVICH. Yes, beneficial nature of the immediate effects, we do not have the right to deny capital punishment. How can society fail to retaliate in kind on such a criminal as...

PYOTR PETROVICH. Are you saying society has to avenge itself?

IVAN VASILYEVICH. Not avenge itself, but the contrary—replace private vengeance with public retribution.

PYOTR PETROVICH. Yes, but then it has to be carried out in forms well defined by the law, and not in exceptional procedures.

IVAN VASILYEVICH. Public retribution replaces that accidental, exaggerated, unlawful, often groundless, and erroneous vengeance to which a private individual might resort.

PYOTR PETROVICH (*angrily*). Then in your opinion this retribution is now never dispensed accidentally, never groundlessly, never erroneously? No, I'll never agree with that. None of your arguments can convince me, nor anybody else, that these exceptional procedures under which thousands are executed and executions continue on and on—that this is or could ever be rational, legal, and beneficial. (*Gets up and paces the floor in agitation.*)

FEDYA (*to his mother*). Mommy, what's Daddy arguing about?

MARYA IVANOVNA. Daddy thinks its wrong to have so many death penalties.

FEDYA. Does that mean killing people until they're dead?

MARYA IVANOVNA. Yes. He thinks it shouldn't be done so often.

FEDYA (*goes over to his father*). Daddy, why do the Ten Commandments say: "Thou shalt not kill?" Doesn't that mean it shouldn't be done at all?

PYOTR PETROVICH (*smiling*). That was said about something else, not what we're talking about. It's about some people not killing other people.

FEDYA. But when they execute, people are still killing, aren't they?

PYOTR PETROVICH. Of course, but you have to understand why and when you can do this.

FEDYA. When can you?

PYOTR PETROVICH. Well, how should I explain it to you? Well, take war, or take a wicked man who kills a lot of people. How can he be left unpunished?

FEDYA. But in the Gospel it says to love everybody, and to forgive.

PYOTR PETROVICH. That would be fine, if it could be that way. But it can't.

FEDYA. Why not?

PYOTR PETROVICH. Because. (*Turns to* IVAN VASILYEVICH *who has been smiling while listening to* FEDYA.) And so, my dear Ivan Vasilyevich, I cannot, cannot acknowledge the benefit of exceptional procedures and trials by court-martial.

Syomka, *13*, Aksyutka, *10*, Mitka, *10*, Palashka, *9*, Vanka, *8.*[6]
(They are sitting by a well after having gathered mushrooms.)

AKSYUTKA. Oh how Auntie Matryona was moanin' an' groanin'! An' the kids—soon's one begun cryin', all the other chimed in.

VANKA. Why were they bawlin'?

PALASHKA. Why? They done went an' took their father away t'jail. Who else d'ya think would bawl?

VANKA. Why t'jail?

AKSYUTKA. Who knows. They come, "Get ready," they said, then grabbed 'im an' took 'im away. We saw it all...

SYOMKA. They took 'im away cuz yuh don't steal horses. He swiped Dyomkin's, an' was in on the Krasnov job. An' our gelding didn't get away from their sticky fingers either. What should they do, pat 'im on the head?

AKSYUTKA. You said it, the only thing is that I'm sorry for the kids. There're four of 'em, yuh know. An' so poor—nothin' t'eat. They come over t'our house today.

SYOMKA. Then don't steal.

MITKA. But he's the one that done it, not the kids. What are they gonna do now, go beggin'?

SYOMKA. Then don't steal.

MITKA. But it wasn't the kids, he done it.

SYOMKA. Yuh keep on sayin' "the kids, the kids." Then why'd he do wrong? Does he have a right t'steal just cuz he has a bunch o' kids?

VANKA. What'll they do to 'im there in jail?

AKSYUTKA. He'll sit aroun', that's all.

VANKA. Will they feed 'im?

SYOMKA. That's why they're not afraid, these dam'd hoss thieves. What's jail t'him. Everythin's taken care of, just sit aroun' an' hang out. If I was the tsar, I'd know what t'do with these hoss thieves. I'd break 'em o' that. This way, what's it t'him. He sits aroun' an' hangs out with the same kind o' bandits like him. They teach each other how t'steal betta. My grandpa told me that Petrukha was a good kid till he spent time in jail, but he came outta there a downright crook. An' that's when it started...

VANKA. So why do they put 'em there?

SYOMKA. Go 'head an' ask.

AKSYUTKA. They put 'im there an' take care of 'im...

SYOMKA (*interjects*). So's he can learn things betta.

AKSYUTKA. An' let the kids an' their mom starve t'death. They're our neighbors, yuh know, I feel sorry for 'em. Whacha gonna do with 'em? They come askin' for bread, yuh hafta give.

VANKA. So why do they put 'em in jail?

SYOMKA. An' what d'ya wanna do with 'em?

VANKA. What? What t'do? Somethin' so's somehow...

SYOMKA. That's just it, somethin', but what yuh don't know. Smarter people than you have been thinkin' 'bout it, but haven't come up with nothin'.

PALASHKA. I think if I was the tsarina...

AKSYUTKA (*laughing*). Well, Tsarina, what would'ya do then?

PALASHKA. I'd do so that nobody'd steal an' kids wouldn't cry.

AKSYUTKA. An' how would'ya do that?

PALASHKA. I'd do so that everybody'd have what they need, an' nobody'd be hurt, an' everybody'd be happy.

SYOMKA. Some tsarina. An' how would'ya do it?

PALASHKA. I'd just do it.

MITKA. So are we gonna go t'where there's lots o' birches? T'other day the girls gathered a whole bunch there.

SYOMKA. Good idea. Let's go, guys. An' you, Tsarina, watch yuh don't drop yer mushrooms, cuz yer too quick.

(*They get up and leave.*)

A LANDOWNER, *his wife, daughter, and six-year-old son,* VASYA, *are sitting on a balcony having tea. The older children are playing tennis. A young* BEGGAR *approaches them.*

LANDOWNER (*to the* BEGGAR). What do you want?

BEGGAR (*bowing*). You know what. Have pity on me, I'm outta work. Got no clothes, nothin' t'eat. I was in Moscow, now I'm makin' my way back home. Please help a poor man.

LANDOWNER. And why are you poor?

BEGGAR. You know why, cuz o' bad straits.

LANDOWNER. If you would work, you wouldn't be poor.

BEGGAR. I'd be glad to, but there's no work now. Everythin's shut down.

LANDOWNER. Why do other people work, and you have no job?

BEGGAR. Honestly, I'd be more than glad t'work. They ain't hirin'. Have pity, sir. It's goin' on two days since I had somethin' t'eat.

LANDOWNER (*looks into the room, to his* WIFE). *Avez-vous de la petite monnaie? Je n'ai que des assignats.*

WIFE (*to* VASYA). Be a good boy and go look in my bag on the little table by the bed, my purse is there—bring it to me.

(VASYA *does not hear his mother and stares intently at the* BEGGAR.)

WIFE. Vasya, did you hear me? (*Pulls him by the sleeve.*) Vasya!

VASYA. What, Mommy?

(*His mother tells him again where to go and what to bring.*)

VASYA (*jumps up*). Okay. (*Exits, still keeping his eyes on the* BEGGAR.)

LANDOWNER. Wait a moment. (*The* BEGGAR *goes off to the side. To his* WIFE *in French.*) It's awful how many of them are out of work. It's all because of their laziness. Still, it's awful if he's hungry.

WIFE. It's an exaggeration. They say it's the same abroad. I read that there were around one hundred thousand people out of work in New York. Do you want some more tea?

LANDOWNER. Yes, but not so strong. (*Begins to smoke. Silence.*)

(*The* BEGGAR *looks at them, shakes his head and coughs, obviously drawing attention to himself.* VASYA *runs in with the purse and looks immediately for the* BEGGAR, *and, handing the purse to his mother, stares at him.*)

LANDOWNER (*taking a ten-kopeck coin from the purse*). Here you go, hey what's your name, take this.

BEGGAR (*takes off his hat, bows, and takes the coin*). Thank you, much obliged even for this. Thanks for feeling sorry for a poor man.

LANDOWNER. I'm mainly sorry that you don't work. If you would work, you wouldn't be poor. He who works shall not want.

BEGGAR (*having taken the coin, he puts on his hat and, turning away, says*). It's true enough, if yuh work for dough, yuh'll get bent low. (*Exits.*)

VASYA. What did he say?

LANDOWNER. He repeated one of those stupid peasant sayings: If you work for dough, you will get bent low.

VASYA. What does that mean?

LANDOWNER. Supposedly that if you work you get a bad back but cannot become rich.

VASYA. Is that wrong?

LANDOWNER. Of course it's wrong. Those who, like him, loaf around and do not want to work, are always poor. Only those who work are rich.

VASYA. But why are we rich and don't work?

WIFE (*laughs*). How do you know that Daddy doesn't work?

VASYA. I don't know, but we're very rich so Daddy must work very, very hard. Does he really work that hard?

LANDOWNER.[7] There are different kinds of work. Maybe the work I do, not many other can do.

VASYA. What is your work?

LANDOWNER. My work is to feed, clothe, and teach all of you.

VASYA. But his is the same. So why should he be so miserable, while here we are so...

LANDOWNER (*laughing*). Here's a natural socialist for you.

WIFE. Yes, they say: *Ein Narr kan mehr fragen, als tausend Weise antworten* (A fool can ask more questions than a thousand wise men can answer.) One should say: *Ein Kind* (not a fool but a child).

"LOVE THEM WHICH DESPITEFULLY USE YOU"

MASHA, *10, and* VANYA, *8.*

MASHA. I'm thinking: I wish Momma would come back now and take us with her, and we would first all go to the stores and then to Nastya's. What would you like?

VANYA. Me? I'd like the same as yesterday.

MASHA. And what was so special about yesterday? Having Grisha beat you up and both of you crying? Not much good about that.

VANYA. No, there was a lot of good. It was so good that nothing could be better. I'd really like that again.

MASHA. I don't understand.

VANYA. Now listen, I'll explain it to you. You remember last Sunday, Uncle P. I.... I like him very much...

MASHA. Who doesn't. Momma says he's a saint. And that's true.

VANYA. You remember last Sunday he told a story about a man who was wronged by everybody, and those who wronged him the most he loved the most. They scold him, and he praises them. They beat him, and he helps them. Uncle said that if someone does this, it would be very good for the one who did. I liked that and wanted to try it out. So when Grisha beat me up yesterday, I remembered this and began to kiss him, and he started crying. And I felt so happy. But I made a mistake yesterday with Nannie: she began to scold me and I forgot what you should do, and was rude to her. So now I want to try again as I did with Grisha.

MASHA. So you want somebody to beat you up?

VANYA. Yes, I'd like that very much. I'd do what I did with Grisha, and I'd feel happy right away.

MASHA. What nonsense! You was always stupid and still are.

VANYA. All right, I'm stupid, but now I know what to do to feel always happy.

MASHA. You awful dummy! Are you sure it makes you happy?

VANYA. Yes, very.

THE PRESS

A study room.

VOLODYA, *a high school boy, 14, is reading and preparing his lessons.*
SONYA, *15, is writing.*

HANDYMAN (*enters with a heavy load on his back, followed by* MISHA, *8*).
Where should I put this here stuff, sir. It's 'bout broken my back.
VOLODYA. Where did they tell you to put it?
HANDYMAN. Vasily Timofeyevich tol' me: Take it t'the classroom 'til he
gets there.
VOLODYA. Then put it here in the corner. (*Goes on reading.*)

(*The* HANDYMAN *puts down his load and sighs.*)

SONYA. What's that?
VOLODYA. It's a newspaper, *The Truth.*
MISHA. What do you mean the truth?
SONYA. How come so many?
VOLODYA. It's for a whole year. (*Continues reading.*)
MISHA. Somebody wrote all this?
HANDYMAN. Yuh could say they was workin', not shirkin'.
VOLODYA (*laughing*). What did you say?
HANDYMAN. Just that. I says they was workin', not shirkin'. Well, I'll be on
my way, please tell 'im I brung it. (*Exits.*)
SONYA (*to* VOLODYA). Why does Dad want all these papers?
VOLODYA. He wants to get Bolshakov's articles.
SONYA. But Uncle Mikhail Ivanovich says that Bolshakov makes him sick.
VOLODYA. Well, that's how it is for Uncle. He only reads *Truth for All.*
MISHA. Is Uncle's *Truth* as big as this one?
SONYA. Even bigger. This is only for one year, and they've been publish-
ing for twenty years or more.
MISHA. Twenty of those and twenty more.
SONYA (*wishing to impress* MISHA). That's nothing. That's only two news-
papers, and there are thirty or more published.

VOLODYA (*not raising his head*). Thirty? Five hundred and thirty in Russia alone, and thousands if you count those abroad.

MISHA. They won't fit in this room.

VOLODYA. In this room?! They won't fit in our street. But please, don't bother me. They're sure to call on me tomorrow, and here you are with your nonsense. (*Goes on reading.*)

MISHA. But I think they shouldn't write so much.

SONYA. Why not?

MISHA. Because if it's the truth, they shouldn't keep saying the same thing, but if it's not, they shouldn't lie.

SONYA. Nice idea!

MISHA. But why do they write so, so much?

VOLODYA (*not looking up*). Without freedom of the press, how would we know the truth?

MISHA. But Dad says the truth is in *The Truth,* but Uncle says *The Truth* makes him sick. So how can they know where the truth is, in *The Truth* or in *Truth*?

SONYA. That's right. I think there are too many newspapers, magazines and books.

VOLODYA. That's a woman for you! Always a scatterbrain.

SONYA. No, I'm only saying you can't know because there are too many of them.

VOLODYA. That's why everyone has their own mind, to judge where the truth is.

MISHA. If everyone has their own mind, they can judge on their own.

VOLODYA. There you've judged with your great mind, but now, please, go somewhere, don't bother me.

REGRET

VOLYA, *8, is standing in the corridor with an empty plate and crying.* FEDYA, *10, runs in and stops.*

FEDYA. Momma sent me to find you. Why are you crying? Did you take the cake to Nannie? (*Sees the empty plate and whistles.*) Where is it?

VOLYA. I... I... I wanted, I... and suddenly... oh, oh, oh. I ate it by accident.

FEDYA. You didn't take it to Nannie, you ate it? Pretty slick. And Momma thought you'd be happy to take it to Nannie.

VOLYA. I was glad... but suddenly... by accident... oh, oh, oh.

FEDYA. You tasted it and ate it all. Slick! (*Laughs.*)

VOLYA. Yeah, it's... all right for you... to laugh, but how am I going to tell... I can't go to Nannie and I can't go to Momma...

FEDYA. Well, Brother, you've really done it... ha, ha, ha. So you ate it all, eh? There's no use crying, you've got to think...

VOLYA. What can I think of? What am I going to do now?

FEDYA. What a mess! (*Tries not to laugh. Silence.*)

VOLYA. What am I going to do now? I've had it. (*Sobs.*)

FEDYA. There's nothing for you to be so upset about. Stop bawling. Just go and tell Momma that you ate it.

VOLYA. That would make it even worse.

FEDYA. Then own up to Nannie.

VOLYA. How can I?

FEDYA. Now listen: stay here, I'll run over to Nannie and tell her, she won't mind.

VOLYA. No, don't. How can I tell her?

FEDYA. That's nonsense! Well, you made a mistake, what's there to do? I'll go tell her. (*Runs off.*)

VOLYA. Fedya, Fedka, wait. He's gone. I just took a little taste, and then I don't remember how, but I did it. What am I going to do now? (*Sobs.*)

(FEDYA *comes running.*)

FEDYA. Stop bawling. I told you Nannie would forgive you. All she said was, "Oh, my little darling!"

VOLYA. She isn't mad?

FEDYA. Not at all. "Who cares about the cake, I would've given it to him anyway," [is what she said].

VOLYA. I didn't mean to do it. (*Cries again.*)

FEDYA. Well, what's the matter now? We won't tell Momma, and Nannie has forgiven you.

VOLYA. I know that Nannie has, she's good and kind. But how am I?... I'm naughty, very naughty. That's why I'm crying

ON ART

FOOTMAN *and* HOUSEKEEPER.

FOOTMAN (*with a tray*). Some almond milk for tea, an' some rum.

HOUSEKEEPER (*knitting a sock and counting the stitches*). Twenty-two, twenty-three...

FOOTMAN. Avdotya Vasilyevna, do yuh hear me? Hey, Avdotya Vasilyevna!

HOUSEKEEPER. I hear yuh, I hear yuh, just a minute. I only got two hands. (*To* NATASHA.) Just a minute, dear, I'll get some prunes for you too. Just lemme give 'im the milk. (*Strains the milk.*)

FOOTMAN (*sits down*). Well, I really got an eyeful. An' they even pay good money for it.

HOUSEKEEPER. So yuh've been t'the teater, have yuh? Why'd it take you so long today?

FOOTMAN. Opera's always long. Yuh just sit an' sit. It's a good thing they let me in. T'was strange.

(*The* BUTLER PAVEL *enters with the cream and stops to listen.*)

HOUSEKEEPER. Yuh mean the singin'?

FOOTMAN. What singin'! They just shout like crazy. Makes no sense at all. "I love her so very much," he says, an' hollers it at the top o' his voice— makes no sense at all. An' then they begun arguin', an' instead o' fightin', off they go singin' again.

HOUSEKEEPER. They say a suscription's expensive.

FOOTMAN. Three hundred roubles for our box for twelve pufformances.

PAVEL (*shaking his head*). Three hundred roubles! Who gets all that money?

FOOTMAN. The person that sings, of course. They say one woman singer gets fifty thousand a year.

PAVEL. Forget about thousands, even three hundred goes a long way in the village, that's a pile o' money. A man can knock 'imself out his whole life an' not make three hundred, not even a hundred.

([NINA], *a senior in high school, comes into the pantry.*)

NINA. Is Natasha here? Why did you disappear? Mama is looking for you.

NATASHA (*eating a prune*). I'm comin'.

NINA (*to the* BUTLER). What's that you were saying about a hundred roubles?

HOUSEKEEPER. Semyon here (*points to the* FOOTMAN) was tellin' 'bout the singin' he heard in the theater, an' how much the singers get paid, an' Pavel was suprised. Is it really true, Nina Mikhailovna, that a singer gets fifty thousand?

NINA. Even more. They invited one singer to America for one hundred fifty thousand. And that's not all. In yesterday's newspapers there was something about a musician who got twenty-five thousand for his finger nail.

PAVEL. They write all sorts of things. Can that really be?

NINA (*with obvious enjoyment*). I'm telling you the truth.

PAVEL. But why twenty-five thousand for a finger nail?

NATASHA. Yeah, why?

NINA. Because he plays the piano and is insured. So if anything happens to his hand and he can't play, they pay him.

PAVEL. That's a deal.

(*Enter* SENICHKA, *a senior in high school.*)

SENICHKA. Looks like you have a meeting here. What's it about?

(NINA *explains.*)

SENICHKA (*with even greater enjoyment*). A fingernail is nothing. In Paris a ballerina insured her legs for two hundred thousand in case she can't work because of a sprain.

FOOTMAN. That's for them, yuh'll excuse me, that work wid no drawers on their legs.

PAVEL. Yuh call that work—an' get paid for it yet!

SENICHKA. Not everyone can do it, you know, and it took her years to learn how.

PAVEL. What'd she learn? T'do good or t'twirl her legs?

SENICHKA. Well, you don't understand. Art is a great thing.

PAVEL. I think it's alotta nonsense. They pay a ton o' money cuz they've got nothin' else t'do. If they had t'break their backs for the money the way we do, there'd be none o' them there hoofers an' songstresses. They ain't worth a damn thing. So what's there t'say.

SENICHKA. That's what I call ignorance. For him Beethoven, Viardot,[8] and Raphael are all nonsense.

NATASHA. An' I think he's right.

NINA. Come on, let's go.

Two high school boys, the FIRST *from a school with a technical curriculum, the* SECOND *from a school with a classical curriculum, and a pair of twins,* VOLODYA *and* PETRUSHA, *8, brothers of the* SECOND *BOY.*

FIRST BOY. Why do I need Latin and Greek if everything that's good or important has already been translated into modern languages?

SECOND BOY. You will never understand the *Iliad* if you don't read it in Greek.

FIRST BOY. But I don't need to read it at all, and what's more I don't want to.

VOLODYA. What's *Iliad?*

FIRST BOY. It's a fairy tale.

SECOND BOY. Yes, but there isn't a better one in the world.

PETRUSHA. What's so good about it?

FIRST BOY. Oh, nothing, it's just a fairy tale.

SECOND BOY. Yes, only you will never really understand antiquity if you don't know these tales.

FIRST BOY. But in my opinion it's all superstition just like religion.

SECOND BOY (*angrily*). Religion is lies and falsehoods, but this is history and wisdom.

VOLODYA. Is religion really fibs?

SECOND BOY. What are you doing here anyway? You don't understand anything.

VOLODYA AND PETRUSHA (*offended*). Why don't we understand?

VOLODYA. Maybe we understand better than you.

SECOND BOY. All right, all right, only don't interfere in the conversation, sit still. (*To the* FIRST BOY.) You say that ancient languages are not applicable to life, but the same thing can be said about bacteriology, chemistry, physics, and astronomy. Why do you need to know the distances of the stars and their dimensions, and all these details which are completely useless to anyone?

FIRST BOY. Why useless? They're very useful.

SECOND BOY. For what?

FIRST BOY. For what? For everything. How about navigation?

SECOND BOY. You can do that without astronomy.

FIRST BOY. But their practical application to agriculture, medicine, industry...

SECOND BOY. But the same information is applied to making bombs, waging wars, and by revolutionaries. If this knowledge would make people live better...

FIRST BOY. And do people really live better from your science?

VOLODYA. What sciences make people live better?

SECOND BOY. I told you not to interfere in your elders' conversation. You keep on talking nonsense.

VOLODYA AND PETRUSHA (*in unison*). Nonsense or not, what sciences make people live better?

FIRST BOY. There aren't any. That you have to do by yourself.

SECOND BOY. What are you talking to them for? They don't understand a thing.

FIRST BOY. Yes, but let me explain. That, Volodya and Petrusha, is not taught in high schools.

VOLODYA. If that's not taught, what's the use in learning?

PETRUSHA. When we grow up, we're not going to learn useless things.

VOLODYA. We'll just live better by ourselves.

SECOND BOY (*laughing*). There's a couple of wise men for you, that's quite an idea.

CIVIL COURT

A PEASANT, *his* WIFE,[9] *his children's* GODMOTHER, FYODOR, *his son, 19, and* PETKA,[10] *another son, 9.*

PEASANT (*enters his cottage and takes off his coat*). It's real nasty outside, I barely made it home.

WIFE. T'ain't 'round the corner, reckon it's 'bout ten miles, no?

PEASANT. It's all o' fifteen. (*To his son* FYODOR.) Go take care o' the hoss.

WIFE. Well now, did the case come out aw right?

PEASANT. Like hell it did. There ain't no justice at all.

GODMOTHER. What's goin' on, Coz?[11] I don't get it.

PEASANT. The thing is that Averyan got hold o' my garden an' kept it, an' I can't find out what's what.

WIFE. We've had it in court now for over a year.

GODMOTHER. I know, I know. Yuh had it in the district court durin' Lent. My ol' man tol' me yuh won.

PEASANT. That's right, but Averyan took it t'the provincial court. An' the provincial court went an' sent the whole thing back. So I went t'the judge. An' the judge gave it back to me. That shoulda been the end of it, but no, they gave it t'him again. Some judges!

WIFE. So what do we do now?

PEASANT. Well he sure ain't gonna keep my property. I'll take it t'the sureme court. I've already talked t'an adtoney.

GODMOTHER. An' if he wins in the sureme court, what then?

PEASANT. I'll go still higher. I'd sooner lose my last cow 'fore I'd give in to that potbellied troublemaker. He'll remember me!

GODMOTHER. Oh, grief, nothin' but grief with these courts. An' if he wins there, what then?

PEASANT. I'll go t'the tsar. I gotta go give the hoss some hay. (*Exits.*)

PETKA. An' if the tsar says no, who can he go to then?

WIFE. There's nobody afta the tsar.

PETKA. How come some judges gave it t'Averyan, an' some t'Daddy?

WIFE. Must be cuz they don't know themselves.

PETKA. Then why ask 'em if they don't know?

WIFE. Cuz nobody wants t'give up what's his own.

PETKA. When I grow up, this is what I'll do: if I argue with somebody 'bout somethin', we'll toss for it. Whoever wins—wins, an' that's the end of it. Me an' Akulka always do it that way.

GODMOTHER. Whacha say t'that, Coz? Makes more sense that way, really. There ain't no harm in it.

WIFE. Sure enough. We've already spent more 'en the garden's worth. Oh, 'tain't right, 'tain't right!

The children: GRISHKA, *12,* SYOMKA, *10, and* TISHKA, *13.*[12]

TISHKA. Cuz yuh don't go sneakin' into another man's grain bin. They'll toss yuh in jail, then maybe yuh'll get wise.

SYOMKA. Well that's aw right if yuh done it, but Gran'pa Mikita[13] says Mitrofan's in jail for nothin'.

TISHKA. Whacha mean for nothin'? Won't they do somethin' to the guy who sent 'im there for nix?

GRISHKA. They won't 'xactly pat 'im on the head. If he goes 'gainst the law, they'll punish him too.

SYOMKA. Who'll punish 'im?

TISHKA. Them that's higher up.

SYOMKA. Who's higher up?

GRISHKA. The big shots.

SYOMKA. An' if the big shots make a mistake?

GRISHKA. Them that's still higher up. An' they can get punished too. That's what the tsar's for.

SYOMKA. An' if the tsar makes a mistake, who'll punish him?

GRISHKA. Who'll punish 'im, who'll punish 'im? Naturally...

TISHKA. God will.

SYOMKA. Then God'll also punish the guy who stole the cow. So let God alone punish everyone who's done wrong. God won't make a mistake.

GRISHKA. No, that won't work.

SYOMKA. Why not?

GRISHKA. Cuz...

PROPERTY

An OLD CARPENTER *is repairing the rail on a balcony. A seven-year-old* BOY, *the son of the landowner, is watching and admiring the* CARPENTER's *work.*

BOY. What nice work you do. What's your name?

OLD CARPENTER. My name? They used t'call me Khrolka, nowadays I'm Khrol, an' even Mr. Khrol Savich.

BOY. What nice work you do, Mr. Khrol Savich.

OLD CARPENTER. Work's gotta be done nice. Why do bad work?

BOY. Do you have a balcony in your house?

OLD CARPENTER. Us? We, little guy, got a balcony that puts yers t'shame. Our balcony got no rail, not even a nail, step in an' off yuh sail. That's the kinda balcony we got.

BOY. You're just joking. No, really, do you have a balcony? I'm serious.

OLD CARPENTER. Eh, little guy, little guy, a balcony! What kinda balcony can folks like us have! We're lucky t'have a roof over our heads—a balcony! I started on my roof this past spring. Tore off the ol' one, but still ain't got the new one on. An' now the house's rotting widout a roof.

BOY (*surprised*). Why?

OLD CARPENTER. Cuz I haven't the strength t', that's why.

BOY. But why don't you have any strength? Here you're working for us.

OLD CARPENTER. Yes I'm workin' for you, but can't for myself.

BOY. Why not? I don't understand that, explain it to me.

OLD CARPENTER. When yuh grow up, kid, yuh'll understand. I can work for you, but can't for myself.

BOY. Why?

OLD CARPENTER. Cuz I need lumber, got none—gotta buy it, but got nothin' t'buy it with. So I do some work for you, an' your momma pays me. Tell 'er t'pay me a bit more, an' I'll go t'the grove an' buy me half dozen poplars for rafters, then I can finish the roof.

BOY. But don't you have a forest of your own?

OLD CARPENTER. Oh, yeah, forests yuh can walk in for three days an' never come to the end. The only trouble is they ain't ours.

BOY. But Momma says that our forest causes her more trouble than anything else; she has nothing but troubles from the forest.

OLD CARPENTER. That's just the problem. Yer momma got troubles cuz she's got too much forest, an' I got troubles cuz I ain't got none at all. Well, enough talkin' with yuh, here I've stopped workin' and they won't say thanks t'us for that. (*Goes back to work.*)

BOY. When I grow up, I'll make sure that I have the same as everyone else—everything will be equal among all.

OLD CARPENTER. Grow up quick, I'd like t'be aroun'. Look here, don't forget. Now what did I do with my plane?

CHILDREN

A LADY *with her children, a* HIGH SCHOOL BOY, *14, and* TANICHKA, *5, are walking in their garden. An* OLD PEASANT WOMAN *comes up to them.*

LADY. What is it, Matryona?

OLD WOMAN. I've come t'Yer Ladyship.

LADY. About what?

OLD WOMAN. Ah, Yer Ladyship-Ma'am, I'm ashamed t'say it, but what can yuh do. Yer godchildren's momma had another baby. God's given 'er a girl. She sent to t'ask yuh if yuh wouldn't mind standin' up at baptism with this one too.

LADY. She had a baby not so long ago, didn't she?

OLD WOMAN. Don't know if I'd say that. 'Twas a year ago last Lent.

LADY. How many grandchildren do you have now?

OLD WOMAN. There's no countin' 'em, Ma'am. I'd give half o' them away. One smaller'n the next. It's terrible.

LADY. How many does your daughter have?

OLD WOMAN. This one's the seventh, Yer Ladyship-Ma'am, an' all alive. If God'd only take some away.

LADY. What are you saying? How can you talk like that?

OLD WOMAN. Well what can yuh do? I'll be damned, yuh just can't help sinnin'. But we're really strapped. What about it, Ma'am, take pity on us, christen the baby. Honest t'God, Yer Ladyship, we can't even buy enough bread t'go aroun', let alone pay the priest. They're all little squirts. My son-in-law's away workin'. So it's just me an' my daughter. I'm old, an' she's either pregnant or nursin'. What kinda work can yuh get outta her? I hafta do it all. An' this gang keeps on askin' for food.

LADY. Are there really seven of them?

OLD WOMAN. Cross my heart, seven. The oldest girl's just beginnin' t'help, but the rest are all little squirts.

LADY. But why does she have so many?

OLD WOMAN. What can yuh do, Yer Ladyship-Ma'am? He comes home on a visit or a holiday. They're young. An' he lives in town, nearby. If only he was a long way off.

LADY. Yes, some complain that they have no children or that they die, but you complain that you have too many.

OLD WOMAN. Too many's right. More 'an we can handle. What about it, Yer Ladyship-Ma'am, can she count on it?

LADY. All right. I've christened the others, and I'll christen this one too. Is it a boy?

OLD WOMAN. A little guy, but a scrappy one, never stops bawlin'...[14] When can you do it?

LADY. Whenever you wish.

(*The* OLD WOMAN *says thanks and exits.*)

TANICHKA. Mama, how come some people have children and others don't? You have, and Matryona has, but Parasha doesn't.

LADY. Parasha isn't married. Children are born when people get married. They get married, become husband and wife, then children come.

TANICHKA. Always?

LADY. No, not always. Our cook has a wife, but they have no children.

TANICHKA. Can't it be done so that a person who wants children would have them, and the one who doesn't, wouldn't have any?

HIGH SCHOOL BOY. What a dumb question.

TANICHKA. No it isn't. I was thinking that if Matryona's daughter doesn't want more children, it could be arranged so that she doesn't have any. Mama, can it be?

HIGH SCHOOL BOY. I'm telling you, you're talking nonsense about things you don't understand.

TANICHKA. Mama, can it be arranged?

LADY. How shall I put it? We don't know that. That depends on God.

TANICHKA. Where do children come from?

HIGH SCHOOL BOY. From a goat. (*Laughs.*)

TANICHKA (*hurt*). It's not funny. I think that if Matryona says it's hard for them because of the children, it should be arranged so that they won't have any. There's our nannie, she doesn't have children and never had any.

LADY. She's not married, she doesn't have a husband.

TANICHKA. Then everyone who doesn't like children should be like that.

It's wrong to have children and have no food for them. (*Mother and son exchange glances and are silent.*) When I grow up, I'll definitely get married and I'll arrange to have a girl and a boy, and no more than that. It's not right to have children and not love them. I'll love mine very, very much. Isn't that true, Mama? I'll go to Nannie and ask her.

LADY (*to her son*). Yes, as they say: out of the mouth of babes... comes the truth. What she says is absolutely true. If people understood that marriage is a serious matter and not a fling, that they should marry not for their own sake but for the children's, there wouldn't be such horrors as rejected, abandoned children, nor would there be, as is the case with Matryona's daughter, children who were not a joy but sorrow.

A HANDYMAN *is cleaning the door locks,* KATYA, *7, is playing with building blocks,* NIKOLAI [NIKOLINKA], *15, a high school boy, enters and tosses his book.*

NIKOLAI. They can go to hell with their damn school.

HANDYMAN. What's wrong?

NIKOLAI. I flunked again. There's going to be another to-do. Damn them! A lot of use I got for that damned geography. Them there Californias. Why the hell know that!

HANDYMAN. What'll they do t'yuh?

NIKOLAI. I'll be left back again.

HANDYMAN. So why don't yuh study?

NIKOLAI. Why? Because I can't study baloney. Ah, the hell with it all. (*Throws himself into a chair.*) I'll go tell Momma. I can't, and that's that. Let them do what they want, but I can't. And if she won't take me out of high school, I'll leave. I swear I will.

HANDYMAN. Where are yuh leavin' to?

NIKOLAI. Away from home. I'll hire myself out as a coachman or handyman, anything's better than that damn baloney.

HANDYMAN. It's also hard bein' a handyman, yuh know. Gotta get up early, chop wood, carry it, get the heat goin'.

NIKOLAI. Whew. (*Whistles.*) That's a vacation. Chopping wood—I like doing that. What's so surprising? It's my favorite thing. No, you just try studying geography.

HANDYMAN. Sure enough. Why d'ya need it? Do they make yuh?

NIKOLAI. Yeah, and you go ask them why. For nothing. That's how it is. They think you can't do without it.

HANDYMAN. So's yuh can go into the service later, get rank an' a salary, just like yer dad, or uncle.

NIKOLAI. But what if I don't want to.

KATYA. Yes, what if he doesn't want to?

(*Enter* MOTHER *with a note in her hand.*)

MOTHER. The principal writes here that you got an F again. That can't go on, Nikolinka. It's has to be one of two things. You either study or you don't.

NIKOLAI. Of course it's one thing: I can't, I can't and I can't. For God's sake, let me quit. I can't study.

MOTHER. Why can't you?

NIKOLAI. I just can't, it doesn't go into my head.

MOTHER. It doesn't go because you're thinking about other things. You have nothing but nonsense in your head. Stop thinking about nonsense, think about your lessons.

NIKOLAI. Momma, I'm serious. Let me quit. I don't want anything, just free me from this horrible studying, this drudgery. I can't.

MOTHER. Then what will you do?

NIKOLAI. That's my business.

MOTHER. No, it's not your business, but mine. I'll have to answer to God for you, I must educate you.

NIKOLAI. But what if I can't?

MOTHER (sternly). What nonsense: "I can't." I'm telling you for the last time, as your mother. I'm asking you to change and to do what is requested of you. If you will not obey me now, I will have to take other measures.

NIKOLAI. I told you I can't and I won't.

MOTHER. Nikolai, be careful.

NIKOLAI. I don't have to be careful. Why are you tormenting me? You don't understand this.

MOTHER. Don't you dare speak to me like that. How dare you! Leave the room! Watch out!

NIKOLAI. I'm going. I'm not afraid of anything. I don't want a thing from you. (Runs out, slamming the door.)

MOTHER (to herself). Ah, he's worn me out. I know where all this comes from. It's all because he's not thinking about what he should, but about this nonsense of his—about dogs and chickens.

KATYA. But Momma, remember, you told me yourself that one can't help thinking about the polar bear.

MOTHER. I'm not talking about that, I'm saying that you have to study when you're told to.

KATYA. But he says he can't.

MOTHER. He's talking nonsense.

KATYA. But he's not saying that he doesn't want to do anything, he just doesn't want to study geography. He wants to work, to be a coachman or a handyman.

MOTHER. If he were a handyman's son, he could be a handyman, but he is your father's son and he has to study.

KATYA. But he doesn't want to.

MOTHER. It doesn't matter what he wants or doesn't want, he has to obey.

KATYA. But if he can't?

MOTHER. Mind that you don't do the same thing.

KATYA. But that's exactly what I want to do. There's no way I'll study something I don't want to.

MOTHER. And you'll be a fool.

KATYA. When I grow up and have children, I'll never force them to study. If they want to, they can, if not, they don't have to.

MOTHER. You won't do that when you grow up.

KATYA. Yes, I certainly will.

MOTHER. No you won't, when you grow up.

KATYA. Yes I will, I will, I will.

MOTHER. Then you'll be a fool.

KATYA. Nannie says that God needs fools too.

The Traveler and the Peasant

1909

A peasant cottage. An old TRAVELER *sits on a bench and reads. Return-ing from work the* PEASANT *sits down to supper and offers some to the* TRAVELER. *He refuses. The* PEASANT *eats his supper. Having finished, he gets up, prays, and sits down next to the old* TRAVELER.

PEASANT. So what brings yuh here?..

TRAVELER (*takes off his eyeglasses and puts his book down*). There's no train till tomorrow. The station's real crowded. I asked your wife if I could spend the night here, an' she said it's all right.

PEASANT. That's fine, stay.

TRAVELER. Thanks. So how's life these days?

PEASANT. How's our life? Worse'n ever!

TRAVELER. Why's that?

PEASANT. Cuz there's nothin' for us t'live on. That's how our life is. It couldn't get worse even if we tried. I've got nine hungry mouths t'feed an' harvested five bushels, go 'head an' live on that. Like it or not, yuh gotta hire yuhself out. An' when yuh do, the wages are down. The rich just do whatever they want t'us. There's a lotta peasants, little land, an' more an' more taxes. Then yuh have rent, the local government, the land, an' bridges, insurance, the police, the army—there's no countin' 'em all—an' priests an' landowners. Everybody's squeezin' us, only the ones too lazy t'squeeze us don't.

TRAVELER. But I thought the peasants have a good life these days.

PEASANT. Yeah, they don't eat for days, that's how good.

TRAVELER. I thought so because they're really throwing money around.

PEASANT. What money? Yuh're talkin like a nut. Folks are dyin' o' hunger, an' he says they're throwin' money aroun'.

TRAVELER. Well according to the papers, last year peasants drank up seven hundred million—and a million, you know, is a thousand thousand roubles—so seven hundred million roubles worth of liquor.

PEASANT. As if we're the only ones who drink? Look how the priests slug it down, like it's goin' outta style, an' the landowners ain't no slouches either.

TRAVELER. That's only a small amount, it's mostly the peasants.

PEASANT. So what, can't we even drink liquor now?

TRAVELER. No, I'm just saying if they can just throw away like nothing seven hundred million a year on liquor, it means they're not doing so bad after all. That's no laughing matter—seven hundred million—can't even imagine it.

PEASANT. Now how can we do widout it? We didn't dream up drinkin', an' we won't be the ones t'stop it; there's church holidays, an' weddins, an' funerals, an' when yuh treat—like it or not, yuh can't do widout it. That's how it is.

TRAVELER. There are people that don't drink, and they live all right. There's no good in liquor.

PEASANT. What's the good if it's bad!

TRAVELER. Then you shouldn't drink it.

PEASANT. Drink, don't drink, there's nothin' t'live on anyways. There's no land. If there was land, we'd be able t'live, but there ain't none.

TRAVELER. What do you mean no land? Wherever you look, there's land all around.

PEASANT. There's land aw right, but it ain't ours! It's close by but outta reach.

TRAVELER. Not yours? Then whose?

PEASANT. Whose? You know whose. The potbellied bastard's. He grabbed seventeen hundred acres for 'imself, an' it's still ain't enough for 'im; an' we're about t'stop keepin' chickens—no place t'let 'em out. We'll have t'get rid o' the cattle soon. There's no feed. An' if a calf or a hoss gets into his field—yuh pay a penalry. Yuh hafta sell what's left an' give it t'him.

TRAVELER. What does he need so much land for?

PEASANT. What does he need land for? You know what for: to sow, harvest, sell an' put money in the bank.

TRAVELER. How can he plow an' harvest such a spread?

PEASANT. You're just like a newborn babe. He's got the money, he can hire hands, an' they do the plowin' an' harvestin'.

TRAVELER. The hands are probably all you folks, right?

PEASANT. Some are, some are from other places.

TRAVELER. But they're all peasants, right?

PEASANT. Sure enough. Who else works but the peasant? Sure they're all peasants.

TRAVELER. And what if the peasants didn't go to work for him...

PEASANT. Work for 'im or not, he won't give it t'yuh anyways. Even if the land lies fallow, give it t'yuh he won't. Like a dog in a manger: it don't eat an' don't let others.

TRAVELER. But how can he keep an eye on his land? It probably runs over three miles, right? Where does he get the time to watch it?

PEASANT. Yuh're talkin' like a nut. He's got guards for that. He just loafs aroun' an' grows a potbelly.

TRAVELER. Look here, are you folks also the guards?

PEASANT. An' who else, sure we are.

TRAVELER. So the peasants work the land for the lords, and what's more they guard it against themselves?

PEASANT. What's there t'do?

TRAVELER. Don't go to work for him, that's what, and don't hire out as guards. The land would be free then. It's God's land and God's people, whoever needs to, go plough, sow, harvest.

PEASANT. Yuh mean, strike? They've got soldiers for that, my friend. They'll send soldiers in—ready, aim, fire—some'll be shot, an' some hauled off. There's no words wasted with soldiers.

TRAVELER. But you folks are also the soldiers, right? Why would they shoot their own people?

PEASANT. Sure they will, that's the oath.

TRAVELER. The oath? What about the oath?

PEASANT. Ain't you a Russian? The oath's the oath, an' that's that.

TRAVELER. You mean, they swear?

PEASANT. You bet. They swear by the cross an' the Gospel t'lay down their life for tsar an' country.

TRAVELER. But to my mind they shouldn't do this.

PEASANT. Shouldn't do what?

TRAVELER. Swear.

PEASANT. Whacha mean shouldn't when it's the law?

TRAVELER. No, it's not the law. Christ's law absolutely forbids this: "Swear not at all," He says.

PEASANT. Is that so? Then what about the priests?

TRAVELER (*takes his book, opens it, looks for the passage, and reads*). "But I say unto you, Swear not at all. But let your communication be, Yea, yea;

Nay, nay: for whatsoever is more than these cometh of evil" (Matthew 5:34 and 37). It means that according to Christ's law it's forbidden to swear.

PEASANT. If they don't swear, there won't be any soldiers.

TRAVELER. And why do you need them soldiers anyway?

PEASANT. Whacha mean why? An' what if some other tsars attack our tsar, what then?

TRAVELER. If the tsars themselves fight, let them sort it out themself.

PEASANT. Come now! How can that be?

TRAVELER. It's as simple as this: whoever believes in God won't kill anyone no matter what you tell him.

PEASANT. Then why did the priest read a decree in church that war's been declared and reservists must muster?

TRAVELER. I don't know about that, but I do know that the sixth commandment plainly says: "Thou shalt not kill." That means it's forbidden for a man to kill another man.

PEASANT. That's at home, yuh know. But how can yuh help it in war? They're enemies, yuh know.

TRAVELER. According to Christ's Gospel there are no enemies, you have to love everyone. (*Opens the Gospel and looks for the passage.*)

PEASANT. Well go on, read some more.

TRAVELER (*reads*). "Ye have heard that it was said by them of old time, Thou shalt not kill; and whosoever shall kill shall be in danger of the judgment: But I say unto you, That whosoever is angry with his brother shall be in danger of the judgment." Furthermore it says: "Ye have heard that it hath been said, Thou shalt love thy neighbor, and hate thine enemy. But I say unto you, Love your enemies, bless them that curse you, do good to them that hate you, and pray for them which despitefully use you, and persecute you" (Matthew 5:43–44).[1]

(*A prolonged silence.*)

PEASANT. So what about taxes? Don't pay 'em either?

TRAVELER. That's up to you. If you're children are hungry, naturally you feed them first.

PEASANT. So I mean, yuh don't need soldiers, do yuh?

TRAVELER. What the hell for? They're taking millions and millions from you folks—it's no joke to feed and dress such a horde. They're about a million of them spongers, and they're only good for not letting you have land and shooting you.

PEASANT (*sighs and shakes his head*). That may be true, but... If only we all do it together. But just have one or two do it, they'll shoot 'em or send 'em off to Siberia, an' that's all there'll be to it.

TRAVELER. Still, there are people even now, young guys, who, by themselves, stand up for God's law and don't go into the military: "I can't," they say, "become a killer, it's against Christ's law. Do whatever you want, but I won't pick up a gun."

PEASANT. So what then?

TRAVELER. They put them in prison and they do time, poor guys, three, four years. But I hear tell they have it pretty good there because the authorities are also human, they respect them. And they even let some guys go: "He's not fit for service, his health's bad," they say. But the guy's as big as a house, and he's unfit because they're afraid to take such a guy, he'll tell the others that the military's against God's law. And they let him go.

PEASANT. Is that so?

TRAVELER. Sometimes they let them go, and sometimes they die there. But they also die while in the military, what's more they can get crippled—lose a leg, an arm...

PEASANT. You sure are an ol' fox. That would be nice, but that's not how things'll work out.

TRAVELER. Why not?

PEASANT. Because...

TRAVELER. Because what?

PEASANT. Because the authorities were given the power.

TRAVELER. But you see, the authorities have power only because you obey them. Don't obey them, and they won't have power.

PEASANT (*shaking his head*). Yuh're talkin' like a nut. How can yuh get on without authorities? Yuh just can't without 'em.

TRAVELER. Naturally you can't. But whom are you going to consider the authority, a policeman or God? Whom do you want to obey, a policeman or God?

PEASANT. There's no doubt about that. No one's greater than God. The first thing is t'live in a godly way.

TRAVELER. And if you live in a godly way, you have to obey God and not people. And when you live in a godly way, you won't drive folks away from another's land, you won't become deputies and bailiffs, or collect taxes, you won't work as guards and policemen, and, above all, you won't go into the military and pledge to kill people.

PEASANT. So what about those mop-headed priests? They know it's 'gainst the law, so why don't they teach properly?

TRAVELER. I don't know about that. They hold their ground, and you hold yours.

PEASANT. Them mop-headed bastards.

TRAVELER. There's no need for that: why curse others. Everyone has to keep himself in mind.

PEASANT. You bet.

(*A prolonged silence. The* PEASANT *shakes his head and grins.*)

PEASANT. So, I mean, yuh're sayin' if all of us together just give it a go as one, a real push, I mean, then the land'll be ours, and there'll be no taxes?

TRAVELER. No, my friend, that's not what I'm saying. I'm not saying that if we live in a godly way, the land'll be ours and we won't pay taxes. I'm saying our life's bad only because we ourselves live badly. If we would live in a godly way, there'd be no bad life. What our life would be like if we lived in a godly way—God alone knows, but one thing's certain, there'd be no bad life. We drink, we curse each other, we fight, we sue each other, we're envious, we're hateful, we don't accept God's law, we criticize people: now potbellied, now mop-headed; but just wave some money at us, and we're ready to do anything: be guards, be policemen, be soldiers, and we're ready to ruin, oppress, and kill our own brother. We ourselves live in a hellish way, and we complain about others.

PEASANT. That's true. But it's hard, real hard! Sometimes yuh just can't take it no more.

TRAVELER. You have to, for the sake of your soul.

PEASANT. You bet! We live badly cuz we've forgotten 'bout God.

TRAVELER. That's the trouble. That's why life's so bad. Look at those strikers who say: "Let's kill these here masters and these here potbellied rich men—it's all their fault—and our life will be good." They killed them before and are killing them now, but not a bit of good has come of it. It's the same with the authorities: "Just give us time," they say, "we'll hang and starve a thousand or two of these people in prisons, then life will be good." And look, life's just getting worse.

PEASANT. You bet. Yuh can't do it the wrong way, yuh hafta do it accordin' to the law.

TRAVELER. That's the point. It's one of two things: either you serve God or the Devil. If you want to serve the Devil—drink, curse, fight, hate, be greedy, don't obey God's law but man's—and life'll be bad; but if you want to serve God—obey God alone: not only don't steal or kill, but don't criticize, don't hate, don't get involved in crooked dealings, and there'll be no bad life.

PEASANT (*sighs*). Well said, old-timer, mighty well, but we don't listen much. An, it'd be different if only they taught us like that more. As it is, they come from town, an' also have their say 'bout how t'set things straight; there's lots o' fast talk, but nothin t'listen to. Thank you, old-timer. Them are good words. So, where'll yuh sleep? How 'bout on the stove? The wife'll get beddin'.

October 12, 1909

Untitled Fragment

1910

The front of a house, a large terrace. Two FOOTMEN, *the older,* SEMYON PETROVICH, *and the younger,* MIKHAILA *[*MISHA*], are setting a large dinner table for ten. Two peasant girls are weeding the flower beds. Enter from around the corner of the house an* OLD PEASANT *wearing a long coat, tightly laced leg wrappings, and bast shoes. He takes off his hat, and, not seeing any of the masters, puts it on again.*

OLD PEASANT (*addressing* MIKHAILA). Howdy, Misha. (*To* SEMYON PETROVICH.) Greetings, Semyon Petrovich, how yuh doin'.

SEMYON PETROVICH. Howdy, howdy. (*Busily lays out the napkins.*)

MIKHAILA (*to* SEMYON PETROVICH). Please take over, Semyon Petrovich. I'll be right back, right back. Looks like Dad's got business with me.

SEMYON PETROVICH. Okay, okay. Yer important business! We know. Just remember, we've got ten place settings today. A general's wife an' 'er children. Go on, go, what's there t'do with yuh.

(MIKHAILA *and his father move on to the proscenium.*)

OLD PEASANT. What a thing, Sonny! The gelding's all done for. Dropped in his tracks. First thing this mornin' went up on the headland, an' never finished ploughin' even that one strip o' land. There's no gettin' 'round buyin'. Tomorrow I'd like t'go with the ol' lady t'the fair. There's no gettin' 'round buyin'. Take at least a couple o' tenners.

MIKHAILA. Oh, he don't like that.

OLD PEASANT. Whacha gonna do. Like it or not, gotta have the money.

MIKHAILA. I'll work it out somehow. They have guests today, no time for it. Well, take a walk here somewhere. I'll get to 'im right after dinner. So, how's Marya?

OLD PEASANT. How's yer Marya, she's still expectin'. Yesterday we thought God [illegible]. Akulka even ran t'get the midwife.

(*Enter from the garden two* YOUNG LADIES *and a* YOUNG MAN. *The* OLD PEASANT *walks behind a bush.* MIKHAILA *goes to the table.*)

The Cause of It All

1910

Akulina

an old woman, 70, still spry, staid, old fashioned

Mikhaila [Tikhonych]

her son, 35, passionate, egotistical, vain, strong

Marfa

her daughter-in-law, 32, querulous, talks fast and a lot

Parashka

10, the daughter of Marfa and Mikhaila

Taras

the village policeman, 50, staid, self-important, speaks slowly

Tramp

40, fidgety, thin, speaks in a lofty manner. He is particularly free and easy when drunk

Ignat [Ivanych/Ageich]

40, a joker, happy, stupid

Neighbor

40, fussy

ACT I

Fall. A peasant cottage with a storeroom.

SCENE 1

AKULINA *is spinning,* MARFA *is kneading bread, and* PARASHKA *is rocking a cradle.*

MARFA. Oh, I've got a bad feelin'. What's takin' 'im so long? It's like t'other day when he took wood t'town. Drank 'bout half the money away. An' everything's my fault.

AKULINA. Why think o' bad things. It's still early, an' town ain't 'round the corner, yuh know. So far...

MARFA. Who says early. Akimych's back awready. He left afta our man, an' ours ain't back yet. Yuh struggle an' struggle, an' that's all the pleasure yuh get.

AKULINA. Akimych just delivered his goods, but ours gotta sell his.

MARFA. I wouldn't worry if he was alone, but Ignat's wid 'im. An' when he gets together wid that blubber-headed mutt, Lord forgive me, no good'll come of it. They're sure t'get drunk. Yuh just work away, work away all the livelong day. Yuh gotta do everythin'. If only somethin' good'd come along. But no, knock yuhself out from mornin' till night, that's all the pleasure yuh get.

SCENE 2

The door opens. Enter TARAS *and a ragged* TRAMP.

TARAS. How yuh doin'? I've brought yuh a lodger.

TRAMP (*bowing*). My respects to you.

MARFA. Yuh put 'em up at our place too often. One stayed wid us Wednesday. Yuh keep on bringin' 'em t'us. Put 'em up at Stepanida's. They don't even have kids. I can't handle my own kin, and yuh keep on bringin' 'em t'us.

TARAS. It's yer turn.

MARFA. My turn, yuh say. I got kids, an' my mister ain't home.

TARAS. He'll stay the night. He won't wear a hole in the bed.

AKULINA (*to the* TRAMP). Come on in, have a seat, make yuhself at home.

TRAMP. I offer my gratitude. I'd like a bite to eat, if possible.

MARFA. He didn't even look aroun' yet an' he's awready askin' for food. Didn't yuh ask aroun' the village?

TRAMP (*sighs*). I'm not used to doing that because of my position. Since I don't have any prodeuce of my own...

AKULINA (*rises, gets a loaf of bread, cuts off a piece, and gives it to the* TRAMP).

TRAMP (*taking the bread*). Merci. (*Sits on the bench and eats greedily.*)

TARAS. So where's Mikhaila?

MARFA. In town. Took a load o' hay there. It's time he was back, but he's not. I keep wonderin' if somethin' didn't happened to 'im.

TARAS. What could happen?

MARFA. Whacha mean what? Nothin' good an' a lotta bad. Soon's he's outta the house he don't give a damn. I'm just waitin' for him t'come back drunk.

AKULINA (*sits down at the spinning wheel. To* TARAS *and pointing at* MARFA). She just can't keep her mouth shut. I've always said, us women fret about everythin'.

MARFA. I wouldn't worry if he was alone, but Ignat's wid 'im.

TARAS (*smirking*). Now when it comes t'drinkin', Ignat Ivanych's more than willin'.

AKULINA. Why should he look at Ignat, huh? Ignat's one thing an' he's another.

MARFA. That's easy for you t'say, Ma. I've had it up t'here wid his drinkin'. (*Indicating her throat.*) When he's sober, he ain't a bad guy, but when he's drunk, you know what he's like. Yuh can't say a word. Everythin's wrong.

TARAS. You women are no bargain either. A man gets drunk. So what, let 'im have a bita fun; he'll sleep it off, an' everythin'll be awright again. But you women just hafta be contrary.

MARFA. Whatever I do he don't like when he's drunk.

TARAS. But yuh hafta understand things, yuh know. We men just can't help havin' a drink sometimes. Yer woman's business is at home, but us men hafta drink either out on business or wid friends. So we drink, there's no harm in it.

MARFA. That's easy for you t'say, but it's hard on us women. Real hard. If only you men had t'do our work for just a week. Yuh'd change yer tune. Go knead, an' bake, an' cook, an' spin, an' weave, an' take care o' the livestock, an' do everythin' else, an' bathe, dress an' feed a bunch o' bare-assed kids. It all falls on us women, an' if somethin' ain't just so, look out, 'specially when he's drunk. Oh, the life we women have...

TRAMP (*chewing*). That's right. It's the cause of it all, I mean all of life's cutastrophes come from liquor.

TARAS. Looks like it got t'you too.

TRAMP. Maybe it did and maybe not, but I've suffered from that too—my life's cureer could've been completely different if not for it.

TARAS. Now to my way of thinkin', if yuh drink with yer head there ain't no harm in it at all.

TRAMP. But I say it has such a power of anergy in it that it can completely ruin a man.

MARFA. That's what I'm sayin': yuh hustle an' do yer best, an' the only comfort yuh get is bein' cussed an' beaten like a dog.

TRAMP. And that's not all. There are people, subjects I mean, who go completely out of their mind because of liquor, and produce entirely inappropriate acts. When he doesn't drink, he won't take anything that doesn't belong to him even if you hand it to him; but when he's drunk, he'll steal whatever he can get hold of. And the beatings, the time in prison! When I don't drink, I'm honest and decent, but when I drink, I mean, when that subject drinks, he just steals whatever he can get his hands on.

AKULINA. An' I think it's all inside yuh.

TRAMP. Yes it is, it is, if you are well, but this is a kind of disease.

TARAS. Some disease! A good thrashin' would take care of that disease real quick. Well, I'll see yuh. (*Exits.*)

(MARFA *wipes her hands and is about to leave.*)

AKULINA (*looks at the* TRAMP *and sees that he has finished his bread*). Marfa, hey, Marfa. Give 'im some more bread.

MARFA. Forget 'im. I'm gonna check the samovar. (*Exits.*)

(AKULINA *rises, goes to the table, takes out the bread, cuts a slice, and gives it to the* TRAMP.)

TRAMP. Merci. I've awakened a real good appetite.

AKULINA. Are yuh a tradesman?

TRAMP. Me? I was a machinist.

AKULINA. Did'ya make much?

TRAMP. Got fifty, and even seventy.

AKULINA. That's quite a bit. So how come yuh went wrong?

TRAMP. Went wrong? I'm not the only one. I went wrong because these days an honest man just can't make it.

MARFA (*brings in the samovar*). Oh Lord, still not back. He's sure t'come home drunk. I can feel it.

AKULINA. He went on a binge, didn't he?

MARFA. That's the whole trouble. Yuh hafta knock yuhself out alone, knead, an' bake, an' cook, an' spin, an' weave, and take care o' the livestock, everythin' falls on me. (*The baby in the cradle screams.*) Parashka, rock the little guy. Oh, the life we women have. An' when he's drunk, nothin's right. Just say one word he don't like...

AKULINA (*making tea*). An' that's the last o' the tea. Did'ya ask 'im t'bring some?

MARFA. Sure did. He was gonna. Will he? Does he think 'bout his home? (*Puts the samovar on the table.*)

(*The* TRAMP *moves away from the table.*)

AKULINA. Why'd yuh leave the table? We're gonna have tea.

TRAMP. I offer my gratitude for your hospitable cordiality. (*Throws away his hand-rolled cigarette and comes to the table.*)

MARFA. What are yuh? You a peasant or somethin' else?

TRAMP. I, Missus, am neither a peasant nor a nobleman. I'm from the double-edged class.

MARFA. Whacha mean by that? (*Gives him a cup.*)

TRAMP. Merci. I mean my father was a Polish count, and besides him I had many more, and I also had two mothers. All in all my biography is troublesome.

MARFA. Have some more tea. Did'ya get apprenticed?

TRAMP. My apprenticeship was also superficial. My godmother, not my mother, turned me over to a smithy. So a blacksmith was my first petagog. And his petagogy amounted to this: that same blacksmith would pound me to such an extent that he wouldn't pound on his anvil as much as on my poor head. Nevertheless, however much he pounded me, he couldn't deprive me of my talents. Then I went to a locksmith. And there I was appreciated and learned the trade—I became a master locksmith. I made the acquaintance of educated people, and was a member of a faction. I was able to master the intellectual verbal arts. And my life could have been elevated since I possessed anormous talents.

AKULINA. Sure enough.

TRAMP. And then disaster struck—the despotic oppression of the life of the people, and I got into prison, I mean into the incarceration of my freedom.

MARFA. What for?

TRAMP. For rights.

MARFA. What rights?

TRAMP. What rights? Rights to keep the burzhwas from endlessly loafing, and for the toiling proletariat to receive a reward for his labor.

AKULINA. Yuh mean 'bout the land also?

TRAMP. You bet. It's in the agramonic question as well.

AKULINA. May the Lord an' the Queen o' Heaven grant it. We hardly have any land at all. Well, what now?

TRAMP. Now? Now I'm heading for Moscow. I'll go to an exploiterer. What can I do? I'll eat humble pie and say: give me what work you have, only hire me.

AKULINA. Well, have some more tea.

TRAMP. Thank you, I mean merci.

(*Noise and talk is heard in the passageway.*)

AKULINA. Here's Mikhaila, just in time for tea.

MARFA (*rises*). Oh, good grief. Ignat's wid 'im. Means he's drunk.

(MIKHAILA *and* IGNAT *stagger in drunk.*)

IGNAT. How yuh doin'? (*Crosses himself before the icon.*) Here we are, god-dammit, made it for teapot time. We went for mass, it was long past; we went for chow, got no eats nohow; we went for booze, got just what we use. Ha, ha, ha. You give us some tea, an' we'll give yuh some booze. How's that? (*Laughs.*)

MIKHAILA. Where'd yuh find this dude? (*Takes a bottle out from under his coat and puts it on the table.*) Get cups.

AKULINA. Did'ya have a good trip?

IGNAT. Couldn't be better, goddammit. We had some fun, did some drinkin', an' even brought some home.

MIKHAILA (*fills the cups and offers one to his mother and then one to the TRAMP*). You have a drink too.

TRAMP (*takes the cup*). I offer my earnest gratitude. Your health. (*Empties his cup.*)

IGNAT. Atta boy, the way he knocked that off, must be an old hand at it, goddammit. On an empty stomach, I reckon it's gone right through 'im. (*Pours another cup.*)

TRAMP (*drinks, to* MIKHAILA *and* IGNAT). I wish you success in all your enterprises.

AKULINA (*to* MIKHAILA). So did'ya make a lot?

IGNAT. Whatever, a lot, not a lot, we drank it all away, goddammit. Right, Mikhaila?

MIKHAILA. Sure did. It's not just t'look at. Once in a blue moon yuh can have some fun.

MARFA. Cut yer showin' off. Ain't nothin' good 'bout it. There's nothin' t'eat in the house, an' look what yuh're...

MIKHAILA (*threateningly*). Marfa!

MARFA. Marfa what? I know my name. I wish I'd never laid eyes on yuh, yuh shameless lush.

MIKHAILA. Marfa, watch out!

MARFA. I don't wanna, an' I won't.

MIKHAILA. Pour the liquor for the guests.

MARFA. For shame, you bug-eyed mongrel, I don't even wanna talk t'yuh.

MIKHAILA. Yuh don't? Oh, you bitch. What'd you say?

MARFA (*rocks the cradle. The children are frightened and come to her*). What'd I say? I said I don't even wanna talk t'yuh, that's what.

MIKHAILA. Have yuh forgotten? (*Jumps up from the table, hits her in the head and knocks off her kerchief.*) There's one for yuh.

MARFA. O-o-o-oh! (*Runs to the door crying.*)

MIKHAILA. I'll get you, you slut... (*Rushes after her.*)

TRAMP (*jumps up from the table and seizes* MIKHAILA *by the arm*). You don't have any full right whatever.

MIKHAILA (*stops and looks with amazement at the* TRAMP). Is it long since yuh had yer ass kicked?

TRAMP. You don't have the full right to subject the female sex to insults.

MIKHAILA. Oh you son of a bitch. D'ya see this? (*Shows his fist.*)

TRAMP. I won't allow you to exercise expletation on the female sex.

MIKHAILA. I'm gonna pletation yuh so's yuh won't know which end's up...

TRAMP. Go ahead, hit me. What are you waiting for? Hit me. (*Sticks his face out.*)

MIKHAILA (*shrugs his shoulders and spreads out his hands*). What if I really do?

TRAMP. I'm telling you, hit me.

MIKHAILA. Well you sure are an oddball, now that I look at yuh. (*Drops his hands and shakes his head.*)

IGNAT (*to the* TRAMP). Yuh can tell right away he's got a thing for them women, goddammit.

TRAMP. I stand up for their rights.

MIKHAILA (*goes to the table breathing hard, to* MARFA). Well, Marfa, yuh'd better light a big candle for 'im. If not for him, I'd o' beaten yuh t'a pulp.

MARFA. What else can I expect from yuh: yer whole life yuh knock yuh-self out, bake an' cook, an' as soon as...

MIKHAILA. Well, nuff o' that, nuff. (*Offers liquor to the* TRAMP.) Have a drink. (*To his wife.*) Whacha snivellin' for? Can't yuh take a joke? Here, take the money: two threes, an' two twenty kopeck pieces.

AKULINA. How 'bout the tea an' sugar I asked for?

MIKHAILA (*takes a package out of his pocket and gives it to his wife.* MARFA *takes the money and goes to the storeroom, silently arranging her kerchief*). Them womenfolk are a brainless lot. (*Offers more liquor to the* TRAMP.) Here, drink.

TRAMP (*declines*). Drink it yourself.

MIKHAILA. Quit foolin' aroun'.

TRAMP (*drinks*). Good luck.

IGNAT (*to the* TRAMP). I guess yuh've seen a thing or two in yer life. But oh, I sure like that jumper yer wearin'. Now that's one slicky jumper, where'd yuh get it from? (*Indicates the* TRAMP's *tattered jacket.*) Don't you fix it up, it's just fine the way it is. I mean, it's been aroun' awhile, but what can yuh do? If I had one like that, the women'd go for me too. (*To* MARFA.) Ain't that right?

AKULINA. 'Tain't nice, Ageich,[1] t'make fun of a man yuh don't even know.

TRAMP. Therefore a lack of education.

IGNAT. I'm just kiddin'. Have a drink. (*Offers him liquor.*)

(*The* TRAMP *drinks.*)

AKULINA. You said yuhself it's the cause of it all, an' that you were in prison 'cause of it.

MIKHAILA. What were yuh in prison for?

TRAMP (*very drunk*). I suffered for expropriation.

MIKHAILA. Whacha mean?

TRAMP. I mean we went up to 'em, t'this potbellied guy: "Hand over the money," we say, "if not look here—a levolver." He hemmed and hawed, but pulled out twenty three hundred roubles.

AKULINA Oh Lord!

TRAMP. We only wanted to dispose of this sum properly. Zembrikov was running things. They pounced on us... those vultures. Immediately we were locked up under arrest in prison.

IGNAT. An' they took the money away?

TRAMP. Sure did. Only they couldn't incriminate me. At the trial the prosecutor put it to me this way: "You stole the money," he says. And I immediately replied: "Crooks steal," says I, "but we executed an expropriation for the party." Now he didn't know what to answer. He hemmed and hawed, but couldn't find any answer. "Take him," he says, "to prison," that means, to the incarceration of free life.

IGNAT (*to* MIKHAILA). He's a slick one, the son of a bitch. Atta boy. (*Offers the* TRAMP *more liquor.*) Have a drink, goddammit.

AKULINA. For shame, what language you use!

IGNAT. I ain't cussin', Granny, it's just some word I use: goddammit, goddammit. T'yer health, Granny.

(MARFA *enters, stands by the table and pours the tea.*)

MIKHAILA. Now that's good. Better 'an bein' sore. I say it's thanks t'him. Marfa, I respect yuh. (*To the* TRAMP.) What d'ya think? (*Embraces* MARFA.) I respect my ol' lady, an' how I do. My ol' lady's, in a word, first rate. I wouldn't swap 'er for anyone.

IGNAT. Now that's good. Granny Akulina, have a drink. My treat.

TRAMP. That's the power of anergy for you. Everyone found themselves in melancholy, and now there's sheer pleasantness and a friendly mood. Granny, I feel love for you and for all mankind. Dear brothers. (*Sings a revolutionary song.*)

MIKHAILA. It's really gotten to 'im on an empty stomach.

Curtain.

ACT II

The same cottage. Morning.

MARFA *and* AKULINA. MIKHAILA *is asleep.*

MARFA (*takes an ax*). I'm goin' t'chop some wood.

AKULINA (*with a pail*). If not for that guy, he'd o' beaten yuh black an' blue yesterday. I don't see 'im. Did he leave? Musta. (*Exit one after the other.*)

MIKHAILA (*climbing down from the stove*). Look at that, the sun's way up awready. (*Puts on his boots and stands up.*) The women musta gone for water. Ah, hurts... my head hurts. I won't go for a pick-me-up, the hell wid it. (*Crosses himself before the icon, and gets washed.*) I hafta harness up.

(*Enter* MARFA *with wood.*)

MARFA. What about the beggar from yesterday? Did he leave?

MIKHAILA. Musta. Don't see 'im.

MARFA. Oh well, who cares. But he seemed pretty smart.

MIKHAILA. He stood up for yuh.

MARFA. So what.

(MIKHAILA *gets dressed.*)

MARFA. Did'ya put away the tea an' sugar from yesterday?

MIKHAILA. I figgered you did.

(*Enter* AKULINA *with the pail.*)

MARFA (*to* AKULINA). Ma, did'ya take a package?

AKULINA. I don't know nothin' 'bout it.

MIKHAILA. I put it on the windowsill yesterday.

AKULINA. I saw yuh do it.

MARFA. Where can it be? (*They look for it.*)

AKULINA. Now that's a shame!

(*Enter* NEIGHBOR.)

NEIGHBOR. What about it, Tikhonych, are we gonna go for wood?

MIKHAILA. You bet. I'll harness up right away. Yuh see we've lost somethin'.

NEIGHBOR. That so? What is it?

MARFA. My mister brought a package from town yesterday, tea an' sugar, an' put it here on the windowsill. I didn't think o' puttin it away. Now it's gone.

MIKHAILA. We're blamin' the tramp, the one that spent the night here.

NEIGHBOR. What's the tramp look like?

MARFA. Skinny, no beard.

MIKHAILA. Coat's all ragged.

NEIGHBOR. Curly hair, hooked nose?

MIKHAILA. That's right.

NEIGHBOR. I just saw 'im. Wondered why we was walkin' so fast.

MIKHAILA. Must be him. Far away?

NEIGHBOR. Reckon he ain't made it 'cross the bridge yet.

MIKHAILA (*grabs his cap and quickly makes for the exit with the* NEIGHBOR). Hafta catch 'im. That crook—it's him.

MARFA. Oh, what a shame, what a shame. No doubt it's him.

AKULINA. An' what if it ain't? Once, 'bout twenty years ago, they also said a man stole a hoss. Folks gathered: one says, "I myself saw 'im puttin' a halter on"; another says, "I saw 'im leadin' it off." It was my uncle's hoss, a piebald, really stood out. So folks gathered an' begun lookin' for it. An' they found that same guy in the woods. "It's you," they say. "I don't know nothin' 'bout it, nothin' at all," he says. "Swear t'God," they say. He swears t'God an' swears by the saints it wasn't him. But they say, "Why should we listen t'him? The women said it was him for sure." Then he said somethin' nasty. Yegor Lapushkin was a hothead—he's dead now—an' widout sayin' a word, he swung aroun' and wham, right in the mouth, "It's you," he says. An' once he hit 'im, all the others jumped in an' begun kickin' an' punchin', an' they beat 'im t'death. An' what d'ya think? The followin' week they found the real crook. That guy wasn't no crook at all, he was just lookin' for a nice tree in the woods.

MARFA. That's right, what if they make the same mistake. He's down an' out, but seemed t'be a good guy.

AKULINA. Yeah, he's way down. What can yuh expect from such a guy?

MARFA. There, they're shoutin'. They're bringin' im' back, I guess.

(*Into the room enter* MIKHAILA, *the* NEIGHBOR, *an* OLD PEASANT, *and a* YOUNG ONE, *pushing the* TRAMP *ahead of them.*)

MIKHAILA (*holding the tea and sugar in his hands, to his wife*). We found this on 'im, the thievin' son of a bitch.

AKULINA (*to* MARFA). It's him, poor guy, look how he's hangin' his head.

MARFA. Musta been talkin' 'bout 'imself yesterday, stealin' whatever he can get his hands on when drunk.

TRAMP (*agitated*). I'm not a crook, I'm an expropriator. I'm a man of action and have to live. You can't understand it, just do whatever you want.

NEIGHBOR. Should we take 'im t'the elder or straight t'the police?

TRAMP. I'm telling you, do whatever you want. I'm not afraid of anything and I'm prepared to suffer for my convictions. If you were educated people, you would understand...

MARFA (*to her husband*). Just let 'im go, for God's sake. We got our stuff back. Why not let 'im go, let's not sin... Let 'im go.

MIKHAILA (*repeating his wife's words*). Let's not sin... let 'im go. (*Becomes thoughtful.*) (*Sternly to his wife.*) "Let 'im go." Thanks for tellin' us. Widout you we dunno what t'do.

MARFA. I feel sorry for 'im, poor thing.

MIKHAILA. Sorry! Go 'head, tell us, widout you we dunno what t'do. Yuh're a damn fool. "Let 'im go." He'll go awright, but I got a few words t'say t' him so's he understands. (*To the* TRAMP.) Now you, monsewer, listen t'what I hafta t'say t'yuh. Even though yuh're down an' out, yuh did a mighty bad thing, mighty bad. Someone else mighta busted yer ribs an' then still took yuh t'the police, but I'll just say this t'yuh: yuh did a bad thing, 'bout as bad as it gets. Only yuh're really down an' out, an' I don't wanna hurt yuh. (*Pauses. All are silent. Sincerely.*) Go, God be wid yuh, an' don't ever do it again. (*Looks back at his wife.*) An' you wanna tell me!

NEIGHBOR. Yuh're wrong, Mikhaila. Oh, yuh're wrong, yuh're lettin' them guys get away wid doin' that.

MIKHAILA (*still holding the package in his hand*). If I'm wrong I'm wrong, that's my business. (*To his wife.*) An' you wanna tell me. (*Pauses, looks at*

the package and, looking back at his wife, resolutely gives it to the TRAMP.)
Go on an' take this, yuh'll have tea on the way. (*To his wife.*) An' you
wanna tell me. Go 'head, I said, there's nothin' t'talk about.

TRAMP (*takes the package. Silence*). You think I don't understand... (*His
voice trembles.*) I understand it in completion. It would have been easier for me, had you beaten me like a dog. Don't I understand what I am?
I'm a cheat, I mean, a degenerate. Forgive me, for the love of Christ.
(*Throws the sugar and tea on the table and quickly exits sobbing.*)

NEIGHBOR. He even cried, poor thing.

MIKHAILA (*to his wife*). An' you wanna tell me.

AKULINA. He was once a man too.

MARFA. Lucky he didn't take the tea, or there'd be none t'make.

Curtain.

Notes

1. A number of the works included here were left unfinished at Tolstoy's death, and none was published in his lifetime.

2. For a discussion of the mix of fiction and autobiography in *Childhood* and a consideration of the dialogue between them, see Andrew Baruch Wachtel, *The Battle for Childhood* (Stanford: Stanford University Press, 1990), 7–20.

3. For the concept of sideshadowing, see Gary Saul Morson, *Narrative and Freedom: The Shadows of Time* (New Haven: Yale University Press, 1994), 117–72.

4. I borrow the term autopsychological from Lidia Ginzburg, who uses but does not define it in *On Psychological Prose,* trans. Judson Rosengrant (Princeton: Princeton University Press, 1991), 198.

5. On January 27, 1900, Tolstoy wrote the following entry in his diary: "Went to see Uncle Vanya and became incensed. Decided to write a drama, Corpse. Jotted down a plan" (L. N. Tolstoi, *Polnoe sobranie sochinenii,* 90 vols. [Moscow, 1928–58], 54:10). Further references to the work of Tolstoy in these notes will be made by reference to volume and page number from this edition.

6. Under nineteenth-century Russian law, in order to receive a divorce with the right to remarry, the innocent party had to prove (or the guilty one to admit) adultery. Thus, for Liza to remarry, Fedya would have had to confess to being an adulterer. And while Tolstoy presents him as a man with many flaws, betraying his wife sexually is not among them. It is, therefore, not surprising that he is loath to take the legal steps necessary to free her.

7. She evidently made attempts to leave Akimov for a number of years before 1890. In 1887 her mother told Tolstoy the whole sad story. Tolstoy's characteristic but not very helpful advice was that "she must live with the husband with whom she is living, loving him as much as she is able and allowing him the possibility of being good to her. And she should leave him only when he tells her directly to leave" (Tolstoi, 64:101).

8. "In my sixteen years at the university I never did meet a student who had not read the famous novel while he was still in school. . . . In this respect, the works, for example, of Turgenev or Goncharov—not to mention Gogol or Pushkin—are far behind the novel *What Is to Be Done?*" The quote is from a pamphlet by P. P. Tsitovich. It is cited in Irina Paperno, *Chernyshevsky and the Age of Realism* (Stanford: Stanford University Press, 1988), 28.

9. In his unfinished comedy *An Infected Family* (see Tolstoy, *Plays*, vol. 1) Tolstoy parodied Chernyshevsky and *What Is to Be Done?*. Although in the 1890s he found a few good things to say about Chernyshevsky's aesthetic program, Tolstoy's attitude toward Chernyshevsky's fiction remained negative. As late as 1910 he said, "I always found Chernyshevsky and his writings unpleasant" (N. N. Gusev, *Dva goda s L. N. Tolstym* [Moscow: 1912], 223).

10. Masha's recollection of the name of the character who fakes suicide in *What Is to Be Done?* is incorrect: she should have said Lopukhov. Her use of the name Rakhmanov instead is extremely suggestive. Clearly the reader or spectator is supposed to realize that she "wanted" to say Rakhmetov (one of the other heroes of *What Is to Be Done?*). The name Rakhmanov does not appear in the novel. It is, however, the maiden name of Fedya's wife, Liza. Masha's "Freudian slip" hints at her hope that Fedya will, in a figurative sense, kill his wife through the act of fake suicide, and thereby be free to marry again.

11. There are other details linking Protasov with Lopukhov, Liza with Vera Pavlovna, and Karenin with Kirsanov. Just before Masha convinces Fedya to fake his suicide, she sees a gun by his side and is convinced that he really intends to take his own life. She exclaims: "What a fool. A regular fool." The first chapter of Chernyshevsky's novel, the chapter that describes Lopukhov's fake suicide, is entitled "The Fool," and that is the "name" that all the people in the chapter give to the mysterious "suicide." When Liza receives Fedya's suicide note (remember, she does not know that the suicide was a sham), she becomes hysterical, decides that she really loved only Fedya, and sends Karenin away. This scene exactly parallels the reaction of Vera Pavlovna when she receives Lopukhov's suicide note and temporarily banishes Kirsanov. In both cases, however, the woman is speedily reconciled with and married to the second husband.

12. When Vera Pavlovna hears that Lopukhov has returned she says to Kirsanov: "It is Easter today, Sasha, so say to Katenka: Verily he is risen" (N. G. Chernyshevsky, *Chto delat'?* [Leningrad, 1975], 332). For a thorough discussion of Chernyshevsky's use of religious imagery in *What Is to Be Done?* see Paperno, 195–218.

13. For Tolstoy's readers (and possibly for Tolstoy himself, although there is no evidence that he knew this work) the connection between fake suicide and revolutionary activity might have been strengthened by the appearance in 1897 of a novel called *Ovod* (originally written and published in 1896 in English under the title, *The Gadfly*) by one E. L. Voynich. In Voynich's novel the main character fakes his own suicide in order to disappear and embark on a career as a professional revolutionary. Voynich was an Englishwoman who was married to an Polish/Russian revolutionary. She translated from Russian to English, and there can be no doubt but that she borrowed the fake suicide motif from Chernyshevsky (whose novel any self-respecting Russian revolutionary knew by heart).

14. This idea of parody draws on the definition proposed by Tynianov: "the parody of a tragedy will be a comedy . . . the parody of a comedy can be a tragedy" (Iu. Tynianov, "Dostoevskii i Gogol' [k teorii parodii]," in *Arkhaisty i novatory* [Ann Arbor: Ardis Reprints, 1985], 416).

15. Tolstoy never actually mentions Sukhovo-Kobylin's play, but, in addition to the connections that will be discussed below, there is a strange coincidence that could have encouraged Tolstoy to think about Sukhovo-Kobylin in connection with *The Living Corpse*. In 1850, when Sukhovo-Kobylin was a young man, he was accused of arranging the murder of his mistress. The case was a cause célèbre at the time, and Tolstoy wrote two letters about it to his aunt (see Tolstoi, 59:64 and 81). The last name of the murdered mistress (which Tolstoy mentions several times) was Simon, by chance the same name as the real-life prototype for Liza in *The Living Corpse*.

16. Of course, both of these themes were old favorites of Tolstoy's, but Sukhovo-Kobylin's play might well have helped him to see how they could be used in a dramatic work. It is, perhaps, not coincidental that Tolstoy was writing *The Living Corpse* just as *Tarelkin's Death* was about to be staged for the first time.

17. In Varravin's last line Sukhovo-Kobylin brings up a folkloric subtext

which Tolstoy fails to actualize in *The Living Corpse*: the Russian tradition of vampirism. According to Slavic folk belief, suicides commonly turn into vampires who "lie in their graves as *undecayed corpses*" (Felis J. Oinas, "East European Vampires," in *Essays on Russian Folklore and Mythology* [Columbus, Ohio: Slavic Publishers, 1985], 112; emphasis mine). According to Oinas the words for werewolf and vampire are frequently interchangeable (p. 111).

18. This is symbolized by the fact that, unlike Lopukhov and Tarelkin, Fedya does not receive a new name after his resurrection.

19. N. F. Fedorov, *Filosofiia obshchego dela,* 2 vols. (London: Gregg International, 1970), 2:203–4. From the above citation it might be imagined that Fedorov meant resurrection to be understood metaphorically. However, from a number of his other articles it is clear that he meant the project to be conceived quite literally. For a general introduction to Fedorov's thought, see S. Lukashevich, *N. F. Fedorov (1828–1903): A Study in Russian Eupsychian and Utopian Thought* (Newark: University of Delaware Press, 1977).

20. F. M. Dostoevskii, *Polnoe sobranie sochinenii v tridtsati tomakh,* 30 vols. (Leningrad, 1972–88), 30:13–15.

21. Actually, the sentence was never really to death, but it was decided to teach the prisoners a lesson by making them believe that it was. For a detailed discussion of the mock execution and its aftermath see Joseph Frank, *Dostoevsky: The Years of Ordeal, 1850–1859* (Princeton: Princeton University Press, 1983), 49–70.

22. Dostoevskii, 4:232. Of course, Dostoevsky uses the same paradigm of prison as a locus for resurrection in the epilogue of *Crime and Punishment.*

23. Tolstoi, 63:80–81. For a detailed discussion of Tolstoy's views on Fedorov, see V. Nikitin, "'Bogoiskatel'stvo' i bogoborchestvo Tolstogo," *Prometeia* 12 (1980): 123–30. Dostoevsky and Tolstoy were by no means the only Russian intellectuals interested in Fedorov. See Irene Masing-Delic, *Abolishing Death* (Stanford: Stanford University Press, 1992), for a thorough discussion of Fedorov's influence.

24. For example, characters by the name of Nikhlyudov appear in "Notes of a Billiard Marker" (1855), "A Landowner's Morning" (1856), "Youth" (1857), "Lucerne" (1857), and *Resurrection* (1899). It does not ap-

pear, however, that readers are expected to connect these various Nikhlyu-
dovs to each other.

25. A. Mar'iamov, "Zhiznenyi sluchai i literaturnyi siuzhet," *Voprosy lit-
eratury* 6 (1970): 117.

26. See Andrew Wachtel, "Death and Resurrection in *Anna Karenina,*"
in *In the Shade of the Giant,* ed. Hugh McLean (Berkeley: University of
California Press, 1989), 100–14.

27. See Richard Gustafson, *Leo Tolstoy: Resident and Stranger* (Princeton: Princeton University Press, 1986) for a different interpretation of this
theme in Tolstoy's work.

PETER THE BREADMAN

1. Cf. Mark 10:21.

2. The entire quotation from Mark 10:21 reads: "Then Jesus beholding
him loved him, and said unto him, One thing thou lackest: go thy way, sell
whatsoever thou hast, and give to the poor, and thou shalt have treasure in
heaven: and come, take up the cross, and follow me."

3. In the original Tolstoy has these slaves as males; however in the course
of the scene it becomes clear that they are females.

AND THE LIGHT SHINETH IN DARKNESS

1. John 1:5.

2. He is an officer in the gendarmerie—an agency in the tsarist government that was a forerunner of what eventually became the KGB after
the Russian Revolution of 1917.

3. Court sentences against indentured peasants were usually reviewed
by the landowner, who, if he disagreed, could pardon the defendant.

4. Ernest Renan (1823–92), French historian, philologist, philosopher,
and scholar of religion, was a controversial figure during his lifetime. His
best known work is *The Life of Jesus* (1863), which was followed by six other
volumes that make up his *History of the Origins of Christianity* (1863–81).
The Life of Jesus offers a sympathetic treatment of the protagonist, who is
simply depicted as a human preacher of moral teachings. It was de-
nounced by the Catholic Church.

5. It would seem that Tolstoy lost track of the number of Saryntsev children. Although seven children are indicated here, the dramatis personae lists only five. The sixth would be the nursing child (Nikolenka). In Act IV we learn of additional children (Natasha and Misha)—which brings the number to eight. Act II seems to corroborate this number since we learn that Marya Ivanovna had had nine children, and has apparently lost one of them.

6. Matthew 5:42.

7. At that time in Russia in-laws were not allowed to marry. Hence, as sisters and brothers, Lyuba could marry Boris or Styopa could marry Tonya; however, after the first couple married, the other could no longer do so.

8. The actual land measure in Russia is a *desyatina,* which is equal to approximately 2.7 acres. In order to make the figures work out, we simply substituted *acre* for the actual measure. This familiar term will be used henceforth.

9. Cf. John 15:13.

10. Tolstoy apparently forgot that no previous argument was noted.

11. Cf. Matthew 23:37 and Luke 13:34.

12. Matthew 18:17.

13. Cf. Acts 15:28.

14. See Matthew 20:1–16.

15. These are characters from the opera *The Barber of Seville,* by Gioacchino Antonio Rossini (1792–1868).

16. Cf. 1 Samuel 16:23.

17. Once again Tolstoy has lost track of the number of Saryntsev children.

18. Apparently Nikolai Ivanovich does not wish to address Father Gerasim as one would a cleric.

19. Cf. Matthew 16:18. The entire passage reads: "And I say also unto thee, That thou art Peter, and upon this rock I will build my church; and the gates of hell shall not prevail against it."

20. Matthew 18:20. The entire passage reads: "For where two or three are gathered together in my name, there am I in the midst of them."

21. This is not a direct quotation from the Gospel. Only the second part of this passage is taken from the opening line of Matthew 7:16.

22. The prohibition against oaths may be found in Matthew 5:34–35; "But I say unto you, Swear not at all; neither by heaven; for it is God's throne: Nor by the earth; for it is his footstool: neither by Jerusalem; for it is the city of the great King." See also James 5:12. This, of course, is founded on the ancient Hebrew tradition, which prohibits using the Lord's name.

23. The powers to which Father Gerasim refers are the secular authorities, or the state.

24. Cf. Matthew 5:21–22.

25. Matthew 5:34.

26. Matthew 26:63. This passage, which the audience would be expected to recognize, reads: "I adjure thee by the living God, that thou tell us whether thou be the Christ, the Son of God." It should also be noted that these words were not spoken by Pilate, but by the high priest, Caiaphas.

27. Christ's verbatim answer to Caiaphas was: "Thou has said." See Matthew 26:64.

28. Cf. Matthew 19:22–23.

29. Cf. Matthew 19:21.

30. Cf. Matthew 5:48.

31. Cf. Matthew 11:25.

32. This statement contradicts what Nikolai Ivanovich said to his wife in Act I, Scene 19, "Take over the estate, then I won't be responsible," and the letter he wrote her (Act II, Scene 2) in which he says he intends to keep some of the land. It has been suggested that this inconsistency reflects the real-life drama that took place between Tolstoy and his wife with regard to the disposition of the former's estate.

33. Cf. Matthew 19:29.

34. This ancient monastery (founded in the fifteenth century) is situated on the largest of the Solovets Islands, which are located in the White Sea in the northern Russian district of Arkhangelsk. From the end of the sixteenth century it also became a place of exile for recalcitrant clerics—a tradition that continued into the Soviet era.

35. In adding the word *sonny* to our translation, we are attempting to capture the disrespectful tone of Boris's reply to the general's patronizing treatment of him. In Boris's reply, the original text italicizes the personal pronoun of the familiar form of you (*ty*), which he returns in kind.

36. Cf. John 15:13.

37. See notes 26 and 27.

38. This is not a direct quotation, but is made up of parts from three separate passages in the Gospel: cf. Matthew 10:18–20. Indeed, the phrasing of the last passage in the King James version had to be altered in our translation in order to maintain a logical sequence.

39. See notes 5 and 17.

40. In adding "Aleksandr Mikhailovich" (the formal form of address) and "Alek" (the familiar form of that name) to our translation, we are attempting to capture the difference between the use of the formal personal pronoun for you (*vy*) and the familiar (*ty*).

41. Cf. Matthew 18:6. The entire passage reads: "But whoso shall offend one of these little ones which believe in me, it were better for him that a millstone were hanged about his neck, and that he were drowned in the depth of the sea."

42. The Rzhanov Hospice was a home for the destitute in Moscow. Tolstoy visited it in 1882, and the character of the drunken Aleksandr Petrovich is modeled on a former resident there, Aleksandr Petrovich Ivanov, whom he employed to copy his manuscripts.

43. Emelyan Ivanovich Pugachëv (1742?–1775), a Don Cossack who declared himself to be Peter III, the murdered husband of Catherine the Great, and led a peasant rebellion against her government from 1773 until he was defeated and executed in 1775.

44. It would seem that the name should read Starkovsky. Apparently Tolstoy has forgotten the surname of Lyuba's fiancé.

45. The Dukhobors (Russian *dukhobori*, "spirit wrestlers") were a religious sect (made up mostly of peasants) that originated in Russia sometime in the mid–eighteenth century (1740?). Because of their beliefs—they rejected the authority of both church and state, the priesthood, and all external sacraments, as well as conscription; they believed in the equality of all men, and in direct individual revelation—and proselytizing activities, they were persecuted from the time of Catherine the Great, and sporadically deported to remote corners of Russia. At the very end of the nineteenth century they were allowed to emigrate, thanks to the intervention of Tolstoy, who managed to get the tsar's approval. A number of Dukhobors made their way to Canada.

1. In the American system of criminal justice there is no equivalent to the *sudebnyi sledovatel,* whose function it is to take depositions and testimony from the accused and then turn them over to the prosecutor. In the English system he is known as the examining magistrate. Our translation attempts to capture his function.

2. We have taken some liberties in translating the names of the various songs mentioned in this vignette. A verbatim rendition would make these songs sound very stilted.

3. This is a welcoming song which, like "Happy Birthday" in English, has a fixed tune and words except for the name. Therefore we have added the sentence "What's his name?" to our translation. It should be noted that, by tradition, the person honored pays the performer(s) of the song.

4. Matthew 6:12.

5. The phrase we find in the text is "acceptance of guilt" (*prinyatiya viny*). Though it may be evident to a Russian audience that this clearly refers to adultery—one of the only grounds (in this case the only) on which a divorce that would allow the innocent party to remarry could be granted—readers of the English translation are in no such position. Fedya has just confessed to being the "guilty" party, but we may surmise from previous scenes that he is not guilty of adultery. Therefore, to translate strictly from the original would leave unclear why Fedya now hesitates to acknowledge guilt and claims he would have to lie in order to do so.

6. A novel by Nikolai Gavrilovich Chernyshevsky written in 1863.

7. There is no such character in Chernyshevsky's novel. The character who pretends to drown himself is Lopukhov. However, the name Rakhmanov brings two things to mind: first, it is clear to anyone who is familiar with this novel that Masha meant one of its other heroes, Rakhmetov; and, second, it is the maiden name of Fedya's wife, Liza. For more details on this, see the introduction.

8. In adding "Viktor Mikhailovich" (the formal form of address) and "Vitya" (the familiar form of that name) to our translation, we are attempting to capture the difference between the use of the formal personal pronoun for you (*vy*) and the familiar (*ty*).

9. The actual drink referred to is *kvas,* a sparkling or fizzing native drink made from water and berries, fruit, or honey.

10. The phrase we find in the text, "take blame on myself," refers to adultery. See note 5.

11. In the text he is simply referred to as Boy. We know his name from the list of characters in the dramatis personae.

12. It will be recalled that in his farewell letter to Liza and Karenin, Fedya requested that they help out the watchmaker, Yevgenyev (Act IV, Vignette 2, Scene 5). Perhaps Karenin was honoring Fedya's last request? Why it is a secret, however, remains unclear.

13. Apparently Tolstoy mistakenly assumed that a case involving bigamy would be decided by a jury. Cases of this sort were actually decided by a panel of judges.

14. Since Simonov has not been mentioned before, it is not at all clear who he is. However, it is possible that Tolstoy may have accidently substituted this name for Yevgenyev, the watchmaker. See note 12.

15. The three-headed dog that guarded the entrance to Hades in Greek and Roman mythology.

THE WISDOM OF CHILDREN

1. Cf. Matthew 5:44.

2. Grushka is a diminutive of the name Agrafena, a form frequently used by peasants.

3. Fedka is a diminutive of the name Fyodor. See note 2.

4. Cf. Luke 3:11.

5. Makarka, Marfutka, and Pavlushka are diminutives of the names Makar, Marfa, and Pavel, respectively. See note 2.

6. Syomka, Aksyutka, Mitka, Palashka, and Vanka are diminutives of the names Semyon, Kseniya, Dmitry, Pelagiya, and Ivan, respectively. See note 2.

7. From here on Tolstoy refers to the landowner and his wife as father and mother. For the sake of consistency, we continue to refer to them as before.

8. Pauline Viardot-Garcia (1821–1910), a French mezzo-soprano who became celebrated throughout Europe for her wide range and excellent

technique. She also composed songs and an opera, and after retiring from the stage, taught at the Paris Conservatory. Those familiar with the personal life of the famous Russian writer, Ivan Sergeyevich Turgenev (1818–83), remember her as his close friend.

9. At the beginning and toward the end of this skit Tolstoy refers to the peasant and his wife as father and mother. For the sake of consistency, we do not change their designations.

10. Petka is a diminutive of the name Pyotr. See note 2.

11. We are using this form of address to indicate that there is a relationship, though not by blood, between the peasant couple and the godmother. Specifically, in Russian *kum* or *kuma* indicates a spiritual relationship between the godmother of a child and the child's actual parents.

12. Grishka and Tishka are diminutives of the names Grigory and Tikhon. See note 2.

13. Mikita is a corrupted form of the name Nikita.

14. Apparently Tolstoy has forgotten that previously the old woman mentioned that the newborn baby was a girl.

THE TRAVELER AND THE PEASANT

1. Only the second quotation is from Matthew 5:43–44. The first is from Matthew 5:21–22.

THE CAUSE OF IT ALL

1. Apparently Tolstoy has forgotten that previously Ignat's patronymic was Ivanych.